CITY OF WELL-

CITY OF WELL-BEING provides a radical and holistic introduction to the science, art and politics of town planning. It starts from the premise that the purpose of planning is the health, well-being and sustainable quality of life of people.

Drawing on current and historic examples it offers inspiration, information and an integrated perspective which challenges all professions and decision-makers that affect the urban environment. It is both authoritative and readable, designed for students, practitioners, politicians and civil society.

The science: summarizing the most recent research, the book demonstrates the interrelationships between the issues of obesity, unhealthy lifestyles, inequality, mental illness, climate change and environmental quality. The radical implications for transport, housing, economic, social and energy policies are spelt out.

The art and politics: the book examines how economic development happens, and how spatial decisions reinforce or undermine good intentions. It searches for the creative strategies, urban forms and neighbourhood designs that can marry the ideal with the real. The relationship of planning and politics is tackled head-on, leading to conclusions about the role of planners, communities and development agencies in a pluralistic society. Healthy planning principles could provide a powerful logical motivation for all.

Hugh Barton is Emeritus Professor of planning, health and sustainability at the University of the West of England, and the author or editor of a series of innovative books including *Sustainable Communities* and *Healthy Urban Planning* (both 2000), *Shaping Neighbourhoods* (2010), and *The Routledge Handbook of Planning for Health and Well-Being* (2015). He is an expert advisor to the World Health Organization Healthy Cities movement. A town planner by training, he has spent most of his career teaching planning, urban design and sustainable development at the University of the West of England, Bristol. His research and consultancy has focused on low carbon urban form, inclusive appraisal processes, and the integration of health and well-being into planning. Since 'retirement' in 2012 he has continued writing, and participating in academic and professional engagements, while devoting time to community activism, music-making, tennis and a growing number of grandchildren.

CITY OF WELL-BEING
A RADICAL GUIDE TO PLANNING

HUGH BARTON

Routledge
Taylor & Francis Group

LONDON AND NEW YORK

First published 2017
by Routledge
2 Park Square, Milton Park, Abingdon, Oxon OX14 4RN

and by Routledge
711 Third Avenue, New York, NY 10017

Routledge is an imprint of the Taylor & Francis Group, an informa business

British Library Cataloguing in Publication Data
A catalogue record for this book is available from the British Library

Library of Congress Cataloging in Publication Data
Names: Barton, Hugh, author.
Title: City of well-being / Hugh Barton.
Description: Milton Park, Abingdon, Oxon ; New York, NY : Routledge, 2017. | Includes index.
Identifiers: LCCN 2016023529| ISBN 9780415639323 (hbk) | ISBN 9780415639330 (pbk) | ISBN 9781315438689 (ebk)
Subjects: LCSH: Urban health. | City planning--Health aspects.
Classification: LCC RA566.7 .B37 2017 | DDC 362.1--dc23
LC record available at https://lccn.loc.gov/2016023529

ISBN: 978-0-415-63932-3 (hbk)
ISBN: 978-0-415-63933-0 (pbk)
ISBN: 978-1-315-43868-9 (ebk)

Typeset in Univers and Gill
by Servis Filmsetting Ltd, Stockport, Cheshire

For my grandchildren:
Claudia, Heather, Merlin, Kaya and Zindzi

CONTENTS

FIGURES

PREFACE

This book is about how to plan settlements as if people really mattered. On the one hand it is a radical call to arms, and on the other, a rounded guide to town (or urban) planning. My hope is to have written a book which is highly accessible, clear about fundamental values, and which gives a real understanding of the relationship between people, cities, planning and design. It is both a text-book for student planners and sets a new paradigm for practicing planners and anyone concerned for healthy urban environments.

The book is not about a specific planning system, though it touches on several. It is about spatial planning as a generic activity undertaken by a range of professionals, not simply those with a formal planning qualification. It is highly relevant, for example, to transport engineers, housing planners, economic development officers and urban designers. It plays into the new agenda of public health, which is at last becoming centrally concerned with the health of the built environment. Students of all these subjects will find a text which gives a holistic understanding of all the social, economic, environmental and political issues faced by those who influence the future of human settlements.

City of Well-being introduces the science, the art and the philosophy of planning. It advocates a return to the roots of modern planning. The dire urban health problems of nineteenth-century cities have gone, but since then we have sacrificed environmental quality for other goals, and thus find ourselves in crisis again – whether personal in terms of unhealthy lifestyles, obesity and increased mental illness, urban in terms of air pollution, congestion, spatial inequities and increased flood risk, or global in terms of climate change and loss of biodiversity.

The book is organized in five parts:

I – Orientation – sets out the argument of the book and a theoretical framework that encourages integrated healthy policy-making.
II – Inspiration – gives a trajectory from historic cities, via the planning pioneers of last century, to current cities that demonstrate what can be achieved.
III – Cognition – deals systematically with the relationship between urban environments and physical and mental well-being, social justice, climate change and sustainable urban ecologies.
IV – Navigation – then provides insight into the market and planned processes of change, evaluates the design strategies for sustainable city regions and healthy places, and introduces the broader issues of strategic planning.
V – Perspiration – examines the knotty political issues surrounding land and property, then the various heroic and humdrum visions of the planning process and the role of planners, before presenting practical guidelines for planning in a pluralist society.

ACKNOWLEDGEMENTS

This book has been on my 'to do' list for many years. It is the result of a professional lifetime, rather than just the time spent writing. So there are too many people – students, colleagues, other professionals and academics – to mention individually. But I must thank people in the WHO European Healthy Cities network, especially the 'healthy urban planning sub-network', for stimulating discussion and mutual support in the first decade of this century; and past and present colleagues with whom I have worked closely on related projects, including Richard Guise, Marcus Grant, Sarah Burgess, Laurence Carmichael, Selena Gray, Adam Sheppard, and Susan Thompson.

On another front I would like to thank the enthusiastic team I worked with recently on the Stroud town centre plan, which features in Chapter 17, especially Leonora Rozee, Camilla Hale and Steve Hurrell.

The production of the book would have been impossible without my two brilliant help-mates: Gill Evans acting as secretarial assistant, and Bruce Winslade as graphic artist.

The biggest thanks have to go to my wife, Val Kirby. She has not only been constructive with comments and ideas, but amazingly tolerant as my period of book purdah extended way beyond that intended.

Images

Unless otherwise stated, all the diagrams, charts and photographs are the author's. Special thanks must go to Marcus Grant and Richard Guise for allowing me to use their diagrams and drawings from Barton *et al.* (2010) *Shaping Neighbourhoods*. The marvellous cartoons are thanks to Rob Cowan. Photographs have been kindly provided by Mike Devereux (fig 3.6), Marcus Grant (figs 5.6, 6.8, 7.3, 9.7, and 13.18), Val Kirby (fig 3.5), Steve Melia (fig 5.6), and Philip Ross (fig 4.3).

1 Orientation

The origins of modern planning in the late nineteenth century were mainly due to health concerns. In Britain and elsewhere, forms of planning were devised to confront the evils of rapid, unchecked industrialization and urbanization – evils evident from the writings of Dickens and his contemporaries. Public health policies and housing design codes led on to early Town Planning Acts. That transition, from rampant, unadorned capitalism to a more socially responsible model, was a critical period in the history of planning. But in the following years of the twentieth century health was side-lined as other issues dominated the planning agenda, and institutional silos were built up.

The aim of this book is to put *people* back at the heart of urban planning. The politics, the economics and the spatial arrangement of cities are interdependent, and shape the social opportunities and well-being of the inhabitants. The urban environment is a reflection of the dominant values, via the development and planning processes. In turn, the environment is a critical determinant of equity, health and climate resilience. The central message of this book is that we ignore the need for 'healthy planning' at our peril.

The Prologue tells the story of three Western cities with different characteristics and a startling variety of approaches to planning. It serves to give a picture to enliven the imagination. Chapter 1 then ranges wide in order to provide a general introduction to the book. It sets out arguments which are then developed later, touching first on the conflicting views of planning in the twenty-first century. It explains the linked 'time-bombs' of public health and climate change, and the relationship of these to the planning of our urban habitat. It presents the case for seeing spatial planning as an inclusive and integrating activity aimed at health and well-being.

Chapter 2 then presents a conceptual framework to assist understanding of the way the planning of the built environment is linked to all aspects of the city: the people, the economy, the place and the wider environment. This framework – the *Settlement Health Map* – has become internationally recognized in the public health field, especially the WHO Healthy Cities network, and provides a motif throughout the book.

CONTRASTING CITY SCENARIOS

Imagine three cities. One has a political philosophy that values the freedom of the individual, of landowners and the market. The second has a similar market orientation, but also a tradition of strong planning policies for conservation and countryside protection. The third has a social market philosophy, valuing equality of opportunity and having an expectation of civic responsibility. The three cities are relatively free-standing, with extensive hinterlands. They enjoy similarly benign climates, geographic context, social structure and strong economic base. To a significant degree they are able to shape their own destinies.

These cities have very different spatial trajectories, and different social outcomes. The first city is car-dependent. People consider it is their right to drive their vehicle from any place to any place else, and park right next to the building, for free. Even the students and staff of the university on their downtown campus do not normally walk more than a block or two, relying instead on the university minibus. Along the suburban 'strip malls' it is impossible to walk from shop to shop because of the absence of sidewalks and crossing places: people drive to the next door shop. Cyclists are rare: if they are unlucky enough to be knocked over by a vehicle, there is no redress, because the owners' insurance does not cover cyclists. Downtown has offices and a university, but has hollowed out for retail and social activities – few people are on the streets, and none apart from the destitute after 5.00 pm. The sedentary lifestyle is reflected in 35 per cent obesity rates, and some of the worst health statistics in the developed world. Income and health inequality are dire, and linked to race and to location. Life expectancy of the substantial minority population is far below that of the majority, and 50 per cent are obese. There is a concentration of poverty in the core city where over 25 per cent of households live below the official threshold. Some parts exhibit market failure, housing a residual population unable to sell and lacking good quality services.

The ability of the city council to tackle poverty is compromised because the rich outer suburbs are in different authorities. The market is buoyant in those outer areas. Development is triggered by new freeway investment. The policy of the authorities is to specify a minimum plot size of quarter acre (0.1 ha) and in that context allow individual property owners to develop their homes and businesses as they see fit. The sprawling suburbs mostly have no facilities within walking distance.

The political agenda of the second city is modified capitalism. There are powerful forces requiring the authority to take care of its built and natural environment. The historic city centre is conserved, partly for its tourist value, and progressive pedestrianization has helped it to maintain its social and cultural roles. Strong greenbelt protection policies have forced the market to look inward to brown-field sites. Land values are high. Larger companies dominate land transactions in both housing and commercial fields. Sale of private greenspace, allotments and school playing fields has reduced access to nature. The subsidized sale of the social housing stock to tenants has meant an increasing reliance on owner-occupied and private rented housing. Houses and flats are traded increasingly as long-term investments rather than simply as homes.

The traditional transport policy of the city has been to try to accom-modate motor traffic. But road improvements have not kept pace with rising demand, especially from the population diaspora beyond the greenbelt, and from the business parks, superstores, leisure facilities, university and main hospital in peripheral campus-style developments. Problems of congestion – with resulting economic inefficiencies and air pollution – have forced a rethink. Some public transport and cycleway investment has begun, though starting from a low base.

In social terms, it is a city of two halves. This becomes starkly obvious when looking at longevity and years of healthy life. The richest quintile (i.e. the top 20 per cent) on average enjoy 70 years of healthy life, and live to 88. The poorest quintile enjoy only 50 years of healthy life, and live to be 75 – so for a third of their shorter lives, they are disabled. The differential is very obvious spatially. Despite policies aimed at diversity of housing, there is concentration of poorer households in particular areas, ghettoized by the housing market, including by gentrification of some inner neighbourhoods. Poorer areas lack investment in housing and the environment. The housing is the least energy-efficient in the city, so heating costs are high, and often homes are cold in winter. Local facilities have atrophied for lack of spending power. Health centres are few and far between. Parks are under-maintained and some have become intimi-dating because of rowdy youths. Bus services are too expensive for many and service frequency is reduced. The job search areas, and access to main shopping centres are limited because of low car availability. Schools, with a concentration of poor children, struggle to combat the lack of parental support. The city has commendable plans to improve the situation, but little power to realize them.

The first city …

'Along the suburban "strip malls" it is impossible to walk from shop to shop because of the absence of sidewalks and crossing places: people drive to the next door shop.'

The second city …

'In social terms, it is a city of two halves. The poorest quintile enjoy only 50 years of healthy life, and live to be 75 – so for a third of their shorter lives, they are disabled.'

By contrast, many of the rich live in flourishing neighbourhoods. High spending power has led to a wide choice of walkable retail facilities, excellent schools, convenient health and leisure centres, beautifully maintained greenspaces, and good bus services. Some rich and average income households live in villages, suburbs and exurbs which have few facilities, so that 80 per cent of trips are by car, forcing high car ownership. Despite the affluence of some of the population, the general well-being of the children of this city gives many causes for concern. According to a UNICEF survey of rich countries, they are, subjectively, the least happy in Europe. They are on average among the least fortunate in terms of material well-being, health and safety, educational well-being, family and peer relationships and risky behaviours, such as being drunk or over-weight. One causal factor may be their lack of freedom to roam. There is suspicion of strangers, a lack of openness, and most parents strictly curtail their children's freedom.

The contrast with the third city is marked. The city adopts a paternalistic approach to its citizens. While in a past age this might have been heavy-handed, it is now a matter of democratic accountability, opening up opportunities for all. The city is able to exert strong control over the land market and land availability, taking over any brownfield or greenfield sites that are needed for development, putting in the infrastructure, then releasing plots to the housing and commercial markets. The housing market is ironically much more open than in the second city: more dwellings are completed, many households build their own homes, housing co-operatives flourish, social providers and local and national house-builders contribute. Public and private sector rents are controlled. The result is a 'social market', with close community and business engagement in decision-making. House prices have remained stable for several decades. Houses and flats are not considered as investments, but purely as homes.

The location and form of urban development are plan-led. The city plan is a long-term one, setting the ground rules for market and institutional investment. The key to the plan is the relationship between transport and land use. All major facilities – large-scale offices, business centres, shopping and leisure centres, hospitals, colleges, stadia, concert halls, theatres – have to be close to a stop on the tram system. The city ensures there are enough convenient sites, recycled or new, to satisfy demand. In many instances, it forms partnerships with developers and residents to facilitate regeneration, planning and design. There are some difficult areas where immigrant minorities are not fully integrated, but even in these areas a sense of community cohesion appears to survive.

What is very striking, visiting the city, is that the roads are rarely congested. Public transport – run by a joint public/private company – requires little subsidy and works superbly to reach all parts of the city region. Walking and cycling are a normal part of everyday life, accounting for the majority of trips. Safe and convenient pedestrian and cycling routes thread through the city. Local facilities and social networks flourish because people are on the street, not so much in their vehicles. Car ownership in some parts of the city

The third city …

'What is striking is that the roads are rarely congested. Walking and cycling are a normal part of everyday life, accounting for the majority of trips. Safe and convenient pedestrian and cycling routes thread through the city.'

is proving unnecessary, releasing household income for other pur-chases or saving in the local community bank – both of which help to support the city economy.

The health of the population is good. The richest quintile has similar life expectancy and years of healthy life as in the other cities. The poorest quintile is much healthier, only about five years behind the richest. There are several reasons for this. First is that the level of daily exercise leads to better diet/exercise balance, and fewer people are overweight or obese. The second is that the poorest are included in society in a way that does not happen in the other cities. They have pedestrian-friendly environments, excellent public transport, enabling easier access to job opportunities, plus afford-able housing, state education and health services – all meaning that with a relatively progressive tax system, they are better off. They can make more choices for themselves. Local facilities flourish. Recreational greenspaces are close and accessible to all, supporting mental well-being.

The well-being of children reflects the general state of affairs. In the UNICEF survey, the children of this city are near the top of the rankings in material well-being, health and safety, educational well-being, family and peer relationships and risky behaviours. Their own subjective assessment suggests they are happy. It is noticeable that parents allow them much greater freedom to roam, there is less traffic danger, and children's attitude to each other and to strangers is more open.

These three cities are not random imaginings. They are based on a study of real places, and should ring bells among professionals and observers of urban planning. The first and second cities draw on experience in the southern United States and the UK respectively. The social democratic city draws on cities in Germany, Denmark, and the Netherlands. The results of the UNICEF study into child well-being have been generalized, as have health statistics from major conurbations in Britain. So while there is some poetic licence, the pictures given are not untypical. Overall then, it is apparent that the people in the city that has *freedom* as its watchword, are less free than the people in the city which espouses equity of opportunity. When liberty is at the cost of equality and fraternity, then it is not liberty at all.

'It is apparent that the people in the city that has freedom as its watchword, are less free than the people in the city which espouses equity of opportunity.'

Reference

UNICEF Innocenti Research Centre (2007) *Child poverty in perspective: an overview of child well-being in rich countries*. Florence: UNICEF. Available at: www.unicef.org.irc

CHAPTER ONE

PUTTING *PEOPLE* AT THE HEART OF PLANNING

We must bring back into society a deeper sense of the purpose of living. The unhappiness in so many lives ought to tell us that success alone is not enough. Material success has brought us to a strange spiritual and moral bankruptcy.

Ben Okri[1]

Introduction: the purpose of planning

What is the purpose of town and city planning? Is it to facilitate economic development and market operation? Is it to create a beautiful environment, a fairer society, or a well-functioning settlement? Is it to combat climate change? Well, yes, to some extent it is all of these things ... but what is the *essence* of it? If we look back through history, from Hippocrates and Hippodamus in ancient Athens, to the great pioneers of modern planning at the beginning of the twentieth century, the best of it has been about the health, well-being and the quality of life of citizens.

The entrepreneurial planners and social reformers a century ago, reacting to the inhumane conditions prevailing in the industrial cities of Europe and America, saw health as central. They were confronted by the devastating effects of infectious diseases. In the overcrowded, unsanitary, air-poisoned slums of the industrial cities, poor health and short lives were endemic. Promoting a healthy environment was not viewed in opposition to economic development. Rather, it was seen as a prerequisite for it, increasing productivity and creativity. In this century we are faced with a rising economic burden from non-communicable diseases and an ageing population. To rely on health care to address these issues is misguided in terms of both medical and economic realities. The UN Habitat report, *Hidden Cities*, sees the health threat facing urban populations as one that could cripple global health care systems.[2]

Yet in many ways we are quite literally building unhealthy conditions into the human habitat. Many urban environments are bad for physical health because, for example, they inhibit daily physical activity, expose people to unhealthy air, provide poor quality housing; they can be bad for mental well-being because of the lack of contact with nature and the decline of local communities offering social support; they can exacerbate inequalities of income and health by inflating the cost of housing, by increasing social segregation, reducing access to facilities and necessitating high car ownership (Figure 1.1).[3]

Central and local government are implicated in this crisis. The early planning ideals of healthy towns were blown away over the latter part of the twentieth century. The segregation of professional and institutional responsibilities, the pressures of technological change (particularly motorization), and the triumph of free market economics, have meant that holistic principles were submerged. With some notable exceptions, silo decision-making predominates. Health planning has become all about providing services for those who are ill, while tacitly ignoring the many societal factors, including environmental conditions, that tend to make them ill. Income inequality has grown even in the recent worldwide recession, reinforced by social exclusion and leading to huge health inequities. The worldwide obesity epidemic is partially due to an environment that prejudices healthy physical activity. Parallel increases in social isolation, mental illness, stress-related cardiac morbidity and respiratory diseases – usually dealt with in separate clinical silos – are all related when considered from a spatial planning perspective.

Rhetoric and reality of sustainable development

The formal international answer to the question, 'what is the aim of planning?' is clear. The United Nations, the European Community, and the UK government all agree: the purpose is *sustainable development* (Figure 1.2). This principle is about achieving economic, social and environmental goals at the same time, finding synergistic solutions to problems, and ensuring that today's policies and projects do not compromise the well-being of future generations.[4] 'Sustainable development' has a good ring to it. Since the United Nations promoted the idea at the Earth Summit in Rio in 1992, it has persisted, representing the accepted international gold standard.

But reality is often very different. The phrase has not caught on as a popular slogan. Politicians do not use it to win votes. Its meaning is often abused, providing a green fig-leaf to cover the ambition of developers and the manoeuvring of governments. The paradox inherent in the phrase undermines its appeal because it plays havoc with a clear sense of direction. 'Development' – assumed by governments to mean rising GDP – relies on increased consumption, while 'sustainability' of local and global ecology and life-support systems, relies on reduced consumption.

Influenced by neo-liberal economic theories and political pressures, most states believe that the purpose of planning is first and foremost to support economic development. Protecting the environment is viewed as a 'constraint' on development; providing for social needs as a cost. The UK government, for example, has phrases in its otherwise generally excellent National Planning Policy Framework that allow it to interpret the 'presumption in favour of sustainable

Fig 1.1 Environments that deter physical activity: an edge-of-town business park, with 95 per cent of trips by car; a recent housing estate with only one facility (a pillar box) in easy walking distance; and a bus shelter cut off from the dwellings it serves – all near Bristol, England.

Fig 1.2 *What is sustainability?*

Source: Courtesy Rob Cowan, available at: www.plandemonium.org.uk

development' to mean a presumption in favour of development per se, unless there are overriding environmental and social reasons against.[5] Profit and politics frequently trump both environmental sustainability and social well-being. In this book, I argue that priority is false, and it distorts decisions on the urban environment in ways that undermine people's health and well-being, compromise global sustainability and in the long run undermine the economy too.

The straightforward answer to the question at the start is that planning is for people. The intention must be to evolve towns and cities that are good for people to live in: not for just some people, but all people, whatever their income or abilities; and not just now, but for a future that is inherently uncertain, especially given climate change. If health and well-being were much more clearly embedded in the science, art and politics of planning, more humane settlements would result. We need a socially equitable environment that opens up opportunities and choices for all, promotes healthy lifestyles and social cohesion; an economically buoyant environment that offers jobs, income and status in society; an environment that safeguards ecological capital, husbands resources, and builds long-term climate resilience.

This may seem like an obvious aspiration but in the context of current mainstream attitudes and actions, putting it into practice is a radical and challenging one. The agenda is entirely compatible with the anthropocentric perspective on sustainable development promoted by the United Nations: 'Development which meets the needs of the present without compromising the ability of future generations to meet their own needs.'

What do we mean by health and well-being?

The classic definition of the World Health Organization (WHO) equates health with well-being (see sidebar).[6] This brave and

'Planning is for people. The intention must be to evolve towns and cities that are good for people to live in: not for just some people, but all people, whatever their income or abilities.'

The WHO declares: 'Health is a state of complete physical, mental and social well-being and not merely the absence of disease or infirmity. The enjoyment of the highest attainable standard of health is one of the fundamental rights of every human being, without distinction of race, religion, political belief, economic or social condition.'[6]

idealistic definition expressly gets away from the conventional inter-pretation of 'health' as being primarily the concern of the medical professions. Instead, many professions are involved in supporting healthy social, economic, physical and environmental conditions. The equation of health with well-being also links the concept to other terms. The United Nations General Assembly passed a resolu-tion in 2011 inviting member countries to measure the *happiness* of their populations. Subsequently *The World Happiness Report* has been produced each year, and compares happiness across coun-tries, analysing the key influences.[7] Happiness is assessed by social survey, and can be defined as 'subjective well-being'. It is equated not so much with transitory pleasure as with life satisfaction. Mental health is the most important determinant of individual happiness. Different cities use various terms to promote policy innovation: in Portland, 'health'; in Freiburg, 'quality of life'; in Bogota, 'happiness'. The New Economics Foundation has chosen five headline indicators to measure progress: (1) good jobs; (2) well-being (here defined as life satisfaction); (3) environment; (4) fairness; and (5) health.[8]

Interpretation of these terms varies, but while not completely inter-changeable, they are essentially different angles on the core concern for people. They get away from the use of GDP and economic growth per se as the arbiters of progress.

Time-bombs of health, climate and urbanization

Health and illness trends

Let us consider the facts. On a cursory examination, worldwide trends in health and well-being are positive. Life expectancy is increasing in low-, medium- and high-income countries. Child mortality has fallen dramatically. These trends are expected to continue. Nevertheless, a series of factors are interacting to create a 'perfect storm', threaten-ing the ability of nations and communities to cope. Increased lon-gevity means a growing elderly population dependent on a falling proportion of wage earners. And while people are living longer, many are subject to disability as a result of chronic conditions such as heart disease, cancer, diabetes and mental illness. Some places exhibit alarming characteristics. In the most deprived English neigh-bourhoods at the turn of the century people experienced 30 per cent of life with a physical or mental disability.[9] Recent data suggests the situation is worsening.[10]

At the same time increased affluence, technological changes and lifestyle choices are all contributing to an epidemic of obesity, evident to varying degrees in almost all countries across the world (Figure 1.3). In the USA, obesity rates increased dramatically between 1990 and 2010, now affecting a third of adults. Being overweight has become the norm.[11] According to the UK Foresight Report, by 2050, Britain could be a mainly obese society.[12] Research suggests that there is a direct relationship between obesity and travel choices: in the USA, each additional kilometre walked per day is associated with a 5 per cent reduction in the likelihood of obesity, while each extra

'Research suggests that there is a direct relationship between obesity and travel choices: in the USA each additional kilometre walked per day is associated with a 5 per cent reduction in the likelihood of obesity, while each extra hour in a car is associated with a 6 per cent increase.'

| 9

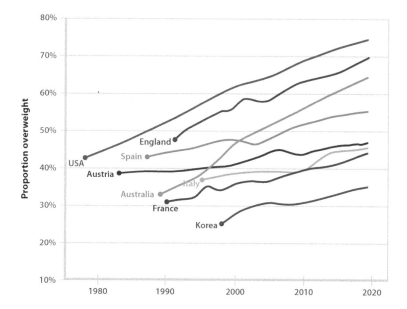

Fig 1.3 *International trends in obesity*

Source: Based upon OECD (2014) Obesity update. Available at: www. oecd.org/health/obesity-update (accessed 28 January 2016).

hour in a car is associated with a 6 per cent increase.[13] In China, the likelihood of being obese is 8 per cent higher for adults in households with vehicles. In India, 50 per cent of those who travel to work by private vehicle are overweight or obese, double the figure for those who walked or cycled. The longer the cycling trips, the greater the reduction in obesity, diabetes and hypertension.[14]

Health inequality is a central concern in this emerging crisis. The Marmot Review in 2010 – *Fair Society, Healthy Lives* – made the point powerfully.[15] Wilkinson and Pickett, in their seminal book of the same year, *The Spirit Level,* demonstrate that, for richer countries, health is unrelated to national income per head, or to health expenditure per head, but is strongly related to income inequality.[16] The analysis of the 'health gradient' between rich and poor in London is salutary: 40 per cent of the poorest groups suffer from a long-term limiting illness, while for the richer groups it is around 5 per cent.[17] We are recognizing that the varied prevalence of non-communicable diseases is a reflection of lifestyle cultures, economic structures and environmental conditions.

The increasing costs of looking after those who are sick are experienced across the world. In the USA, health care expenditure is claiming a larger and larger share of Gross Domestic Product (GDP) – up from 5 per cent in 1960 to 17.5 per cent in 2014, predicted to reach almost 20 per cent – one-fifth of total national income – by 2024.[18] Some 75 per cent of US health expenditure is attributed to treating chronic disease. With the coincidence of an ageing population, increasing obesity and the remorseless rise of chronic illnesses, the ability of services to cope, and society to pay, is increasingly problematic. The WHO concludes that the triple threat to urban health from infectious diseases, injuries and violence, and non-communicable diseases has the potential to cripple health care services – yet most countries give scant attention to the social and environmental determinants of health.[19] In Britain, for example, the National Health Service is not primarily about promoting health, it is about coping with illness – it is a National Illness Service.

Environmental determinants of health

The scope of environmental impacts on health is remarkably broad. The WHO European Healthy Cities programme, in the year 2000 guide to *Healthy Urban Planning,* identified 12 key health determinants and related them to planning policy areas. They range from the influence on lifestyle and physical activity to the threat of climate change, and in between include social cohesion; housing quality; access to work, services, healthy food and open space; safe and equitable environments; healthy air, water and soils.[20] Subsequently, other authors taking a holistic, ecological approach have strongly reinforced this message.[21, 22] Recent research – into fields such as mental well-being and place, health and nature, active travel and urban form, and air quality – has blossomed this century, providing a wealth of substantiating evidence. It has become clear that spatial planning and design affect many aspects of human health and well-being.

Health determinants

Chapters 6–10 explore the science of healthy planning: what are the critical health and ecological problems? In what ways is the environment a determinant of health? How can planning policy influence those determinants?

Climate change

The interdependence of humans and environment becomes self-evident when we consider climate change. Global warming and sea-level rise represent the biggest risks to health in the world, according many authoritative sources,[23] and as detailed by the reports of the Intergovernmental Panel on Climate Change (IPCC) (the most recent being 2013).[24] The main threats to health come from regional weather changes – with consequent heat stress, flooding, water insecurity and food production implications – and from sea-level rise, with huge implications for coastal settlements, economic dislocation, forced migration and disease.

Accepting the seriousness of the threat, there are two kinds of response to climate change: (1) mitigation (i.e. reducing the severity); and (2) adaptation (i.e. making the human habitat more resilient to changing climate). Both require urgent action through spatial planning of settlements and the wider environment. Settlements are profoundly implicated in the causes of climate change. The main greenhouse gas, carbon dioxide, is emitted through energy use. One calculation suggests that in the UK 'at least 70% of energy use is affected to some degree, at some time, by planning policy'.[25] Land transport, for example, which is influenced by land use and transport planning, accounts for 28 per cent of end user CO_2 emissions, and is tending to rise.[26] There are signs of hope of concerted international action following the Paris conference (December 2015), but the 2 per cent temperature rise limit set by the IPCC remains problematic.

The crisis of cities

The title of the book uses 'city' as a shorthand term to mean urban settlement. Towns and cities are the great artifacts of

Fig 1.4 *Taking the easy option*
Source: Courtesy Rob Cowan, available at: www.plandemonium.org.uk

humankind – remarkable, complex structures that provide, for better or worse, the habitat for a growing majority of the human race. They are profound reflections of human culture, dominating economic activity and societal identity, linked by trade, tourism and virtual connections to the 'global village'. Most cities across the world are experiencing rapid urbanization. This is associated with an alarming increase in those – mainly the urban poor – affected by natural disasters, and at risk from flood or inundation as climate and sea level change.[27] At the same time the growing affluence and numbers of the urban middle class, seeking car ownership and suburban living on the American model, are contributing to appalling levels of air pollution. Irrespective of wealth or size, the spatial impacts – 'ecological footprints' – of cities extend far beyond their boundaries, influencing regional and global metabolism.

Human urban settlements do not happen by accident. They happen because of geographical and economic advantage, as perceived by markets, governments and migrating people. But the outcomes of urban change do often seem accidental, the unintended consequences of action and inaction (Figure 1.4). No-one *intends* to create urban smog, or an environment without nature, or one that inhibits walking, but these are often the unfortunate side-effects of decisions taken for altogether different reasons.

'Most cities across the world are experiencing rapid urbanization. This is associated with an alarming increase in those – mainly the urban poor – affected by natural disasters, and at risk from flood or inundation as climate and sea level change.'

Planning at the crossroads

The challenges for spatial planning are huge. The need for effective strategies to combat health, social and climate problems is self-evident, and spatial planning has a part to play. Part of the problem is the sheer complexity of decision-making on the environment. Figure 1.5 illustrates the range of issues and scales which interact and where consistency of policy is needed if the challenges are to be met. Different levels of government, many agencies and many interests are involved.

There is also sometimes a suspicion of government per se. In countries that have experienced the excessive control exercised by communist governments, planning is a contaminated principle. This is also the case in many parts of the USA where the sanctity of private land ownership, and of private development rights, dominate political decision-making. In the UK, planning is primarily pursued in the interests of supporting economic growth and conserving built and natural environmental assets. In the last few decades the rhetoric of the free market, and the purely economic valuing of land – sidelining social, cultural and ecological value – has tended to compromise traditional planning approaches. Decisions on land development are seen through the lens of market interests and economic growth, not 'sustainable development', let alone 'health and well-being'.[28]

Conversely, in some European countries, such as Denmark and Sweden, the social democratic model means that urban planning is an essential tool of social, economic and environmental policy. In the Netherlands, much of which is below sea level, planning is essential for survival.

The future role of spatial planning is therefore contentious. On the one hand, there are hopes that planning will prioritize healthy and sustainable living environments: fulfilling international obligations on air quality, climate change and biodiversity; responding to issues of population change, housing need, employment, congestion and obesity; satisfying public aspirations in relation to environmental quality and heritage. On the other hand, there are powerful societal moves, evident in many countries, to 'lift the burden' of planning off the back of the market, trusting in competition and consumer choice to produce the environment we want.[29]

It would be embarrassing for decision-makers to argue for an urban environment that compromises health – and foolish for them to promote policies that increase the costs of health and social care. Yet that is what they have been doing in most countries. Until this century it was possible to sideline such concerns because, except in specific areas like air quality, the evidence was missing, or at least equivocal. That is no longer the case. There has been an explosion of academic studies across the full range of relevant issues. It has become increasingly clear what works for people and what does not. Some cities have been ahead of the game, and demonstrated the way forward. There is no longer any excuse for persisting with practices that create unhealthy environments.

The difficulty of changing direction is considerable. There is inertia in business, professions and politics. Ignorance is certainly part of

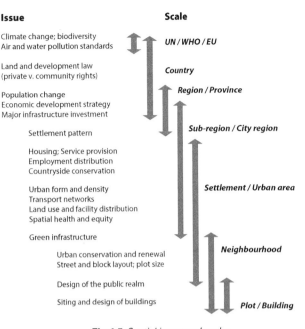

Fig 1.5 *Spatial issues and scales showing the range of issues relevant to spatial planning from building plot to globe*

'*There are powerful societal moves, evident in many countries, to 'lift the burden' of planning off the back of the market, trusting in competition and consumer choice to produce the environment we want.*'

Is planning necessary?

Some economists and politicians imply that 'planning' is unnecessary. This stance is examined in Chapter 15, where it is argued that planning happens whether we like it or not. The real issues are: who is doing the planning, and why?

**Examples of UK anti-
health measures since
2010**

- The abolition of regional
planning which previously
was giving momentum to
local housing supply.
- Undermining the
mechanisms for delivering
and funding affordable
housing.
- The promotion of 'fracking'
to produce shale gas, while
drastically cutting support
for energy efficiency and
renewables.

the reason. Planning can go one of two ways: either it can fulfil the neo-liberal ideal, acting instrumentally to support market development and protect amenity. Or it can do much more – recover its health ideals, and recognize that planning is for *people*.

Planning in a pluralist society

Urban planning in modern capitalist, democratic societies is tricky. Planners do not have a free hand. They work to the briefs set them by commercial clients and politicians. Those briefs have economic or political objectives that do not generally prioritize the long-term health and well-being of the population. Nevertheless public sector planners are charged with co-ordinating the diverse agencies involved in spatial decision-making: responsibility without power. If healthy and sustainable environments are to be achieved, then the conventional equation of 'planning' with local state activity, specifically planning departments and the local politicians they advise, is fallacious. The key decisions are often taken by landowners, developers, transport authorities, housing departments, water and energy companies, hospital authorities, and major industrial and commercial enterprises. The decision of the transport authority, for example, to construct a new highway is a huge town planning decision that is going to affect the spatial evolution far into the future. People's daily options and life chances will be affected. Merely because the decision is not taken by 'town planners' does not mean it is not town planning. Equivalently, when a house builder constructs and markets a new housing estate, with or without the close involvement of the local authority, he is changing the quality, shape and efficacy of the town. People's health and well-being will be affected, for good or ill. So too will the landscape, wildlife, air quality, and the level of greenhouse gas emissions.

Many problems arise because these influential agencies do not sufficiently recognize wider responsibilities. The transport authority and the house builder in these examples are making decisions on the basis of their own specific remit – mobility, on the one hand, and profit, on the other – and assuming that others will cope with the fall-out. They only take what they see as 'externalities' into account when forced to by government regulations, or public/ political outcry.

If cities are to be healthy and environmentally sustainable in a pluralistic society, where decision-making power is distributed among many actors, then all have to accept responsibility. They are all, in a sense, planners. Central government departments, public agencies, housing providers, retail giants, industrial behemoths ... all need an ethical approach. This is recognized in the employment and consumer fields. Their public profiles could benefit from taking social and environmental responsibilities seriously. Agencies could feel good about seeing their own spatial planning decisions as supporting health and well-being. Governments need to reinforce good motives with clear rules and guidance – as already with building regulations and air quality.

So planning is defined here in the broadest possible way, encompassing decisions about the change and development of human

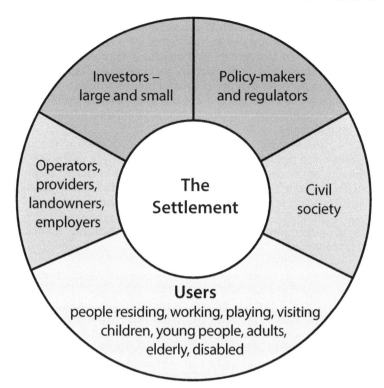

Fig 1.6 *Stakeholders in planning the urban environment*

Source: Barton et al. *(2015) (see further reading).*

settlements in their ecological context. It is about *spatial* (or *urban*) planning as a generic activity, involving not only the state but also market and community interests which have an impact, or a stake, in the creation of the human habitat (see Figure 1.6). In a pluralist society, the diversity of actors means that a process of effective town planning is necessarily about mutual engagement and co-operation, not centralized diktat, on the one hand, or sporadic market decisions, on the other.

'Planning is defined broadly: it is about spatial (or urban) planning as a generic activity, involving not only the state but also market and community interests which have an impact, or a stake, in the creation of the human habitat.'

Reflection

It is intuitively evident that the built environment affects our well-being. You only have to think of the pleasure to be had from a walk on the common, or a visit to a street market, bumping into people you know. Or, on the downside, the danger of crossing a busy road, or cycling behind a diesel bus. But despite this intuitive recognition, there is a widespread assumption that biology is more important than ecology in determining our health and well-being. This assumption is manifest, for example, in the degree of blame we may attach to our genes and the degree to which we assume the remedy for bad health is medicine, or surgery. We spend huge amounts of scarce resources on curative medicine, and our preventive measures are largely biological as well, i.e. inoculation. All the while we are paying scant attention to the social and environmental conditions which are, on some calculations, at least equally important.

The biological assumption is strangely paralleled by commonly held views when Hippocrates (the 'father of medicine') was alive. In his treatise 'On airs, waters and places', published around 2,500 years ago, Hippocrates used evidence from various places in Europe and Asia to refute the prevailing belief in divine affliction and providence. Instead he advocated an ecological perspective, noticing the effects of air and water, climate, housing conditions, social patterns and cultural norms, on health and well-being.[30]

Hippocrates was right. So were the pioneers of modern planning. We ignore the influence of the urban environment on health and well-being at our peril. The inalienable purpose of spatial planning must become the health, well-being, quality of life and happiness of people. If we are to move in the right direction, we need:

- to understand the human environment holistically, seeing the relationship of people, place, and planet – no longer 'through a glass darkly, but face to face';[31]
- to challenge cultural attitudes, commercial myopia and political dogma that conflict with humane decision-making;
- to recognize the shared ethical responsibility of all the agencies that over time create the urban environment;
- to cultivate the professional wisdom and skills necessary to transfer healthy theory to healthy practice – clarity of vision, coherent strategy, quality of design, collaborative decision-making, consistent implementation.

Further reading

Inspirational books from two ages (there are many others):

Gehl, J. (2010) *Cities for people.* Washington, DC: Island Press.

Jacobs, J. (1962) *The death and life of great American cities.* Harmondsworth: Penguin.

Books covering the broad field of planning and health:

Barton, H. and Tsourou, C. (2000) *Healthy urban planning: a WHO guide to planning for people.* London: Spon Press. Prepared for the WHO European Healthy Cities network as part of the launch of the 'healthy urban planning' initiative, this has been called a 'landmark publication', and is available is seven languages.

Barton, H., Thompson, S., Burgess, S. and Grant, M. (eds) (2015) *The Routledge handbook of planning for health and well-being.* London: Routledge. Comprehensive and authoritative review of the research and practice across the world.

Dannenberg, A., Frumpkin, H. and Jackson, R. (eds) (2011) *Making healthy places: designing and building for health, well-being and sustainability.* Washington, DC: Island Press. A wide-ranging review of the research in the field – mainly from an American perspective.

Ross, A. and Chang, M. (2013) *Planning healthier places: report from the Reuniting Health with Planning Project.* London: Town and Country Planning Association. A report making the economic and political argument for the UK.

Notes

1 Okri, B. (2008) 'Our false oracles have failed. We need a new vision to live by', *The Times*, 30 October.

2 WHO Centre for Health Development (2010) *Hidden cities: unmasking and overcoming health inequities in urban settings* (Kobe: WHO Centre for Health Development).

3 Barton, H., Grant, M. and Guise, R. (2010) *Shaping neighbourhoods: for local health and global sustainability* (London: Routledge).

4 World Commission on Environment and Development (1987) *Our Common Future (The Brundtland Report)* (Oxford: Oxford University Press).

5 Department for Communities and Local Government (2012) *National Planning Policy Framework (NPPF)* (London: DCLG).

6 WHO (1946) *Constitution of the World Health Organization* (Geneva: WHO).

7 Helliwell, J., Layard, R. and Sachs, J. (2013) *The World Happiness Report 2013* (New York: Oxford University Press).

8 New Economics Foundation (2014) *Five headline indicators of national success* (London: NEF).

9 Marmot, M., Allen, J., Goldblatt, P. *et al.* (2010) *Fair society, healthy lives: the strategic review of health inequalities in England post-2010 (The Marmot Review)* (London: Department of Health).

10 Office of National Statistics (2014), as reported in the *I* newspaper, 2 May 2014.

11 Butland, B., Jebb, S., Kopelman, P., *et al.* (2007) *Tackling Obesities: Future Choices: Project Report* (London: Government Office for Science).

12 Ibid.

13 Frank, L., Schmit, T., Sallis, J. *et al.* (2005) 'Linking objectively measured physical activity with objectively measured urban form: findings from SMARTRAQ', *American Journal of Preventative Medicine*, 28: 117–125.

14 Millett, C., Agrawal, S., Sullivan, R. *et al.* (2013) 'Associations between active travel to work and overweight, hypertension and diabetes in India: a cross-sectional study', *PLoS Med*, 10(6): e1001459.

15 Marmot *et al.* (2010), op. cit.

16 Wilkinson, R. and Pickett, K. (2010) *The spirit level: why equality is better for everyone* (London: Penguin).

17 Ibid.

18 See www.cms.gov/research-statistics-data-and-systems/nationalhealthstatistics (accessed 11 February 2016).

19 WHO Centre for Health Development (2010), op. cit.

20 Barton, H. and Tsourou, C. (2000) *Healthy urban planning: a WHO guide to planning for people* (London: Spon Press).

21 Corburn, J. (2009) *Towards the healthy city: people, places and the politics of urban planning* (Cambridge, MA: MIT Press).

22 Dannenberg, A., Frumpkin, H. and Jackson, R. (eds) (2011) *Making healthy places: designing and building for health, well-being and sustainability* (Washington, DC: Island Press).

23 WHA (2008) *World Health Assembly Resolution on Climate Change and Health*, WHA 61.19 (Geneva: WHO International); Costello, A., Abbas, M., Allen, A. *et al.* (2009) 'Managing the health effects of climate change', *Lancet*, 373: 1693–1733.

24 IPCC (2013) *Climate change 2013: the physical science basis – summary for policy-makers* (Geneva: Intergovernmental Panel on Climate Change).

25 Barton, H. (1990) 'Local global planning', *The Planner*, 26 October.

26 DEFRA (2008) *The environment in your pocket* (London: DEFRA).

27 Hague, C. (2015) 'Rapid urbanization, health and well-being', in H. Barton, S. Thompson, S. Burgess, and M. Grant (eds) *The Routledge handbook of planning for health and well-being* (London: Routledge).

28 In Britain, this observation is commonplace.

29 The Thatcher government in the UK produced a White Paper entitled 'Lifting the burden'.

30 Hippocrates, quoted by Laurence, R. (1999) 'Urban health: an ecological perspective', *Reviews on Environmental Health*, 14(1).

31 In the Bible, Paul's letter to the Corinthians 13.12.

CHAPTER TWO

A FRAMEWORK FOR UNDERSTANDING

Introduction

The Enlightenment, with its pursuit of reductionist scientific philosophy – i.e. an approach that dissects reality in order to understand it better – has been a mixed blessing. It has brought great strengths of clarity and analytical rigour, but sometimes at the cost of holistic understanding. In the planning field, the separation of both analysis and action into compartmentalized silos, has meant the loss of a coherent integrated view. Whether in relation to transport modelling, retail forecasting, conservation or air pollution, increased expertise and specialization have been accompanied by loss of synthesis. As has been said about the new science of synthetic biology: 'For eighty years we have been taking life apart. Now we want to put it back together again.'[1]

The views of professional planners and academic commentators about what planning is, reflect this. Here are a few, kept short to make the point, from the past 50 years:

> The application of scientific method to policy-making.
>
> (Faludi, 1973)[2]

> The institutional process of making decisions about the future use of land and buildings in order to achieve social ends.
>
> (Oxford Polytechnic planning course, 1968)[3]

> The mediation of space, the making of place.
>
> (Royal Town Planning Institute strap line)

> A means by which society collectively decides what urban change should be like and how to try to achieve it.
>
> (Rydin, 2011)[4]

How satisfactory are these definitions? The first stems from a view of planning as a rational scientific process. The second ties that process to official bodies. The third implies a negotiating process and a design process. The fourth suggests a collaborative, political process of decision-making. None of these is sufficient, though each tells part of the truth. Except for the Oxford version, they focus on the way decisions are taken, the *how* of planning, rather than the *what* or the *why*. What is not clear is the *substance* of planning, and its essential aim.

The aim of this chapter is *synthesis*. A conceptual model of human settlements is developed which takes as its starting point the centrality of planning for human health and global sustainability. The model encourages us to see the relationship of one part of city function to another, to understand the relevance of varied disciplines and professions, and to see the human habitat in a holistic way.

'The purpose of this chapter is synthesis. A conceptual model of human settlements is developed which takes as its starting point the centrality of planning for human health and global sustainability.'

The model is called the *Settlement Health Map*. It is constructed so as to integrate theories of human ecology with theories of the determinants of health, and was first widely publicized in 2006.[5] Here I explain it more fully than has been possible before, showing how the perspective of health and well-being can provide a unifying theme linking the economic, social and environmental goals of planning – often perceived as at odds with each other – and consistent with the overarching principle of sustainable development. I suggest how the model can be helpful for professional practice, analysis, research and the education of planners, and argue that planners can recover an underlying sense of ethics and purpose if – phoenix-like – health is again put at the heart of planning.

Towards an ecosystem model of cities[6]

In searching for a simple conceptual model of human settlements, there is a danger in using vivid images that ignore critical aspects of the complex reality. In his 1981 book, *A Theory of Good City Form*, Kevin Lynch examines the relationship between human values and the physical form of the city.[7] He evaluates some of the favoured concepts of the day: the city as a machine for living in, the city as an organism. He rejects both of these as inadequate, concerned more with image and metaphor than actuality. The idea of the city as machine, promoted by Le Corbusier, sees the settlement in engineering terms, a system of man-made physical structures, ignoring the people living there and the wider environment.[8] It does not get us very far. The idea of the city as an organism has the merit of integrating people and place. Lewis Mumford and others have advocated it, because it recognizes the metabolism of settlements, growing and changing, consuming resources, expelling wastes.[9] We use this idea in casual conversation, for example, when we talk about the heart of the city, or traffic as the life-blood of the city. It is a powerful metaphor, but still treats the human settlement as distinct from its environment. It also implies a controlling mind, guiding development, when in fact there are many minds, often at cross-purposes.

Lynch's solution is the theory of the urban ecosystem. Building on earlier work by Geddes and others, his theory recognizes the complexity of an open system with living (biotic) and non-living (abiotic) elements, cyclic processes and complicated networks of relationships. The abiotic elements are the buildings, streets, the physical infrastructure we together create, and the land, air, water, and environmental assets which are thereby impacted. The biotic embraces all the people living in the region, but also species besides mankind, the flora and fauna of the city and its bioregion. The ecosystem approach recognizes that the urban habitat involves the co-evolution of many diverse species in the same terrain. The settlement is not seen as a free-standing system, an island, sufficient unto itself, but tangled and interdependent with the wider world. The bioregion provides basic life support in terms of water, air, energy and soil. Cities, through their energy use, carbon emissions, food and mineral consumption, are connected to the global ecosystem.

The urban ecosystem is not only about the human/environment interplay, but also the complex web of social, cultural and economic relationships. The economy depends on knowledge exchange and trade with other settlements far and near. The social networks, in this age of high mobility and virtual communications, may be very local, or city-wide or reach anywhere on Earth. Culture (and behavioural norms) varies between groups within a city; also between cities and between countries.

Many subsequent commentators have advocated an ecosystem approach. Herbert Girardet popularized the idea of *urban metabolism*, as an integrated perspective on all the processes at work in human settlements. He drew a distinction between 'linear' and 'circular' processes; the former being typical of industrialized societies, exploiting the environment, then polluting it with wastes; the latter being a sustainable pattern of reuse and symbiosis, mirroring natural ecosystems.[10] The EU Expert Group on the Urban Environment observed many techniques of analysis springing from the ecosystem idea: quantification of resource flows, environmental indicators, energy and water budgets, ecological footprint studies and state of the environment reporting.[11] The guide to *Sustainable Settlements* used the ecosystem approach to underpin principles of satisfying human needs while maximizing urban feedback loops and building robustness and adaptability into the environment.[12]

The ecosystem approach stems from ecological theory. In 1985, Trevor Hancock made the conceptual leap to link human ecology to *theories of human health*. He saw that the public health analysis of the social and environmental determinants of health mirrored the environmental analysis, from a different starting point, and wrote 'The mandala of health: a model of the human ecosystem' (Figure 2.1).[13] Building on his work, Whitehead and Dahlgren devised a diagram of the main determinants of health, encompassing a range of factors from individual age, sex and heredity through lifestyle, social influences, living and working conditions, to the broader societal and environmental influences, that has been widely reproduced in health circles.[14] The 'health map' that I have devised with Marcus Grant uses the agenda set by these authors, adapting it so as to clarify the relationship of different elements and to encompass the concept of sustainable development.

'In 1985, Trevor Hancock made the conceptual leap to link human ecology to theories of human health. He saw that the public health analysis of the social and environmental determinants of health mirrored the environmental analysis.'

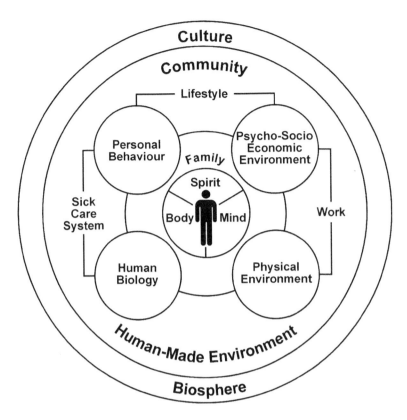

Fig 2.1 *The mandala for health*
Source: Hancock (1985). (note 13).

One way of conceiving 'sustainability' is illustrated by Figure 2.2. Human society and economic activity depend on the global environment, and in the last resort are limited by its resources and ability to cope with human detritus. Society (human population) is in the middle, and the economy mediates the relationship with the environment.

The Settlement Health Map

The Settlement Health Map (Figure 2.3) follows other diagrams in placing human health and well-being at the heart, representing the central purpose of policy, and around that in a series of concentric rings all the social, economic and environmental elements of a settlement, set within the wider global and societal context. The map resonates strongly with public health professionals concerned about the structural significance of the built environment for healthy behaviour. It has been widely welcomed and used by the WHO Healthy Cities movement across the world, has been translated into many languages, quoted in UK government documents, and referred to in many plans and health impact assessments.[15,16]

The sequence of spheres reflects the strength of association between each sphere. All the eight spheres around *people*, in the centre, exert an influence on their health and well-being. Spheres 1–7 constitute the settlement ecosystem – people and their habitat.

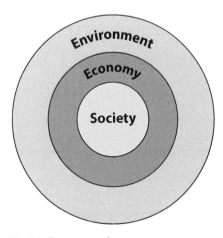

Fig 2.2 *The concept of sustainability*

Fig 2.3 *The Settlement
Health Map*

*Source: Adapted from Barton and Grant
2006 (note 16), p.11.*

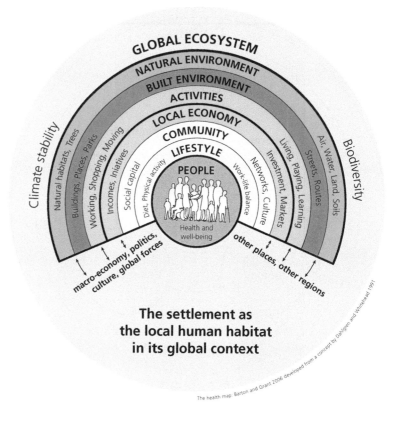

The health map: Barton and Grant 2006 developed from a concept by Dahlgren and Whitehead 1991

It could be a village, an urban neighbourhood, a town, a city or conurbation depending on the scale under consideration. The relationship to other settlements is represented, as are the wider economic,
political and cultural factors. Encompassing everything, as sphere 8,
is the global environment, the ecosphere.

The 'built environment' (sphere 6) is the field where spatial planners, designers and decision-makers have *direct* impact, thereby an
indirect influence on the other spheres. The 'built environment' is
defined so as to include all the human-made elements of settlements,
not simply buildings and physical infrastructure but the gardens and
greenspaces too. Other professionals, investors and politicians have
direct responsibilities in relation to other spheres. The map gives a
common agenda for considering the impact of decisions, and a base
for collaborative decision-making.

Thus, the map includes the human, the constructed and the natural
dimensions of the neighbourhood, town or city under consideration.
It avoids the poisonous duality of man and environment by seeing
human activity as part of nature.

The health map as an analytical tool

The health map can be used to analyse the knock-on effects of policy
and development. By way of example, consider a proposal for a new

business park on the edge of the city, on green fields near a motorway junction. It is an initiative within the *built environment* sphere, directly aimed at contributing to the *local economy*, and thereby influencing the pattern of *activities* – working and travelling. Its construction will have an impact on the landscape and biodiversity, and – through the materials used and the construction process – on natural resources and climate emissions (spheres 7 and 8). When in use it will typically foster more and longer car trips, discouraging daily healthy active travel (sphere 2), generating extra congestion, pollution and accident risks. If most of the firms simply move from existing premises in the town, then some people may find they cannot access the new location because of their restricted mobility. Work communities may be formed, while old ones vanish. It is clear that every level of the map is touched by the proposal. There will be some benefits if new jobs are created or firms become more efficient, but also many costs, mainly because of the inappropriate location for major office development.

There will be impacts on health and well-being, presented below in the form of general questions, working from sphere 2 out to sphere 8:

- How are lifestyles affected? Does the proposal facilitate healthy choices, or is there likely to be a reduction in levels of physical activity?
- Is social exclusion increased or decreased, especially for less mobile groups – the options people have available to them, the social networks and the sense of community?
- How is economic activity affected, especially the range, quality and accessibility of job opportunities, and the quality of those jobs?
- How is travel affected, with related risks of accidents? How is the availability of services likely to be affected – public transport, retail, health, education, social and leisure?
- Is the resulting quality of the public realm likely to have a positive or negative impact on people's well-being, especially in relation to the street environment, greenspace and nature?
- What impacts will there be on biodiversity, habitats, air quality, water quality, ground water supplies, flood risk, soil erosion and non-renewable resources?
- Will carbon and other greenhouse gas emissions be reduced or increased? Does the proposal build resilience to climate change?

Thus, the diagram gives an agenda for analysis of the direct and indirect impacts of spatial policies and projects, so that assessment processes are more holistic in their scope, recognizing the interplay of social, economic and environmental variables in achieving a healthy, sustainable human habitat.

'The diagram gives an agenda for analysis of the direct and indirect impacts of spatial policies and projects, so that assessment processes are more holistic in their scope, recognizing the interplay of social, economic and environmental variables in achieving a healthy, sustainable human habitat.'

The professional value

The health map helps to bridge gaps between professions, and demonstrates how they relate to health and well-being and to decisions in the built environment. Staff at the WHO Collaborating Centre for Healthy Urban Environments at UWE[17] have used the map at inter-professional seminars, asking participants to locate their own responsibility on the map: doctors and social workers directly with the individual or family; public health professionals with group behaviour and lifestyle; community development officers with the community; economic development officers and members of the Chamber of Trade with the economy, and so on. Each participant can see how he or she impinges on the whole. Professions which directly affect the built environment begin to appreciate their role more fully. Elected representatives and commercial developers are encouraged to recognize that their decisions are not taken in a vacuum.

The political value

Politicians often find themselves under pressure from vested interests, articulate minorities and the media. Decision-making tends to be driven by short-term advantage. They need clarity of argument if such pressures are to be deflected, or co-opted. The promotion of health and well-being is a noble, easily understood, aim with public appeal. It provides a rationale for policy synthesis in relation to climate change, local environment, healthy lifestyles, community equity and development, job creation, accessibility to facilities and a safe, attractive townscape. It is also amenable to scientific evidence, not just rhetoric. Few politicians, planners or developers would be happy to promote policies for neighbourhoods, towns or cities that are openly evaluated as *unhealthy*.

The research value

Researchers normally belong to specific discipline groups: planning theorists, environmental scientists, public health researchers, etc. Each group tends to form international clubs with their own conceptual frameworks, language, conferences and journals. Despite the recognition that everything is connected, reductionist traditions persist. The health map helps to contextualize specific research programmes, acting as a prompt to integrated thinking (Figure 2.4).[18]

The educational value

The Settlement Health Map puts the main academic 'ingredient' disciplines that are important for settlement planning in the context of an integrated conceptual model, so that relevance for education and training is clear. Psychology, public health, sociology, economics, politics, urban systems theory, urban geography and ecology all find a place. The map helps to define what aspects of those disciplines are most relevant to spatial planning; namely, the aspects that relate to the health and well-being of people, to the relationships between spheres, and to the spatial pattern of activities and the environment. In relation to economics, for instance, macro-economics is much less important than urban economics: land and property markets,

'The promotion of health and well-being is a noble, easily understood, aim with public appeal. It provides a rationale for policy synthesis in relation to climate change, local environment, healthy life-styles, job creation.'

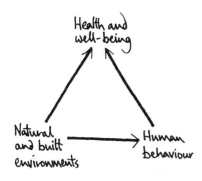

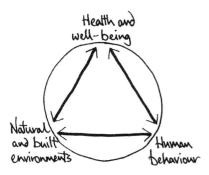

Fig 2.4 *Piecemeal and integrated research. The upper diagram indicates the dominant directions of current research. The lower one shows an integrated conceptual framework.*

Source: Adapted from Lawrence (2015).

location theory, the dynamics of urban growth and decline, changing market and employment patterns, and the effectiveness of local/central government interventions.

Interpretation of the Settlement Health Map

This final section of the chapter explains each of the spheres of the map to help orientation, introducing the subject matter of Chapters 6–10, where much more detail, evidence and references are provided (Figure 2.5).

Sphere 1: People – their characteristics, health and well-being

- 'People' are at the heart of the map because they are our prime concern. All the outer spheres impact on people's well-being.
- There are differential impacts on health – inequalities of health – according to age, gender, race, income, education, mobility, neighbourhood character and location.
- Health inequalities are due to the structure and planning of the human habitat as well as to social and economic factors.

Sphere 2: Lifestyle – levels of physical activity and dietary choices

- Lifestyle is a personal thing. Each individual, family or household has a degree of freedom to choose their lifestyle. Hence the position on the diagram next to 'People'.
- Lifestyle choices are heavily implicated in the prevalence of illness – lack of exercise and unhealthy diet often lead to obesity, which increases the risk of type 2 diabetes, hypertension, cardiovascular disease (stroke, heart attack) and some cancers. Obesity can also impair a person's sense of well-being and learning ability.
- Lifestyle choices are shaped to a significant degree by the general culture of a city or country, by social and economic conditions, and by the character of the built environment.
- The built environment has a strong influence on levels of active travel and active recreation. In specific situations it has some impact on diet.

Sphere 3: Community – social interaction, networks and capital

- Social interaction and social networks (meeting people, belonging to social groups) are important for mental well-being, avoiding the sense of isolation and loneliness.
- The culture of a group or community affects lifestyle choices. Communities may be based on propinquity, family or tribe, shared interests and activities or shared cultural background. They may be very local or very widespread.

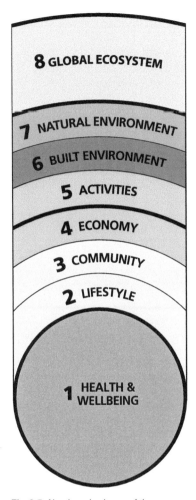

Fig 2.5 *Numbered spheres of the Settlement Health Map*

- The built environment influences the degree of local social interaction, through the accessibility of local facilities, through the design of places and streets.
- Social capital is a broader concept, including active engagement and ability to take action in political, cultural or community affairs. Policy-making for the built environment can influence social capital for good or ill through empowering (or disempowering) local people.

Sphere 4: Economy – local economic activity, markets in land and housing

- Employment is a critical determinant of health and well-being, in terms of the income that results, the enjoyment (or not) of work, and the status that having a job gives.
- Conversely unemployment, especially if prolonged, damages health. Poverty resulting from lack of work or poor pay is associated with shorter lifespan and fewer years of healthy life.
- The level of economic activity is a main driver of demand for housing, retail and leisure activities. It thereby affects the price of land and property and the pace of urban development.

Sphere 5: Activities – residing, working, shopping, learning, playing, moving

- The availability, quality and accessibility of social, recreational and economic activities and services affect well-being and quality of life.
- The activities of households, businesses and institutions create the dynamic of the city. They need space (see the next sphere) and may be suppressed if the competition for space leads to high prices/rents.
- The way people move is related to locational and route options, and to lifestyle choices. It has implications for health, for community and economic activity.

Sphere 6: Built environment – buildings, spaces, routes, utilities

- The built environment is the sphere over which spatial decision-makers have direct influence. It is the *supply* side, while spheres 4 and 5 represent *demand* and *need*. If there are not enough houses, or no parks, then some people suffer.
- Direct health and well-being factors include the quality of housing (dampness, energy efficiency, space standards, sound insulation); the quality and layout of streets/localities (road safety, crossing points); access to nature – trees and greenspace.
- Places can also be important to people for their cultural and historic associations, their familiarity and beauty – helping to give a sense of identity and belonging.

- Urban form at strategic and local levels affects the viability of service provision and accessibility of jobs/services to residents, with knock-on effects on lifestyles, social networks and employment prospects.

Sphere 7: Natural environment – land, soils, air, water, wildlife habitats

- The natural environment (geology, land form, soil conditions, drainage, water courses, aquifers, flora, fauna, air quality, local climate) is continuously affected by human action. In that sense, it is not natural.
- Clean water, air and soil, freedom from destructive floods, are vital for basic life support. In many parts of the world these cannot be taken for granted. Even in 'developed' countries, air pollution is a major cause of premature death.
- Ecosystem services may occur within and around built-up areas (urban trees, drainage systems), or in broader bioregions (water supply, fresh fruit and vegetables). The term 'green infrastructure' expresses the interdependence of settlements and nature.
- Urban development may reduce the carrying capacity of the natural environment on which people depend; for example, through reducing resilience to flood. Conversely, it can increase carrying capacity through holistic planning and design.

The cultural, economic and geographical context

The seven spheres of the settlement shown on the map represent a complete geography of settlements. But no city is an island. The diagram provides reminders of context. There are neighbouring places and regions which interact with the city in terms of people (e.g. commuting to and fro, moving house), the economy (import/export of goods and services), and the environment (input/output of environmental resources and wastes). There are also national and international factors that shape the behaviour and performance of a city: these include macro-economic trends, globalization, fiscal policies, legal and political contexts, governance structures, broader social trends and cultural attitudes. It is salutary to recognize the degree to which any particular city has freedom of action.

Sphere 8: The global ecosystem – climate, biodiversity, land and sea

- The final, all-embracing, global ecosphere, is on a different scale altogether, like the outermost sphere of the fixed stars in mediaeval cosmology. Planning must be concerned with the global commons as well as the local.
- Human metabolism, in particular the emission of carbon, is leading to climate change and sea-level rise which together

The science of planning

Part III of this book is structured around the spheres of the map. It provides a review of all the health and sustainability issues in relation to the urban environment.

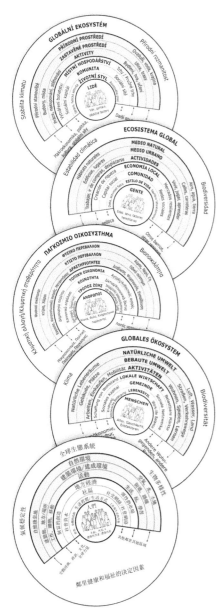

Fig 2.6 *The Health Map goes international: a selection of translated versions.*

are considered by the WHO to be the greatest health risk. Built environment policies and related urban activities are implicated.

- Desertification and soil erosion problems are being exacerbated by both climate change and inappropriate industrial and farming practices.
- We are doing a poor job as stewards of Earth's biodiversity. Habitat loss and species decline are due to the nature of urbanization, lifestyles, food and energy production, all compounded by climate change.
- Mineral reserves – energy resources, metal ores, rare earths – are vital to our current version of civilization, but over-exploited. Built environment practices on materials, construction and transport can help reduce demand.

Conclusion: ethics for planners

What I have endeavoured to show in the first two chapters is that by giving pre-eminence to the goals of health, well-being, happiness and quality of life we provide a sound motivation for spatial planning. A focus on health and well-being ties in positively with other key aspirations such as economic growth, social justice and environmental sustainability. It is entirely consistent with the integrating principle of sustainable development, but has the advantage of being more 'user-friendly', appealing to common-sense politics. At the rhetorical (political and media) level, advocacy of a healthy urban environment can also be sold on the basis that it will be fairer, will increase economic productivity and cut long-term health and social care budgets.

At the professional level, an emphasis on health and well-being can provide an integrating principle which knits together the various, often competing, goals of planning. The Settlement Health Map places relevant professions, and the academic disciplines they relate to, in a relationship to each other and the environment they affect. The map emphasizes an integrated, holistic view. Healthy places make for healthy people and a healthy planet. The microcosm is related to the macrocosm. A place which cultivates excellent accessibility for all to a wide range of jobs and facilities, that promotes active travel and recreation, community well-being, strong place identity, and environmental risk reduction, will also be doing its bit to promote urban resilience and moderate the threat of climate change.

If the logic of this is accepted, then it implies a sea-change in the role of planners and other colleagues in the built environment. No longer a tacit acceptance of purely instrumental decisions, based on narrow commercial or institutional interest, rather a reinforced professional ethic: responsibility for making clear to decision-makers the degree to which their decisions will promote or compromise health and well-being. This provides spatial planners with a bottom line of acceptability which can be strongly held. Just as engineers provide clear guidance on safe building structures, so planners can offer clear guidance on healthy towns and cities.

The implications are profound. Planning education and retraining have to embrace the science of healthy settlement planning. That is part of the purpose of this book – to provide an introduction to the whole agenda: the science, the art, the politics. There are plenty of potential allies in every profession. The public health agencies can help to change the mindset of decision-makers. As George Bernard Shaw declared: 'The problems of the world cannot be solved by sceptics and cynics. Now more than ever we need people who can dream about things that never were, and ask themselves, why not?'

'A reinforced professional ethic: responsibility for making clear to decision-makers the degree to which their decisions will promote or compromise health and well-being.'

Further reading

Barton, H. (2005) 'A health map for urban planners: towards a conceptual model for healthy, sustainable settlements', *Built Environment*, 31(4). Discusses the genesis and logic of the map, though before its final form evolved.

EU Expert Group on the Urban Environment (1995) *European Sustainable Cities Part II*, ESDG XI, Brussels: EU Commission. An influential European review which stressed the ecosystem approach to city planning.

Laurence, R. (1999) 'Urban health: an ecological perspective', *Reviews on Environmental Health*, 14(1).

Notes

1   BBC Radio 4 broadcast on synthetic biology, July 2013.
2   Faludi, A. (1973) *A reader in planning theory* (Oxford: Pergamon Press), p. 1.
3   The definition given to me and my fellow students, which felt satisfying at the time.
4   Rydin, Y. (2011) *The purpose of planning* (Portland, OR: The Policy Press), p. 12.
5   Barton, H. and Grant, M. (2006) 'A health map for the local human habitat', *Journal of the Royal Society for the Promotion of Health*, 126(6): 1–2.
6   The discussion here draws on my first paper on the subject: Barton, H. (2005) 'A health map for urban planners: towards a conceptual model for healthy, sustainable settlements', *Built Environment*, 31(4).
7   Lynch, K. (1981) *A theory of good city form* (Cambridge, MA: MIT Press).
8   Le Corbusier: the most influential Modernist architect of the twentieth century, but one who had a disastrous, sterile impact on mid-century urban design.
9   Mumford, L. (1961) *The city in history* (Harmondsworth: Penguin).
10 Girardet, H. (2004) 'The metabolism of cities', in T. Beatley (ed.) *The sustainable urban development reader* (London: Routledge), pp. 125–132.
11 EU Expert Group on the Urban Environment (1995) *European Sustainable Cities Part II*, ESDG XI (Brussels: EU Commission).
12 Barton, H., Davis, G. and Guise, R. (1995) *Sustainable settlements: a guide for planners, designers and developers* (Luton: Local Government Management Board, and Bristol: University of the West of England).
13 Hancock, T. (1985) 'The mandala of health: a model of the human ecosystem', *Family and Community Health*, April 8(3): 1–10.
14 Barton, H., Thompson, S., Burgess, S. and Grant, M. (eds) (2015) *The Routledge handbook of planning for health and well-being* (London: Routledge), p. 11.
15 Whitehead, M. and Dahlgren, G. (1991) 'What can be done about inequalities of health?' *Lancet*, 338: 1059–1063.
16 Barton and Grant (2006), op. cit., has remained for many years one of the most downloaded articles on the University of the West of England website, with demand coming from all parts of the world. Building on note 14 above.
17 The WHO Collaborating Centre for Healthy Urban Environments, in the Faculty of Environment and Technology at the University of the West of England, Bristol.
18 Figure 2.4 is adapted from Lawrence, R. (2015) 'Mind the gap: bridging the divide between knowledge, policy and practice', in Barton *et al.* (2015), op. cit., p. 82.

II Inspiration

The questions arise: how does the planning happen? Who does the planning? What kind of city results? What kind do we want?

It may seem perverse to look for inspiration for current urban planning in patterns from the past. But many of the essential ingredients of towns have not changed as fundamentally as one might think. Towns flourish because of their geographical setting and location. They require an economic or political *raison d'être*, are often the focus of communication in a region and a market place for the exchange of goods and services; they offer employment, social and leisure opportunities to their inhabitants; they provide life support in terms of shelter, food, water, energy sources, waste treatment. Mechanical transport may have transformed the feasible scale of cities. Electricity and telecommunications may have hugely extended the range of possible human activity. Yet many elements of life are constant.

We can learn from the past. Chapter 3 is a highly selective sampling of town planning history, from classical, mediaeval and modern times, taking us up to industrial model towns of the Victorian era. It examines historical examples that can give inspiration and insight to contemporary practice. The chosen people and places demonstrate a concern for human ecology, health and well-being.

Chapter 4 takes up the story at the point where public health and town planning were reinvented in the late nineteenth century. It draws mainly on the British experience up to and including the new towns in the mid-twentieth century. During this period Britain was considered a world leader. Many of the insights and policy tools of the period are still influential today.

Chapter 5 then brings us up to date by looking at four city exemplars – Copenhagen, Kuopio, Freiburg and Portland – which demonstrate what is possible with vision and commitment, in varied cultural settings.

CHAPTER THREE

SHAFTS OF LIGHT FROM THE PAST

Introduction

The principle of consciously planning the form of cities is probably as old as cities themselves. Towns may originally have grown up as spontaneous accretions around markets for agricultural surpluses. Kostoff, in his eloquent book, *The City Shaped*, argues convincingly that these would have been temporary settlements.[1] For them to become permanent, it required chiefs and rulers to adopt them. Early cities in Egypt, Mesopotamia, China and the Indus valley were not so much accidents of economic geography, as deliberate expressions of political power – reflecting military might and defensible strongholds. Religious identities – the locus of rites and sanctuaries that expressed the deepest traditions of a tribe – were also important. The findings by archaeologists in ancient cities such as Ur, Uruk and Babylon (in Mesopotamia) and Mohenjo-Daro and Harrapa (in the Indus river valley) suggest intentional planned urban development, within city walls, with graded thoroughfares and lanes, often on an orthogonal (grid) basis. The apparent care taken to create integrated settlements around the palaces and temples suggests a concern for the well-being of the subjects – whether this was due to altruism we have to doubt. More likely, it was motivated by enlightened self-interest, prestige, military requirements and economic benefit.

The sequence of selected examples in this chapter is as follows:

- Ancient Greek planning: Hippodamus and the city of Priene;
- Roman theorist: Vitruvius;
- Mediaeval design principles and the city of Siena;
- Grand designs of the Renaissance and the Baroque – and Napoleon III's Paris;
- Ethical entrepreneurs and Saltaire.

This brings us up to the middle of the nineteenth century, before the partnership of town planning and public health was invented. The conclusion draws out the varied agencies involved in planning, their commitment to humane planning, and the range of spatial principles adopted.

Hippodamus and the city of Priene

Greek and Roman city planners and writers (two or three millennia after the earliest cities) were quite explicit about social and health principles in city planning. Hippodamus, credited with being the 'father of town planning', provides the starting point. He lived in the fifth century BC (498–408), the classical Greek era, coinciding with Pericles' Athens and the construction of the Parthenon. He was an architect-planner, physician and philosopher. He would have known Hippocrates, the 'father of medicine' who was born about 40 years later on the Greek island of Kos, and was equally long-lived. We know nothing about Hippodamus through his own writings but only through the writings of others, in particular, the great Greek philosopher Aristotle.

Hippodamus' reputation as the father of town planning rests on his advocacy of a simple orthogonal grid for the street pattern of towns, with careful placing of principal public buildings and spaces to provide for markets, meeting places, temples, theatres, gymnasia, and civic halls. He believed the city should reflect the social order and through its form promote social cohesion. He re-planned his home town of Miletus, in Ionia, on these principles, winning such renown that he was employed by Pericles to plan the new Athenian port of Piraeus. He and his followers designed Greek colonies around the Mediterranean. Hippodamus was by no means the first to apply the grid idea to town planning, but he developed it in such a way that the 'Miletian grid' became very influential across the Greek and then the Roman world (Figure 3.1).

Many settlements lacked such a clear structure. They had grown incrementally over centuries, often with narrow, winding streets clustering around aristocratic, religious and civic institutions. Hippodamus, reacting to his own experience, found them inefficient. He considered they were problematic for wheeled traffic such as carts and chariots to negotiate; it was difficult to develop and redevelop buildings because of awkwardly shaped plots; and it was almost impossible to deal with sewage effectively.

His younger colleague, Hippocrates, made the link between environment and health explicit in his treatise, 'On airs, waters and places'. Hippocrates refuted the commonplace assumption of his time, that illness stemmed from the intervention of the gods, arguing that the social and environmental conditions explained the patterns of disease, health and well-being. He adopted what we might call an *ecological* perspective, seeing life and place in the round.[2] Plato agreed. In *Critias*, he chastised the Greeks for destroying the fertility of the soil, the reliability of the water supply and the temperance of climate through over-exploitation of the land and the forests.[3]

The city of Priene,[4] in Ionia, designed on the Miletian pattern, escaped the ravages of war and the substantial reconstruction in

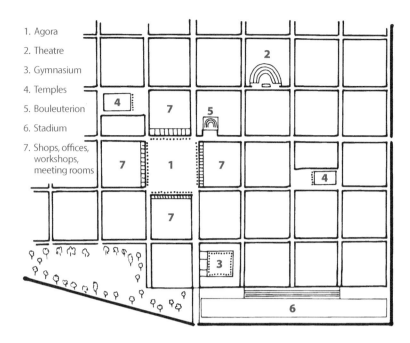

1. Agora
2. Theatre
3. Gymnasium
4. Temples
5. Bouleuterion
6. Stadium
7. Shops, offices, workshops, meeting rooms

Fig 3.1 *An illustrative town plan based on Hippodamus' principles*

Priene's population

6,000 is the figure often quoted but it is not at all clear whether this total included slaves as well as free men and their families. The fact that the theatre held 6,500 indicates to me that the total population may well have been substantially greater, at least for a time.

Roman, Byzantine and Turkish eras which affected many greater cities. It may well be the best-preserved Hellenistic city. Priene's village origins are uncertain, but from the fifth century BC, it was an Athenian colony, a trading centre on the Aegean Sea. It was rebuilt around 350 BC. Alexander the Great supported its construction as a model city, following Hippodamus' principles.

Priene flourished as a port and religio-political focus for the 12 cities of Ionia, with a population believed to be around 6,000–10,000 people, thus more comparable in our own day to a small market town or urban neighbourhood (Figure 3.2). The city is built on four broad terraces on the side of a hill, with river wharfs at the bottom, and the acropolis at the summit of the rocky outcrop above. The orthogonal grid of streets was laid down across the terraces, with steps between levels. The grid creates adaptable development blocks circa 60 x 60 metres. The site is now pleasantly green, but beneath the trees you can see something of the quality of the place. The marble, peristyle (i.e. courtyard) houses on the main terrace were generous in size, some with two storeys, many with direct water supply, indoor toilets and connection to the city sewer system. Elsewhere the less affluent population was no doubt in wooden or wattle and daub houses, which have left few traces. The streets were stone-paved, with water fountains and sculptural features.

At the heart of the city, within easy walking distance of the whole, is the agora – a substantial square providing for markets and events, surrounded by colonnaded buildings serving as offices, shops and meeting rooms, creating the social hub of the city. Nearby is the splendid, well-preserved theatre, with seating for 6,500 people curved into the hillside – large enough for all or most of the inhabitants. On either side of the city are the upper and lower

Fig 3.2 *An imagined aerial view of Priene*
Source: Author, photo of an on-site display board.

gymnasia, offering physical activities and baths for all, and schooling for children. Next to the lower gymnasia is the stadium, with
seating tiered up on one side, nearly 200 metres long. Towering
over all, on the top terrace, is the temple to Athena, the largest of
several temples in the city.

The rigid grid might be expected to contradict the natural lie of the
land, but in fact responds well to the steep contours of the hill, some
streets lying more or less along the contours, others stepped down
across them, reflecting the terrace levels; the tilt of the site affords
superb views – not least from the agora. The streets themselves
have a domestic, small-scale character, contrasting with the grand
principal buildings.

All this suggests a society which was surprisingly affluent, but
more than that, planned for the well-being of its members – their
physical, social, cultural and spiritual well-being. Few present-day
settlements of equivalent size offer the same level of service. We
know that there was inequality: a powerful aristocracy, women disenfranchised, a society reliant on slavery. Yet decision-making, following the Athenian tradition, was based on a form of participatory
democracy, involving all adult propertied men. This becomes visible
at the Bouleuterion, the council chamber (Figure 3.3). It has seating
space for 500, and these men were able to determine much of

Fig 3.3 *Priene: the council chamber; and a street*

the policy for the city, and appoint the secretariat. The city was from time to time absorbed within conquering empires, but it seems to have survived as a political entity, only fading as a city when the port silted up in early Byzantine times.

We can see many echoes of the Miletian grid and the coherent planning of Priene in subsequent eras: the Roman forts and cities, including London, follow similar principles; the bastides (military towns) of mediaeval France, the colonial cities of North and South America, Asia and Australasia – wherever, in effect, new settlements or rapid expansion call for a clear urban framework.

What, then, do we learn from Hippodamus and Priene?

- The town planners of Priene, inspired by Hippodamus, saw the city as a whole, and produced a remarkable and civilized habitat, which can still act as a model for contemporary designers.

'The town planners of Priene, inspired by Hippodamus, saw the city as a whole, and produced a remarkable and civilized habitat, which can still act as a model for contemporary designers.'

- The economic *raison d'être* of a town is very important in deciding the location. When the original site of Priene proved non-viable, by 350 BC, because of river changes, the city moved. It then flourished for as long as its port remained viable.
- The street pattern of a town is one of its most permanent features, outlasting individual buildings, shaping the development sites, still visible after 2,000 years.
- The Miletian grid can, if well planned with squares and public facilities, provide a simple and effective structure for urban development, offering excellent permeability and the possibility of incremental renewal as needs change.
- The agora provides a model for the heart of a town: space for markets and events, buildings for many purposes, colonnades providing communal shelter from sun or rain, the whole designed to encourage social interaction and a sense of shared identity.
- The motivation of decision-makers is critical – and in the case of Priene, the evidence suggests they were concerned with the well-being and quality of life of the residents. Priene demonstrates that coherent town planning does not have to depend on centralized autocratic power – municipal democracy can deliver exemplary results.

Vitruvius: Roman theorist

Vitruvius, living in the Roman world in the first century BC, was another multi-talented designer: engineer, architect and planner. He produced one of the seminal books on design, the multi-volume work *De Architectura*, and is famous for specifying three principles of good design: durability, utility and beauty.

Vitruvius was explicit about the siting and design of human settlements. He wrote that it was vital to choose a healthy site, neither too hot nor too cold, neither exposed to frost nor to foul mists from stagnant marshes, nor to risk of flooding or poor drainage. He emphasized the importance of good water quality and farmland. He saw the city as being part of the landscape. It should be located where

'Vitruvius' three principles of good design: durability, utility and beauty.'

excellent communication by sea, river and land was possible, and good defensive walls could be constructed.

His design principles within the town show the same awareness of environment. Streets, alleys and house plots were arranged with regard to climatic conditions: for example, in hot climes ensuring that cool rooms were available facing away from the sun, to store grain and wine; and that the courtyard dwellings shut out the cold winter winds while offering shade in summer. Public buildings should be carefully sited – central in the town if inland, close to the harbour if on the coast. In contrast to the Miletian grid, Vitruvius advocated star-shaped cities, with streets radiating from the centre, giving optimum access. He believed, like today's public health professionals, that walking in the open air is good for you, giving both healthy exercise and contact with nature. He suggested that colonnades and walking routes should be embellished with greenery, helping to purify the air, with groves of trees providing resting places. Some colonnades should be covered, so athletes can run in winter protected from the elements.

With the exception of the radial as opposed to grid form, all that Vitruvius advocated was consistent with the Hippodamian principles visible in Priene, and with the ecological view of Hippocrates. His influence has extended through subsequent ages, particularly when his works were rediscovered in the Renaissance. His principles of durability, utility and beauty are as relevant now as then.

The mediaeval city: Siena

On the face of it mediaeval settlements appear very different from the ordered cities of the Greek and Roman worlds. The mediaeval cores of many modern cities in Europe and the Middle East show a much more organic tangle of urban development. Streets wind, alleys are narrow, often impassable for vehicles. Grand mansions, churches and town halls rear up unexpectedly in bustling streets, and only in the market square, or where a cathedral is close, or by the river, does the town open up to give a sense of bigger space.

This informal layout, often influenced by the terrain, is now considered attractive, even romantic. The great writer on cities, Lewis Mumford, eulogizes the unpredictable character, the variety, verticality and sense of surprise of mediaeval cities. He sees them as works of art, the setting for pageants and ceremonies, finding delight in the blocked vistas, soaring spires, sharp gables, and sense of urban enclosure balanced by productive open fields immediately around.[5] Gordon Cullen, who coined the term *townscape*, constructed a whole language of urban design to express the character and sense of place of mediaeval streets and spaces.[6]

But it would be a mistake to think of such towns as unplanned. Town building was one of the great enterprises of the Middle Ages, at least until the Black Death. State, church and trade interests all took a hand. The influence of the kings and nobles was paramount in many settlements, with castles and city walls and the main gates defining shape. Awe-inspiring cathedrals – still in many cities today the largest structures – dominated the sense of place. The monastic orders commandeered space around cathedrals and elsewhere, often constructing buildings for social purposes: hospitals, schools, foundling homes, alms-houses. The rising merchant class formed trade-based guilds competing with the traditional powers, founding their own mutual-help institutions, and influencing the priorities for street planning.

The town council, elected by the burgers of the town, was commercially oriented. The broad market streets and squares, the town hall, the main streets giving access to and from the rural hinterland for produce, relied on agreement and co-ordination. In many places building ordinances determined the shape of building plots and width of streets. We would call these ordinances *design codes.* Frontages onto the streets were strictly controlled to allow trading possibilities to as many households as possible – hence the narrow mediaeval ('Burbage') plots we still see in old towns. The town buildings themselves were linked to form terraces, with common frontage, though heights and styles could vary greatly. Design codes were instituted in London in 1200, following a disastrous fire. They specified minimum street widths, building lines and materials to reduce future fire risk.[7]

The siting of towns responded to markets, defensive needs, landscape and the availability of water. Building ordinances, plot controls, street design codes, combined with the pre-emptive power of the king, barons, church and monastic authorities, meant that the European mediaeval city – however organic it may feel – was subject to many plans. Sometimes, indeed, it seems the layout was based on an intentional aesthetic effect, with subtle decisions being made about the form of market squares and street alignments designed to delight users and frame views, indicating creative minds at work. Siena is one city that excites admiration.

'Design codes were instituted in London in 1200, following a disastrous fire. They specified minimum street widths, building lines and materials to reduce future fire risk.'

Siena

Visiting this Tuscan city now, one is immediately aware of the degree to which the form of the place, and many of the buildings, reflect its mediaeval flourishing. Later ages have not subdued it. It is still a hill town, with close-knit, intense development extending along the ridges, culminating in the central piazza, with green valleys between. The streets are narrow and gently curving, with buildings of several storeys fronting directly on to them. The plots have in many cases been almost completely filled with buildings, severely restricting light access and garden opportunities in the inner courtyards. But the green valleys – with allotments, fields and recreational facilities – are close by, allowing the city to breathe. The Piazza del Campo, at the heart of the city, is a miraculous space (Figure 3.4). Shaped like a scallop shell, completely surrounded by civic and multi-use buildings, it has a curved sloping surface that invites relaxation and focuses visual attention on the tall city tower at the lower side. People linger there, drawn by the social ambience, the street-opening cafés and the sheer quality of space. It is a place for planned and spontaneous meetings, chance encounters, hatching plots, flirtations, dreams. Every year it hosts the famous Palio, where tribal neighbourhood groups compete in wild horse-racing.

Fig 3.4 *Aerial photograph of Siena*
Source: Google images, downloaded 1 Feb. 2016.

The glory days of Siena, as a centre of power competing in importance with Florence, were the later Middle Ages. The city became
a self-governing commune in the twelfth century, with nobles and
commoners sharing influence. In the following century the city implemented a series of projects: the cathedral, the university, the Piazza
del Campo and new streets giving centrality to the Campo.[8] The city
council had a clear vision, valuing the sinuous interplay of the streets,
paving the main thoroughfares and the Campo in brick, insisting that

> It redounds to the beauty of the city of Siena and to the satisfaction of
> almost all the people of the city, that any edifices that are to be made
> anew anywhere along the public thoroughfares … proceed in line with
> the existing buildings, and one building not stand out beyond another,
> but they shall be disposed and arranged equally so as to be of greatest
> beauty for the city.[9]

How far health and well-being were drivers of Siena's development
is difficult to say. The council emphasized aesthetic quality, economic and social opportunity, and strong city identity – all important
for health – but probably greatly underplayed the importance of
clean water and sewage treatment. Siena illustrates the strengths of
the organic approach to planning. The shape of the city, the alignment of streets and the slope of the Campo follow the landscape

Fig 3.5 *The Siena Campo and close-knit streets*

(Figure 3.5). Change occurred not through some grand plan, but through incremental decisions, responding to problems, pressures and opportunities as they arose, creating a unique place. Many other mediaeval towns in their own context echo the elements and principles visible in Siena.

Sixteen hundred years separate the planning of Priene and Siena. Despite the formality of one and the informality of the other, both exhibit characteristics that are humane, practical and attractive. Both seem designed for quality of life. Both had city-state powers and a significant degree of citizen involvement (proto-democracy) at key stages of development. Unlike the views expressed by thinkers like Vitruvius and Mumford, one city design is not *right* and the other *wrong*. We can learn a lot from both.

Grand designs

Formality of design was not lost in the Middle Ages. The fortified bastides in France illustrate the persistence of grid layouts, modelled on Roman originals, when kings were establishing or re-establishing authority over territory. But it was during the Renaissance, and even more the Baroque, as the power of monarchs, counts and earls increased, that a new imposed grandeur affected city form.

The architect Alberti, working in Florence at the birth of the Renaissance, reworked Vitruvius' treatise on design. He enjoyed the curved streets of mediaeval towns, with their ever-changing views giving interest to the traveller and vitality to the town. But for major centres of power, he advocated formal grandeur. 'The principal ornament of a city,' he said, 'is the orderly arrangement of streets, squares and buildings according to their dignity and their function.' Later Italian designers, following this lead, sometimes equated order with an idealized pattern – such as a circular walled city, radial ceremonial routes leading from city gates to the imposing central space and a perfect spider's web of lesser streets. This was, perhaps, more a question of playing with designer patterns than town planning. Alberti's own approach was more nuanced, recognizing context and valuing variety.

The noble visions of Renaissance designers – grand squares and circuses, linked by wide straight streets and bold diagonals, with vistas culminating in monuments and civic/religious buildings – evolved into the Baroque. In London, following the Great Fire, there were brave attempts at city planning by Christopher Wren and John Evelyn. Their motivations were not simply inspired by the new aesthetics, but by the need to create a city that reduced fire risk and allowed healthy air circulation. Their ideas foundered on the complexities of land ownership and private rights, but post-fire London established patterns of regulated city planning that helped to shape the city we see now. Subsequently plans for other capitals often employed the Baroque palette – in Washington, St. Petersburg, Delhi and Canberra. London's grandest example, eventually, was Nash's urban renewal project, with Regent Street integrated into the older street network and linking through to the new royal Regent's Park. In the eighteenth and early nineteenth centuries, enterprising entrepreneurs applied Baroque order on a more domestic scale for the fashionable classes. London squares, with their grand town houses and generous recreational greens, had both aesthetic and health appeal.

British Baroque

There are many famous examples of Baroque civic design in Britain. Edinburgh New Town, Bath's Crescent, Circus and Square, and London's Regent's Park and Regent Street stand out.

Paris re-imagined: Baroque planning with a human face

A late – and famous – flourishing of Baroque design occurred in Napoleonic France. Paris as we know it now, within the Périphérique, was largely created in the nineteenth century, following the radical principles pursued by Napoleons I and III. The great boulevards, wide public spaces, extensive parklands, substantial housing blocks and noble buildings at key locations – all succeed (with a little help from the French lifestyle) in making central Paris a dream city, a city of romance. But the vanity of emperors was not the only motivation. Re-making the city was a radical response to the squalid, diseased conditions experienced by the populace.

Some of the most famous landmarks, such as the Champs-Elysées and the Arc de Triomphe, were constructed early, responding to the grandiose pretentions of Louis XV and Napoleon Bonaparte. But the key driver of the Parisian Renaissance was Napoleon III, in the mid-nineteenth century, partnered by the engineer, Baron Haussmann. One reason for his innovations was the need to police the streets effectively after the 1848 riots, but his writings reveal that he recognized the need for a new approach to the development of the city that could combat the overcrowding, pollution and disease. Remarkably his insight had been previewed early in the revolutionary period. The *Plan de la Commission des Artistes* (1793) was inspired by the revolutionary principle of making a city fit for all, a city people could enjoy. Patrick Abercrombie called this plan 'one of the most remarkable pieces of town planning in existence'.[10]

Napoleon III lived for many years in exile in England in the 1830s and 1840s. It was an experience that had a profound influence on his approach to Parisian planning, both negatively and positively. Negatively he was shocked by the appalling conditions in which the new industrial working classes found themselves living. Positively, he was impressed by the way London had well-regulated estate development – Bloomsbury, Mayfair, Belgravia – and was planning new thoroughfares and parks.

In 1848, Napoleon was back in Paris when 18,000 Parisians died of cholera. It was evident that poor housing and poor sanitation were to blame. He launched Paris' earliest social housing project, which set the pattern for much of what happened later as the low rise slums were cleared: town houses/flats of five or six storeys built round a courtyard, with a concierge. He commissioned a new Parisian drainage system, learning from Victorian London. Haussmann was appointed to manage urban change – expressly to convert Paris into a 'ville verte' (green city). New parks, such as the Bois de Boulogne and the Parc Monceau, were created, following the English landscape tradition, and in 17 years more than 600,000 trees were planted.[11] Haussmann co-ordinated the replacement of the mediaeval street pattern by boulevards, new extensions of the city and the construction of many more houses than were demolished. He instituted building regulations and helped to establish the design codes and conventions that made the Paris of today (Figure 3.6). Critics pointed to the loss of historic streets and to social disruption, but the improvement of living conditions and health of the poor was a considerable achievement.

In all this, Napoleon, guiding the process, had a very clear philosophy. He saw city planning as an integrated, strategic activity, supporting social, economic, environmental and aesthetic ends. The prestige and economic success of the city depended on its attractiveness and healthiness. He successfully used the market pressures for stylish new quarters to subsidize the creation of parks for all, and saw the tremendous ecological and recreational value of green open space. In some ways, he can claim to be the first modern planner.

Ethical entrepreneurs

In nineteenth-century Britain, most urban expansion was controlled by the new industrial barons – concerned with profit, exploiting natural and human resources mercilessly. But there were exceptions. Some capitalists recognized the inequities of the new industrial system sooner than others. One of the first, lighting a utopian beacon that would influence later nineteenth-century tycoons, was Robert Owen. He was horrified by the unhealthy cellars and garrets of

'The Plan de la Commission des Artistes (1793) was inspired by the revolutionary principle of making a city fit for all, a city people could enjoy. Patrick Abercrombie called this plan "one of the most remarkable pieces of town planning in existence".'

Fig 3.6 Paris: *grand courtyard blocks; and urban parks*

the Scottish tenements. He became a social reformer, believing that environmental and material conditions, health and education facilities, access to good food, all managed through mutual co-operation, would improve the character of the poor and promote well-being. The ideal industrial village of New Lanark, on the upper River Clyde (providing power), exemplified his principles. Under the guiding hand of this paternalistic autocrat, children were brought up with 'good habits', 'rationally educated' and subsequently their labour was 'usefully directed'.[12] Mutuality and shared facilities ensured that social distress and pauperism were banished.

Saltaire was a mid-century industrial village (almost a town) that took these ideas a stage further. Titus Salt – an innovative industrialist and devout Congregationalist– rose from the bottom to own a series of mills in Bradford, making worsted from Alpaca wool. In 1848, he became Lord Mayor of Bradford, concerned about the dire health consequences of the poor housing, open sewers, dung heaps and swill tubs. A year later he decided to escape the city grime, moving all his factories to one giant new building to the north, and creating the model settlement of Saltaire. His motivation seems to have been a combination of concern for the welfare of his workers and enlightened self-interest. He is quoted as saying, 'I will do all I can to avoid evils so great as those resulting from polluted air and water, and hope to draw around me a well-fed, contented and happy body of operatives.'[13]

The town was located in pleasant countryside, next to the River Aire and straddling the Leeds and Liverpool canal, not much more than an hour's walk from the centre of Bradford. It was designed as a compact grid of streets with generous terraced houses, for the most part without gardens. The whole emphasis was on shared facilities: a wash-house powered by steam engines for washing and drying; public baths; a range of shops; assembly hall, library, hospital, school and gymnasium; social rooms for smoking, billiards, art, science; alms-houses; allotments within a couple of hundred metres of all residents; five varied places of worship (of a strictly puritan persuasion); and around the residential area and the factory buildings, parks with floral displays and space for play: cricket, croquet, bowls, encouraging recreational activity – all this for a population that might have been not much more than 5,000 souls.

Saltaire was a factory town. The mill was one of the largest in the world, the length of St Paul's in London, with a formidably tall chimney taking the fumes away. The residents' daily lives were shaped by the vision of one man. Salt acted in a way we might now consider tyrannical: no advertising, no washing to be hung on lines outside the dwellings, no alcoholic liquor (no pub!). But the houses were all of superior quality, designed to last. Salt was perhaps the first to conduct a survey of workers' actual housing needs, and on that basis built a range of sizes/styles to suit different families and income levels.

'Salt acted in a way we might now consider tyrannical: no advertising, no washing to be hung on lines outside the dwellings, no alcoholic liquor (no pub!).'

Conclusion

It is evident from these examples that town planning is an ancient skill, not a recent invention. The planning may be by public authorities, powerful vested interests, or established custom. In the case of Priene, the decisions were taken, as far as we know, by a democratic council; in Sienna, by civic and religious elites; in Paris, by Napoleonic diktat; in Saltaire, by a powerful industrialist. This diversity makes the point that planning is not just done by civic authorities.

There are contrasting mechanisms of planning. In the case of Priene, the Miletian grid with its central agora and social provision provided the framework within which domestic and commercial activities could evolve, with buildings renewed as necessary. The mediaeval approach, despite the more organic forms of growth, also allowed progressive renewal within a strong design code. The Baroque vision was of a much more integrated, finished design, intended to impress.

In all the cases here, the well-being of residents was a prime consideration, even while other political and commercial priorities were also pursued. Priene is astonishing in its apparently careful and comprehensive planning for human well-being. Titus Salt went further, attempting to shape the morality as well as the health of his employees. In all cases – most notably in Parisian reconstruction – the relationship of urban dwellers to the natural environment was valued. The ancient theorists, from Hippodamus and Hippocrates to Vitruvius, had a profound understanding of the relationship of cities to the land and to climate. They understood human ecology in a way substantially lost in recent centuries, only now being rediscovered.

Further reading

Kostoff, S. (1991) *The city shaped: urban patterns and meanings through history.* London: Thames and Hudson. A tour-de-force survey of varied urban forms and designs through history, copiously illustrated.

Mumford, L. (1961) *The city in history: its origins, transformations and prospects.* London: Penguin. The classic, if dated, text on city evolution and planning, from the earliest times. Full of insight.

Notes

1 Kostoff, S. (1991) *The city shaped: urban patterns and meanings through history* (London: Thames and Hudson).
2 Laurence, R. (1999) 'Urban health: an ecological perspective', *Reviews on Environmental Health,* 14(1).
3 See a translated extract of *Critias* in Barton, H. and Bruder, N. (1995) *A guide to local environmental auditing* (London: Earthscan), p. 6.
4 The analysis of Priene is my own, drawing on a site visit and a wide range of book and internet sources.
5 Mumford, L. (1961) *The city in history: its origins, transformations and prospects* (London: Penguin).
6 Cullen, G. (1961) *Townscape* (London: Architectural Press).
7 For more information on mediaeval town building, see Marshall, S. (ed.) (2011) *Urban coding and planning* (London: Routledge); and

Gironard, M. (1990) *The English town* (New Haven, CT: Yale University Press).
8 For an excellent potted history of Siena, see Wikipedia.
9 As quoted in Kostoff (1991) op.cit. p. 70
10 Abercrombie, P. (1912) 'Paris: some influences that have shaped its growth', *Town Planning Review,* 2(4), quoted by planning historian Michael Devereux in lecture notes (pers. comm.).
11 De Moncan, P. (2009) *Les jardins de Haussmann* (Paris: Les Editions des Mecène), p. 9, quoted by Mike Devereux in lecture notes (pers. comm.).
12 Owen (1813), quoted in Cherry, G. (1988) *Cities and plans: the shaping of urban Britain in the nineteenth and twentieth centuries* (London: Edward Arnold), p. 8.
13 Salt (1849), quoted in Bell, C. and Bell, R. (1969) *City fathers: the early history of town planning in Britain* (London: Barrie and Rockliff, the Cresset Press), p. 188.

CHAPTER FOUR

THE EMERGENCE OF MODERN PLANNING

Chapter 3 took us in giant steps across nearly two and a half thousand years, showing that town planning was an ancient art pursued for many practical reasons, and sometimes with the well-being of residents as a powerful motivation. The last two examples, in France and Britain, were responding to the Industrial Revolution and urbanization in the nineteenth century. This chapter takes up the story, more in terms of institutional, professional and policy development. It draws mainly on the British experience from the mid-nineteenth to the mid-twentieth century, up to and including the new towns. While other countries were innovating during the same period, Britain was leader of the pack. Many of the insights and policy tools of this period are still influential today.

The public health revolution

In the nineteenth century, Britain was the workshop of the world. The population was growing and cities were burgeoning at the kind of pace now seen in parts of Asia, Africa and America. Awareness of the dire conditions in which the working classes lived in Britain was widespread. The causes of death were widely recognized for the first time in the middle of the nineteenth century and the public health movement gained momentum.

Commentators such as Frederick Engels described in graphic detail the 'Condition of the working class in England' (1845). Novels by Charles Kingsley, Elizabeth Gaskell and especially Charles Dickens – for example, *Bleak House* (1853) and *Little Dorrit* (1857) – challenged the conscience of the nation. Most significant from the official view-point was a voluminous report commissioned by the House of Lords: the *General Report on the Sanitary Conditions of the Labouring Classes of Great Britain, 1842.* Written by Edwin Chadwick, the report

A COURT FOR KING CHOLERA.

Fig 4.1 *At the court of King Cholera*

Source: Google images

demonstrated the relationship between the urban environment, sanitary conditions, overcrowding and health (Figure 4.1). It revealed the shockingly brief life expectancy in some urban areas by comparison with rural life, and the discrepancy between social classes. Typically labourers in the cities lived only half as long as gentry in the same city and as labourers in the country.[1]

It took some time for legislators to accept limits on the free market. The inability of municipalities to tackle the basic life support issues of squalid housing and poor sanitation was shocking. But there was tremendous resistance to any extension of public regulation and taxation. Then, in 1867, the Second Reform Act extended voting for the first time to the male working classes, tripling the electorate and gradually transforming the way political leaders thought and acted. Public Health Acts in the 1870s made urban local authorities fully responsible for sanitation, able to impose standards on developers and co-ordinate sewage systems effectively. It became possible for municipalities to adopt model by-law building codes, stipulating minimum housing standards, street widths and natural lighting requirements, that began to tackle not just sanitation but construction, air quality, space and overcrowding. The result was a progressive improvement in living conditions, though by-law housing became a by-word for monotonous, regimented streets of identical dwellings.

In parallel with concern for housing quality and sanitation, there was a movement for open space within cities, to compensate those living in narrow courts and confined streets. The motivations were fresh air, the opportunity for healthy physical exercise and the enjoyment of nature. Initially private donors, and eventually public authorities (following legislation), began to provide parks, pleasure gardens and botanic gardens. Britain had an unrivalled tradition of landscape gardening, for the rich and privileged. The Victorian parks, such as Phillips, Queens and Alexandra Parks in Manchester, reinvented this great tradition for the urban setting, establishing green lungs in areas that have since become inner cities – and the envy of many continental cities.

Thus, on a number of fronts, concern for a civilized, healthy environment led to innovation in law and practice during the manic urban growth in nineteenth-century Britain. Professional expertise grew in relation to the linked areas of public health, environmental health, town planning, landscape design and architecture. But most features of town development were still lacking in co-ordination. The pattern of industrial and residential development was a haphazard patchwork, with one development often at odds with its neighbours, lacking adequate connections and integration. The railway companies ran their new lines roughshod over existing communities. Pollution from coal fires and industrial processes poisoned the air. Homes were overcrowded and streets congested; extreme poverty and poor health existed alongside unprecedented wealth and well-being. Stimulated by the radical politics of socialists, anarchists and the Arts and Crafts movement, there was the expectation of strong public action: for the voracious landlords to be regulated, for land to be nationalized. Even an establishment figure like Winston Churchill was moved to declare, much later: 'In this country we have long enjoyed the blessings of Free Trade and untaxed bread, but against these inestimable benefits we have the evils of an unreformed and vicious land system.'[2]

In this context, the Housing and Planning Act of 1909 was an inadequate response. Yet from the healthy environment perspective it broke new ground. It was the first legislative instrument to use the new-fangled term 'town planning'. Planning was explicitly related to health, seeing the purpose of planning as creating an environment where all people could enjoy a healthy and fulfilling life. It was legislatively less adventurous than the rhetoric, but did encourage and allow municipalities to work with landowners to produce planning schemes for the development of new suburbs.

'Winston Churchill was moved to declare: "In this country we have long enjoyed the blessings of Free Trade and untaxed bread, but against these inestimable benefits we have the evils of an unreformed and vicious land system."'

Ebenezer Howard and Garden Cities

The prophet of the new planning was Ebenezer Howard. He interpreted the pent-up social radicalism of the time into practical spatial proposals which influenced the emerging planning profession not only in Britain but internationally. His most important contribution was to recognize that cities needed to be planned on a city region scale – creating new settlements to relieve the pressure on the polluted, overcrowded industrial towns. His vision was of 'garden cities' that combined excellent train access to the mother city, with excellent local services and interaction with the productive countryside:

> There is not only – as is so constantly assumed – town life and country life, but a third alternative in which all the advantages of the most energetic and active town life, with all the beauty and delight of the country, may be secured in perfect combination.
>
> (Howard, 1902, quoted in Cherry, 1988 see further reading)

This was not primarily an aesthetic vision, however. Howard's motivation sprang from concern for social justice – the possibility of a good life for all. His garden city was to provide for all classes, including the poor, the old and the destitute. Land reform, to counteract the inequities of the market, was essential. The countryside around the town was to provide opportunities for allotments, small-holdings and recreation for the town dwellers; for convalescent homes and therapeutic farms; for production of perishable foods, wood and building materials. This echoed the utopian ideals of William Morris, the influential thinker and designer, who dreamt of egalitarian communities living in a rural/urban idyll, at one with their natural environment.[3]

Howard's famous schematic diagram of the garden city model (Figure 4.2) was quite explicit about spatial scale. The tributary towns should be around 1000 acres (400 hectares) and cater for 32,000 people.

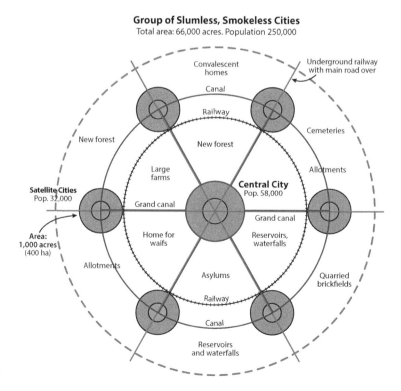

Group of Slumless, Smokeless Cities
Total area: 66,000 acres. Population 250,000

Fig 4.2 Howard's garden city model (as interpreted by the author)

His design ensured that everyone lived less than 800 metres from the town centre, industrial areas, railway station *and* open country, and less than 200 metres from open greenspace. In these insights he was building on his own experience but also being remarkably prescient. Howard's strategy and standards remain relevant today – promoting green, convivial, sustainable and healthy cities.

Letchworth Garden City

Howard's ideas rapidly became the catalyst for a remarkable movement. His book, *Tomorrow: A Peaceful Path to Real Reform,* which came out in 1898, was substantially revised as *Garden Cities of Tomorrow* in 1902.[4] Garden Cities Associations sprang up in Britain and a number of other countries. Howard was preaching a gospel whose time had come, catching people's imagination across the world.

In 1903, the site of what was to become Letchworth Garden City, to the north of London, was purchased by a specially formed company. The concept owes much to Howard, but the physical form owes more to the earlier developments at Bourneville and Port Sunlight. Letchworth has a laid-back, spacious layout: detached and semi-detached housing with generous gardens; ample open space and communal facilities; a mixed-use town centre right next to the train station giving regional access; streets curving in sympathy with the topography and landscape features. In reaction to the serried ranks of Victorian terraces, the town had a new visual quality given by the informal layout and a vernacular style of architecture, influenced by the Arts and Crafts movement (Figure 4.3).

Ironically, Letchworth's plan does not follow Howard's scheme. Where Howard's model imagined high density small towns within the garden of the food-producing countryside, the design for Letchworth made the town itself into a garden.

The Letchworth planners had a powerful social impetus. The private ownership of land was abolished. All land was held in trust for the community through a 'Co-operative Land Society'. Rental income from homes and businesses gave a secure income to the town, which paid for services, maintenance and improvements – a revolutionary principle. It was feasible to provide a good stock of affordable housing, and poorer residents were enabled to avoid the conventional landlord/tenant relationship through co-partnership housing and self-management. This approach was designed to give a greater sense of control over their own environment to tenant families, enhancing confidence and well-being, and building what we might now call 'social capital'.

Sadly this admirable system has not been sustained because of the late twentieth-century (Thatcherite) policy of selling off council homes to long-standing tenants. In time those new owners sell on to others at a premium price, reflecting the high quality environment. Affordability has been sacrificed on the altar of home ownership. This has also resulted in loss of income to the Letchworth Trust from housing land – though the Trust retains ownership and income from commercial developments.

'The Letchworth planners had a powerful social impetus. The private ownership of land was abolished. All land was held in trust for the community through a "Co-operative Land Society".'

Fig 4.3 *Letchworth: the town as garden, spacious residential streets and public spaces setting a trend for later suburbia*

Subsequent garden cities and suburbs improved on some aspects of Letchworth but lost others. Hampstead Garden Suburb, for example, was on one level impressive – a refined realization of the functional and picturesque aspects, retaining initial affordability and co-operative principles. But the mere fact of being a suburb, not a free-standing town, deserted Howard's original impulse. It was a pragmatic acceptance of the inevitability of contiguous urban growth, and as such gave an admirable vision of suburban quality. But it was also a dangerous precedent – setting a trend for suburban sprawl (rarely of equivalent quality) for a century to follow.

The pioneers in Britain and America

Raymond Unwin was one of the key players in the garden city movement in the early days in Britain. He was influential as the chief
planner of both Letchworth and Hampstead, and one of the first
people to call himself a 'town planner'. He trained as an engineer,
was profoundly affected by socialist and co-operative ideas, and
impressed by innovative German approaches to the planning of
town extensions: powers of land assembly, balancing private ownership rights with community rights.

Unwin articulated principles of good civic design, producing
the first modern primer in 1909: *Town Planning in Practice: An
Introduction to the Art of Designing Cities and Suburbs.*[5] He aimed
to raise the debate about town planning above the political arguments over the protection of private property rights. The book was
translated into French, German and Russian. One principle he set
out for new housing – a density (excluding roads) of 12 houses to
the acre (30 to the hectare) – was adopted by the 'Homes for Heroes'
programme after the First World War, and followed by generations
of planners and suburban developers. His logic was that 12 dpa
(dwellings per acre) gave a fair level of accessibility to facilities while
allowing gardens of sufficient size to be of food-growing value to
tenants.

There were flows of ideas both ways across the Atlantic. In America,
as in Britain, the challenge was to humanize the rapid growth of
cities. Unwin was very impressed with Daniel Burnham's 1909 plan
for Chicago. This was a comprehensive spatial plan for a conurbation (one of the first) following 'City Beautiful' principles. Burnham
believed economic renaissance would be triggered by the creation of
a beautiful urban environment, and succeeded in bringing together
business leaders, politicians and public officials in partnership. His
plan led to the creation of the iconic Chicago waterfront, community
centres and playgrounds within half a mile of every house, spacious
parks, and a green girdle around the city designed to purify the air,
grow food for the city, and provide recreation opportunities.

Patrick Geddes

Another figure of the early twentieth century who bestrode planning practice was Patrick Geddes (1854–1932). He was a brilliant and
original thinker, garnering ideas from many spheres of knowledge,
converting them into coherent practical principles, and inspiring
a generation of planners. He pioneered an understanding of the
relationship of human activity to the natural environment, applying
biological theories to human settlements. The city, he said, was an
organism. As such, its metabolism was dependent on the wider
environment – its habitat. Geddes distilled his conception of the city
into three words: *place, folk, work.*

His reputation was established in Edinburgh. Geddes lived in a
slum tenement in the Old Town. He tried to work out how to achieve
synergistic solutions to the overlapping problems of public health,
poor housing, overcrowding and social segregation. Rather than the

*'Geddes distilled his conception
of the city into three words:
place, folk, work.'*

kneejerk reaction of demolish and rebuild, effectively dispossessing the existing residents, he promoted rehabilitation. He raised money and worked out how to renovate the slums – involving residents and volunteers in a painstaking process of piecemeal renewal, retaining the existing population while introducing student halls of residence to diversify the social milieu and stimulate cultural development.

Later, working across the world as a planner, he continued to pursue the principle of working with people to find solutions. He relied on local knowledge and co-operative schemes, and what we might now call 'appropriate technology', for example, in relation to water supply and sewage treatment in India. Sometimes, as the planning guru under pressure to produce instant solutions to huge problems, his plans may have been less than thoroughly researched. But he was ahead of his time in seeing settlements in their setting as ecosystems (a word not yet invented!), in looking for integrated solutions to intractable problems of social and physical renewal, and working with and through the people involved.

The 'wonder drugs' of planning

The first half of the twentieth century was the time when many of the most deep-seated, long-lived policies in town planning were devised in various countries. The Netherlands developed methods of integrated land planning in response to flooding risks and population growth in the low-lying lands of Holland. Germany developed the principle of zoning – land use segregation so that the foul fumes and noise of industry did not pollute residential areas. American planners picked up the idea – zoning was perceived as 'a wonder drug of the planners, the balm sought by lending institutions and householders alike'.[6]

'Zoning was perceived as "a wonder drug of the planners, the balm sought by lending institutions and householders alike".'

Another concept developed in the USA, building on the British garden city movement, was that of the neighbourhood unit. The neighbourhood was conceived as a protected, walkable environment around a primary school and other local facilities, with a population of 5,000–6,000. Part of the motivation for design was the rising tide of traffic. Neighbourhoods might have busy roads around them, but within them there was relative calm and safety. One influential design – that of Radburn, New Jersey – segregated pedestrian and vehicle networks, so that people locally could walk to shops, schools and churches without traffic danger, and children could play in the public realm more freely.

In England, with the highest density of population among major countries, there was popular and political concern with the loss of countryside. Ribbon development out from towns along rural highways, blocking the view of the countryside, became a pet hate. Protection of the open countryside from further development and the idea of a green belt or *cordon sanitaire* (healthy girdle) around the major cities became priorities.

What we see in the interwar years is the creation of a language of planning, increasingly shared between countries, which then dominated policy debate for the rest of the century. Land use zoning, neighbourhood units, green belts, satellite 'garden' towns, countryside protection, became the core tools of planning policy. The ostensible motive of the planners remained similar to that of the pioneers – a concern for the quality of the environment, for the health and well-being of everybody. But in this they were at odds with the dominant political ethos of the time, which was about the rights of landowners (corporate and individual) to do what they wanted to with their own land. In the USA, for example, local authorities zoned new suburbs with minimum house plot size, effectively excluding low-income households who were priced out of the market. Planning tools that had been conceived as egalitarian became instruments for entrenching privilege. In parallel, the transport engineers in the USA were devising ways of managing the huge growth in vehicle traffic, inventing freeways without direct access or conflicting traffic movements, making the free flow of traffic a fetish of city planning.

Two things were happening, which undermined continued progress towards more healthy cities. First, the 'wonder drugs' of planning were becoming institutionalized – becoming ends in themselves rather than means to ends. Second, the professions were each establishing their own territory. Planning was separated from public health; housing, community development, economic development, civil engineering, transport, ecology and environmental health, all gained their own professions. In many countries design skills, including architecture, were separated from planning. Expertise and training followed professional and institutional logic and applied blinkered remits. 'Every profession,' said Bernard Shaw, the Oscar-winning Irish playwright, 'is a conspiracy against the laity.' And despite good intentions, there is much truth in that. The most serious split was between town planners and transport planners, sowing seeds of dissention for the future.

Abercrombie and the London Plan

Patrick Abercrombie (1879–1957) was one of a generation of planners who followed on from the pioneers. An architect by training, he rapidly colonized the new arena of town planning, and, according to one biographer, grew to be the best known town planner in the world.[7] Perhaps the main reason for that was his authorship, during the war, of the *Greater London Plan 1944*.[8] The need for such a plan, for what was – at that time – the greatest city in the world, had become self-evident. Abercrombie's plan was the first attempt at a systematic strategic plan for such a metropolis. At the outset he stressed the need for co-ordination across the many local authorities and agencies responsible within the London region, and was concerned to develop a planning 'machine' or system capable of implementing the plan.

It is fascinating and highly instructive to read this 1944 document. It is a spatial plan, with much analysis, broad strategic diagrams and action area masterplans. The strongest theme is the idea of community. Abercrombie was very concerned that the new speculative suburbs burgeoning all round London during the interwar years lacked facilities or community focus. He sought to plan integrated neighbourhoods and new settlements that would provide for local needs locally and cultivate mutual warmth and social support.

'It is highly instructive to read this 1944 document. It is a spatial plan, with much analysis, broad strategic diagrams and action area masterplans. The strongest theme is the idea of community.'

At a wider level, Abercrombie was concerned about the over-crowded, poor housing conditions in the inner areas, and the imbalance between housing and employment across the region. He noted the growing polarization of the population, with the rich living in the outer city while the poor lived in the inner city, undermining the sense of London as a city-wide community. He proposed the reconstruction of inner areas so that open spaces could be provided alongside better housing, together with the diversification of outer suburbs, the expansion of suburban towns and the creation of a ring of new satellite towns to take a million people from the conurbation. At the same time the green belt was to be extended to provide green lungs to the city and recreational opportunities for the inhabitants.

What is most striking about the document is its directness and readability. In an early chapter it provides a succinct analysis of the issues facing London, and an explanation of the logic of the plan. It deals not in rhetoric, weasel words and legalese, but in a clear-eyed strategic vision combined with practical mechanisms for achieving it – such as zoning and standards for local accessibility and open space. Where it is less impressive is in the evidence base for social, economic and ecological issues – conspicuous by its absence. It is not that these issues were ignored – on the contrary, they were treated as fundamental – questions of social equity, health, and economic change were so self-evident that they did not require specific study.

Planning as civic design

The physical emphasis of Abercrombie's plans was taken further by others, until gradually the social purposes of planning became subsumed. The dominant view of town planners in the first two decades after the Second World War was of planning as design: civic design of places and spaces; strategic design of towns and cities. The distinctive skill of the planner was to understand and plan the interaction between different land uses and routes in an urban area and (at a more detailed level) to design the layout of residential and commercial areas. This emphasis came about partly because many of the new planners were architects and civil engineers whose business was design. Town planning was seen by many as big architecture.

'Le Corbusier claimed to be applying rationality and human scale to city planning – the brave new world of functional, machine logic. To modern eyes, the vision is of an inhuman environment.'

One hugely influential prophet of this view was the Modernist architect Le Corbusier. He claimed to be applying rationality and human scale to city planning – the brave new world of functional, machine logic. However, in his two utopian tracts, *Ville Contemporaine* (Contemporary City) and *Ville Radieuse* (Radiant City),[9] he set out aesthetic visions of serried ranks of monumental tower blocks set in parkland, with freeways between and long vistas. To modern eyes the vision is of an *inhuman* environment. It is more an exercise in Brobdingnagian sculpture than a functional human environment.

A generation of architects, inspired by these images and the impressive buildings of the Modernist movement, designed clusters of tower blocks for lower-income groups on outer estates and bombed sites. Civil engineers planned urban motorways through areas of high density and supposedly 'obsolete' housing – Le

Corbusier's vision rising from the rubble of post-war Europe. For a while, well into the 1960s, these policies were politically fashionable and expedient – presumed to be the answers to the pressing problems of housing and mobility. Later, of course, they were castigated as huge planning mistakes.

Planning, as it became institutionalized, was in danger of losing its soul. The focus on physical solutions to social problems often paradoxically ignored the social realities. Even Lewis Keeble's seminal work of the 1950s – *Principles and Practice of Town and Country Planning*,[10] which examined design principles at all levels, and emphasized a logical process of plan-making – failed to grapple with social issues. Nigel Taylor, reviewing the development of planning theory, elegantly sets out the critique of design-led planning. He called the almost exclusive focus on physical planning 'social blindness'.[11] Planners, architects and renewal authorities were so fixated on the need to remedy the ills of the physical environment that they did not register the social networks which flourished in the slums, and did not anticipate how those would die in the splendid new neighbourhoods.[12]

This social blindness, and reliance on design formula such as the slab block, the neighbourhood unit and free-flow roads, were symptomatic of a paternalistic approach – well-meaning arrogance which assumed the designer knew best. Sociologists castigated planners for being 'physical determinists', i.e. assuming that the environment would determine behaviour.[13] There was little involvement of people in the plans that affected them.

The most influential attack on the design conventions came from Jane Jacobs in 1961. Her book, *The Death and Life of Great American Cities*,[14] was a devastating broadside on the conventional wisdom. She challenged the grandiose single use uniformity of Modernist development, with resulting dead street frontages, instead advocating mixed uses, small blocks and active frontages. In a country (the USA) where car use was the dominant means of travel, and streets were becoming deserted, she stressed the streets were for people. They should be designed to, and bounded by activities that, ensure a critical number of pedestrians to keep the street safe, to foster casual social contact, to provide surveillance for children's play, to create an interesting urban environment. Jacobs recognized that she was not only lambasting the formalist instincts of designers, but the workings of the market. She advocated 'zoning for diversity' that would ensure that low-rent-paying activities were protected and thrived, despite the desire of landowners to maximize values.

This was prescient stuff. Working from observation and logic, Jacobs anticipated many of the planning principles of our present era. But it is fair to say that in her time planning policy was a contested affair. In his analysis of American planning history, Corburn[15] points to three contrasting movements in the emerging planning profession. First, there were the 'sanitarians' concerned with healthy environments and social justice; then there were the members of the 'City Beautiful' movement, who emphasized aesthetic quality and can be linked with the European Modernists; third there were the technocratic planners, who were more concerned

The issues around 'social blindness' and social capital are explored in Chapter 7. Chapter 8 homes in on spatial disparities. Neighbourhood planning is discussed in Chapter 13.

'Working from observation and logic, Jacobs anticipated many of the planning principles of our present era.'

with sophisticated analytical tools – particularly complex mathematical transport models. The different traditions co-existed.

The British new towns

'The New Towns can be an experiment in design as well as living.' (Lewis Silkin, Minister for Town Planning, House of Commons debate on New Towns Act, 1946)

The three traditions linked arms in creating the post-war British new towns. In a phase of tremendous experimentation, a series of new and expanded towns were developed. The planners designed and tested, first theoretically, then in practice, a wide range of alternative approaches and designs. The movement was distinctive in its clarity of purpose and degree of logical analysis. All the plans were intended to promote the public good – though health and well-being were often implicit rather than explicit aims. The diversity of town designs was almost like a 'natural experiment'. We can observe and contrast the results now. By way of illustration, one first-generation and several second-generation new towns are briefly described below.

First-generation new town: Harlow, Essex

Harlow is often taken as an archetypal 'first-generation' new town. It was designated in 1947 as part of Abercrombie's vision for the London region. Harlow New Town commission was appointed by government, and given a land area to develop. Since compensation to landowners was paid at existing use values, it was possible for the Commission to make a surplus through urban development, supporting infrastructure provision, and eventually paying a handsome profit to the Treasury.

Sir Frederick Gibberd, the designer of Liverpool's Roman Catholic Cathedral, was probably more important as a planner than as an architect. He led the design team for Harlow, and on that basis wrote *Town Design*.[16] Harlow was designed as a balanced town, with population matched by employment and service levels (not always achieved). It incorporated an old market town and seven villages, helping to give a connection to local history, and the whole design was based on neighbourhoods, each with a primary school, local facilities and pub. The neighbourhoods were grouped into districts, sufficient to support a good range of jobs and facilities, including secondary schools. The principle of zoning was reflected in separate industrial and town centre zones (Figure 4.4).

Gibberd believed in the importance of a safe, convenient and equitable environment with a strong sense of place. Harlow boasted the first pedestrian precinct, and the first extensive cycle network. The public realm was enlivened by many distinctive sculptures. A third of the town was public open space, wrapping round each neighbourhood and with a major park by the town centre. Thus, while the planning process was design-led, it was strongly based on ethical principles of equity, convenience and quality of life. It has been criticized for its lack of provision for rising car ownership, its suburban character, and failing to offer a more urban choice of accommodation that would appeal to some middle-class residents.[17] To his credit, Gibberd lived in the town he masterminded.

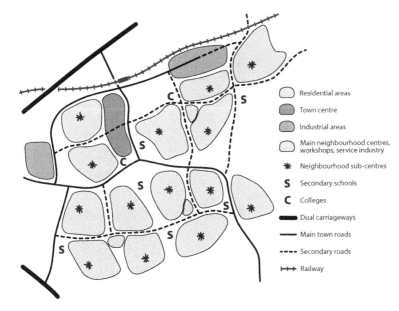

Residential areas

Town centre

Industrial areas

Main neighbourhood centres,
workshops, service industry

✳ Neighbourhood sub-centres

S Secondary schools

C Colleges

Dual carriageways

Main town roads

- - - - Secondary roads

╟┼┼┼┤ Railway

Fig 4.4 *Harlow: a town of distinct neighbourhoods. Designed by Gibberd.*

Source: based on Gibberd 1953 (note 16).

Second generation: Runcorn, Peterborough, Milton Keynes and Hook

The designers of the second-generation new towns, designated during the 1960s, all provided for high car use. The Runcorn team devised a 'figure of eight' plan, with distinct inward-looking neighbourhoods supporting primary schools strung out along a segregated busway that linked them to the town centre and industrial areas. The expanded town of Peterborough created large linear townships, well adapted to bus efficiency, able to support district-level facilities. By comparison, the Milton Keynes kilometre grid of dual carriageways created a much more dispersed, flexible structure, but militated against both public transport efficiency and walking. Hook, at the opposite end of the spectrum, was designed as a unified high density town with local pedestrian and cycling high streets leading into the strong centre (Figure 4.5).[18]

Each of these new towns had a clear planned relationship between land use and transport, each with a different emphasis, demonstrating the variety of designs possible. All were successful (except for Hook, which was never built), with generally low unemployment, and below-average outward commuting. Runcorn, however, suffered because of a high proportion of social housing and its overdependence on one firm – ICI. Milton Keynes and Peterborough, by contrast, with diversified economies, have outgrown their original plans, and are among the fastest-growing towns in Britain.

According to a recent review of new towns, there are some important lessons to learn. These include:

* the critical importance of good location and economic diversity in town success;

'Each of these new towns had a clear planned relationship between land use and transport, each with a different emphasis, demonstrating the variety of designs possible. All were successful (except for Hook, which was never built).'

Hook: a concentration of meeting places on a central pedestrian spine

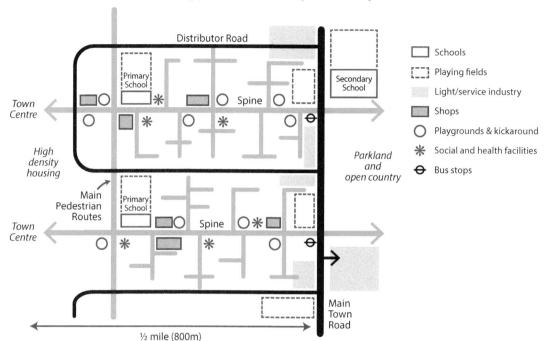

Fig 4.5 *Hook plan (part): pedestrian spine neighbourhoods. Radical ideas, a high point of new town planning, but never realized as population pressures eased*

Source: based on Bennett and GLC colleagues 1961 (note18).

- the importance of effective co-ordination of the many agencies involved in funding and infrastructure delivery;
- the value of achieving overall social mix through a balance of housing tenures, offering plenty of affordable housing without over-dependence on social renting;
- recognition of the time taken to build a new town – the process of town development outlasts many buildings which make up the town – places age slowly.[19]

Gaining the country but losing the plot

Planning has come a long way since the early pioneers. For half a century, the purpose of planning was clearly a better quality of life for people in general. But the ability of local authorities to take an integrated view was strictly limited. In Britain, the 1947 Town and Country Planning Act was a great leap forward. Other countries followed suit, adapting to their own cultures. Settlement planning by local authorities suddenly became the rule, not the exception, backed by strong public support for state planning in the aftermath of the Second World War. Basic life support systems were institutionally embedded: clean water, effective sanitation, including indoor toilets and bathrooms, better air quality as a result of industrial zoning and the Clean Air Act. The new towns, paid for by the increase in land value when rural land is converted to urban, realized something of Howard's ideals, and became an inspiration to the world.

The intentions were noble. But inexperience showed in the post-war settlement. The planning profession expanded overnight, with architects, surveyors and engineers getting on the bandwagon, each bringing their own assumptions and professional orientations. The values of the planning pioneers of the previous half-century were watered down. In the commonplace world of local authorities, convention, expediency and prejudice held sway. Two brief (British) examples must suffice. The first concerns the widespread policy of *maintaining the amenity of the area*. It sounds innocent enough, but local people in more affluent areas, and politicians representing them, interpreted it to mean maintaining the exclusivity of affluent neighbourhoods: no low cost housing, no apartments, no communes. This policy contributed to progressive social polarization and ghettos of the poor. A second example was about urban renewal and road building. It was the assumption that any modest terraced housing over 60 years old was 'redundant' – and therefore could be demolished for road construction, uprooting communities with minimum compensation. Too often, thus, planning became a set of professional and political dogmas that worked against well-being.

In America, Corburn noted the parallel erosion of the explicit focus on health and well-being. He suggests that this was due to the rise of an assertive free market, and an anti-federal orientation, which undermined centralized support for health-oriented policies. In both countries a combination of professional, institutional and political factors have undermined the centrality of health, well-being and quality of life in the lexicon of planning. But of course, the Anglo-American axis is not the whole world. Planners in some other countries in Europe did not lose their central concern for people. Chapter 5 paints a more optimistic picture.

'Inexperience showed in the post-war settlement. The values of the planning pioneers of the previous half-century were watered down. In the commonplace world of local authorities, convention, expediency and prejudice held sway.'

Further reading

Cherry, G. (1988) *Cities and plans: the shaping of urban Britain in the nineteenth and twentieth centuries.* London: Edward Arnold.

Cherry, G. (1996) *Town planning in Britain since 1900: the rise and fall of the planning ideal.* Chichester: John Wiley & Sons, Ltd.

Corburn, J. (2009) *Towards the healthy city: people, places and the politics of urban planning.* Cambridge, MA: MIT Press.

Freestone, R. and Wheeler, A. (2015) 'Integrating health into town planning: a history', in H. Barton, S. Thompson, S. Burgess, and M. Grant (eds) *The Routledge handbook of planning for health and well-being.* London: Routledge. pp. 17–36. Traces the history of modern planning through a public health lens, from the late nineteenth century to the present day.

Morris, E. Smith (1997) *British town planning and urban design: principles and policies.* London: Longman.

Town and Country Planning Association (2014) *New towns and garden cities: lessons for tomorrow.* London: TCPA. A handy summary booklet.

Notes

1   A chart showing these startling inequalities is found on p. 25 of Cherry, G. (1988) *Cities and plans: the shaping of urban Britain in the nineteenth and twentieth centuries* (London: Edward Arnold).

2   Churchill, W. (1910) *The people's land*, quoted in Large, M. (2010) *Commonwealth: for a free, equal, mutual and sustainable society* (Stroud: Hawthorn Press).

3   Morris, W. (1890, Reprinted 1993) *News from Nowhere* (Harmondsworth: Penguin).

4   Howard, E. (1898) *Tomorrow: a peaceful path to real reform* (London: Garden Cities and Town Planning Association, UK); Howard, E. ([1902], reprinted 1946) *Garden cities of tomorrow* (London: Faber and Faber).

5   Unwin, R. (1909) *Town planning in practice: an introduction to the art of designing cities and suburbs* (Charleston, VA: Nabu Press).

6   Scott, M. (1971) *American city planning since 1890* (Berkeley, CA: University of California Press), p. 192, quoted in Corburn, J. (2009) *Towards the healthy city: people, places and the politics of urban planning* (Cambridge, MA: MIT Press), p. 44.

7   Dix, G. (1981) 'Patrick Abercrombie 1879–1957', in G. Cherry, *Pioneers in British planning* (London: Architectural Press).

8   Abercrombie, P. (1944) *Greater London Plan 1944* (London: HM Stationery Office).

9   Le Corbusier (1967) *The radiant city* (London: Faber and Faber).

10 Keeble, L. (1952, 1969) *Principles and practice of town and country planning* (London: Estate Gazette Ltd).

11 Taylor, N. (1998) *Urban planning theory since 1945* (London: Sage Publications).

12 Willmott, P. and Young, M.D. (1957) *Family and kinship in East London* (Harmondsworth: Penguin).

13 See, for example, Gans, H. (1968) *People and plans: essays on urban problems and solutions* (Harmondsworth: Penguin).

14 Jacobs, J. (1962) *The death and life of great American cities* (Harmondsworth: Penguin).

15 Corburn (2009), op. cit.

16 Gibberd, F. (1953) *Town design* (London: Architectural Press).

17 Tetlow, J. and Goss, A. (1965) *Homes, towns and traffic* (London: Faber and Faber).

18 Based on Bennett, H. and GLC colleagues (1961) *The planning of a new town* (London: HMSO).

19 Alexander, A. (2009) *Britain's new towns: garden cities to sustainable communities* (London: Routledge).

CHAPTER FIVE

BEACONS OF HOPE

It is not enough to avoid the mistakes of the past. Our responsibility, as we see it, is rather to conduct an essay on civilization. By seizing an opportunity to design, evolve and carry into execution for the benefit of future generations the means for a happy and gracious way of life.

Lord Reith[1]

Introduction: WHO Healthy Cities

Lord Reith was talking about the first-generation British new towns, but his comment is equally applicable now. Town planning is about creating the spatial opportunities for people to thrive. Cities in rich countries have that opportunity, if national and local politics allow. This chapter aims to inspire and trigger understanding by studying four cities which have seized the initiative – three from Europe and one from America. To a greater or lesser extent they were influenced by the activities of the *Healthy Cities* movement.

In 1986, the WHO Healthy Cities movement was launched, as part of the WHO *Health for All* programme, initiated by two physicians, Trevor Hancock and Leonard Duhl. Their ambition was to raise the profile of public health among decision-makers and empower local authorities to take concerted action.[2] Initially the focus was on the traditional concerns of smoking, drugs and alcohol abuse, sexual diseases, healthy eating and exercise, working with individuals and communities to improve behaviour. In 1997 Agis Tsouros, Director of the European Healthy Cities Programme, launched the 'healthy urban planning' initiative, commissioning myself and Catherine Tsourou to write *Healthy Urban Planning: A WHO Guide to Planning for People*.[3] This 'landmark publication'[4] was subsequently translated into many languages, and supported the progressive reintegration of health and planning in the Healthy Cities movement.[5, 6] A group of pioneer cities, including Rotterdam, Glasgow and Milan, became trail-blazers for the new approach.

Of the four cities examined in this chapter, the first – Copenhagen – was a founder member of the Healthy Cities movement and has long been a beacon of good planning. The second – Kuopio, in

Healthy Cities in Europe

In 2015, a hundred cities, from many countries, were full members of the WHO European network. In addition, 20 national networks were accredited (another 10 aspiring) with 1137 local authorities involved, having a total population of 156 million.[7]

Finland – has been a key member of the pioneer group of WHO cities, the *healthy urban planning sub-network*. The third – Freiburg, in Germany – while not part of the Healthy Cities network, has a huge reputation for planning for quality of life. The final example – Portland, in Oregon, USA – has used health and well-being as a motive for breaking out of the traditionally car-oriented planning regime dominant in America.

The approach to the case studies is mainly descriptive, illustrating the nature of spatial policies pursued, based on personal visits and documents available. In Freiburg and Portland, detailed discussions with key people have allowed insights into the process of decision-making.

Copenhagen: city of cyclists

Copenhagen, the capital of Denmark, is one of the most attractive and welcoming cities in Europe. It is an elegant historic city of canals and waterways, where streets are filled with people walking and cycling, and the atmosphere is relaxed and friendly. It is one of the most livable cities in the world, and according to the *World Happiness Report*, Denmark is the happiest country in the world.[8] Health, well-being and climate change are key drivers of policy, leading to innovative transport, land use, energy and neighbourhood policies.

Copenhagen started early. In 1947, the city developed the *Finger Plan* for the expansion of the city (see Figure 5.1).[9] This was before car ownership became common in Europe. The plan formalized what had been happening through the market as radial tram systems extended out from the centre and businesses and households located close by, creating a stellar pattern of development. The finger plan allowed further outward growth of the city along public transport routes in a series of neighbourhoods, with green wedges penetrating into the city between the urban fingers, thus maintaining good access both to open spaces and to jobs and facilities. As rising car ownership freed up locational requirements, facilitated by road investments, it became difficult to maintain the ideal continuity of open land, but nevertheless Copenhagen has been remarkable in generally sustaining its strategic vision.

The clarity of purpose shown by the finger plan persisted. The issue of climate change was and is taken seriously, with scarce energy resources being used with maximum efficiency. Combined heat and power (CHP) stations, many using waste materials, achieve twice the efficiency of conventional generation, and the heat mains serve 98 per cent of properties. Denmark leads the world in wind power, and aims to provide 50 per cent of electricity from wind by 2020. Even more ambitious, the city intends to be carbon-neutral by 2025. All this is not imposed by government on a reluctant population, but achieved by partnership between people, government and commercial interests. Many of the projects are owned and run by community co-operatives. The decentralized community-oriented approach applies to housing, schooling and green projects as well as energy.

Transport policy is radical. The city authority determined that pedestrians and cyclists should be given preferential treatment. Their

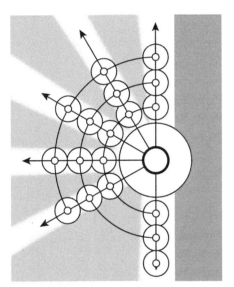

Fig 5.1 *Diagram of Copenhagen's 'finger plan'*

Source: Adapted from (note 9).

reasons are many: to encourage healthy activity, to offer cheap and efficient movement options, to promote social activity, to reduce pollution and greenhouse gas emissions. The city centre now boasts a remarkably convivial and leisured atmosphere as key streets have been elegantly pedestrianized. Car parking has been progressively reduced to make way for people walking, talking, looking, relaxing. The cost of creating beautiful streets and squares has brought environmental benefits of reduced traffic danger, noise and fumes, and economic benefits in terms of increased spending in shops and cafés.

Cycling has become a dominant means of travel, accounting for 36 per cent of commuting trips to work and study. This has not only brought lifestyle and environmental benefits, but has meant much more efficient use of limited road-space, allowing the city to grow with less pain. A major policy driver is the net economic gain to society. One study shows the mortality of adults commuting daily by bike is reduced by 30 per cent. The city estimates that there are DKK534 million (c. £53m) health care savings per year.10 Other economic benefits accrue from improved productivity, cycling-based firms, increased tourism, reduced congestion and lower road maintenance costs.

The early cycle routes in Copenhagen were often on low-trafficked side streets, but they did not prove very popular because many cyclists refuse to deviate from direct routes. Only when the city decided to install curbed cycle lanes on main roads (thereby constraining other traffic in some instances) did cycling take off (Figure 5.2). Safety has become a key issue. The city is now creating 'green' routes, through parks and quiet streets, to encourage the less intrepid cyclists who baulk at the busy main routes. Car ownership and use are now among the lowest of any city in Europe. The cycle strategy for 2011–2025 is ambitious. It intends to improve

'Cycling has become a dominant means of travel, with 36 per cent of commuting trips to work and study. One study shows the mortality of adults commuting daily by bike is reduced by 30 per cent.'

Fig 5.2 *Bikes galore in Copenhagen. Vehicles learn to give way*

Source: Federation of European Cyclists, 31 January 2016.

cycle travel times and cycle track maintenance, drastically reduce injuries, and increase the commuting share to 50 per cent.

From a low point in the early 1980s, when the city was suffering economic stagnation and suburbanization, Copenhagen has transformed itself. Regeneration and new-build projects have enhanced the distinctive character of the city and increased the population. One major scheme is Orestad – a suburban linear development, partly on old military land, linking the city centre to the international airport. It provides mixed commercial, university and residential areas all served by a new metro, which also serves adjacent older suburbs. Everyone is within 600 metres of a station, and 70 per cent of commuters use public transport. Canals, lakes, wetlands and parks percolate through the area, providing a model of integrated ecological development.

Copenhagen is only one of a number of Scandinavian cities, including (but not only) Stockholm, Malmö, Helsingborg (Sweden), Sandnes (Norway), Odense and Horsens (Denmark), which demonstrate the potential for healthy, environmentally conscious development when politicians, business and civil society work together to achieve positive change. All these have been or are members of the WHO Healthy Cities network.

Kuopio: city of lakes and forests

Another long-time member of WHO European Healthy Cities network is Kuopio, in the heart of Finland, a small city in a land of lakes and forests. Kuopio was an influential member of the healthy urban planning sub-network during the first decade of this century, contributing innovative ideas for driving policy forward. Leo Kosonen, former chief architect-planner, has written extensively about his approach, and this section draws on his recent writings.[11, 12]

The aim of Kosonen's 'three fabrics model' of urban form is to promote the recognition and regeneration of three different kinds of urban habitat: (1) the walking city fabric; (2) the transit city fabric; and (3) the car city fabric (Figure 5.3). Each of these has different

Three city fabrics

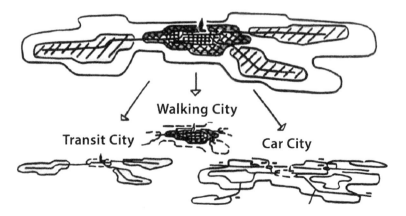

Fig 5.3 *The city as a combination of three fabrics*

Source: Kosonen 1996 and 2015 (notes 11 and 12).

characteristics and priorities in terms of planning for health and well-being. In smaller cities, the car fabric is usually much the most extensive. In larger cities, the older areas are mostly oriented towards public transport, but the extensive hinterlands are car-dominated. The purpose of planning strategy is to progressively extend the walking and transit fabrics so that more people can benefit from the wider modal choice, healthy travel options and a more inclusive environment – incidentally contributing to lower transport carbon emissions. The idea is so simple in essence that it can become a widely understood indicator of progress, through which politicians can be held to account.

The fabrics can be defined by a combination of mapped analysis and observation – as well as public debate. In Finland, the 'inner walking fabric' is defined as being within 1 kilometre of the heart of the city. The 'outer walking fabric' is within 2 kilometres. The inner transit fabric is taken as the area well served by local tram and bus services, normally up to 8 km from the centre, while the outer transit fabric may extend up to 30 km away and depends on trunk bus or train services, sometimes with feeder buses serving sub-centres with their own walking fabric zone. The rest of the city region is the car city fabric, i.e. areas where the car is the only realistic option for most journeys for most people.

The walking city habitat is quite compact, wrapped around the city centre and major sub-centres (Figure 5.4). In Kuopio, a priority network for pedestrians has been progressively enhanced by closing narrow lanes to traffic, providing new pavement treatment, greenery and public art. New connections for pedestrians and cyclists (for example, bridging the river) have allowed new areas to be brought within the walking city. Regeneration of old industrial sites for housing has increased the number of housing units in the centre by 2,000. Some of these dwellings are designed for car-less households. Others have car parking under courtyard gardens which are thereby free for children to play or adults to relax.

The transit fabric in Kuopio has been extended by new bus-links, pushing fingers out from the city and triggering regeneration of isolated neighbourhoods. The most dramatic of these new links is the 'Street of Islands' – a busway and cycle/walkway bridging between islands in the lake, transforming car city pockets, short-circuiting the route into the city centre, and effecting a massive transfer of trips from car. The Street of Islands is predicted to halve transport emissions over the next 50 years by comparison with the business-as-usual alternative without the bridge. The street, passing through green and blue environments, has also created a popular linear recreational area. Local shops and services in the new transit neighbourhoods have revived around the central squares as more people walk to the bus stops or cycle.

The car fabric extends in sporadic low-density estates around the walking and transit fabrics, accounting for the majority of the city region. It offers little choice of transport mode and is innately more energy-intensive. Where good transit services are not viable, and distances deter walking, it is still vital to plan for healthy lifestyles – hence the promotion of bikeways, allowing people to cycle to work,

'The purpose of planning strategy is to progressively extend the walking and transit fabrics so that more people can benefit from the wider modal choice, healthy travel options and a more inclusive environment.'

Fig 5.4 *Varying densities and character in Kuopio: above, the walking city fabric; and below, the car city fabric.*

school and facilities. There is also plenty of land for greenspace, so another priority is easy, safe access for active recreation.

The Kuopio approach is being rolled out across Finland. It offers a very tangible way of selecting priorities and assessing progress towards a healthier, more sustainable settlement.

Freiburg: city of short distances

Freiburg is a university city of just over 200,000 people in South-West Germany, at the edge of the Black Forest. It has established an enviable reputation as *the city that did it all*,[13] attracting planners and designers from all over the world, hoping to find inspiration. I have led two such pilgrimages from South-West England, including chief planners and chief public health officers. We were all immensely impressed by the atmosphere of the city, the quality of the urban environment and by the process for managing change. The city has 'done it all' in the sense of taking a holistic approach to spatial planning at every scale.

The motivation for a coherent approach stemmed initially from the devastation of the Second World War, when Allied bombers destroyed most of the ancient town centre, with the conspicuous exception of the *Munster*. In common with many European cities, Freiburg decided to rebuild a carbon copy of the old city on the mediaeval street pattern, but with up-dated interiors and some street widening to assist trams and traffic. The city responded to rising car ownership by developing a network of high capacity roads, causing high pollution levels and the dispersal of city functions to locations easily accessed by vehicle. The planners in the 1960s, realizing the risks of that direction, began the process of changing expectations and behaviour by the pedestrianization of the city centre, winning people over to a safer, cleaner, walkable environment. The big momentum for change came in the 1970s. The threat of a nuclear power station close to the city, imposed by the central government, galvanized the population. A group of ex-students won power on a radical green agenda. Building on links between university, industry and the city, they promoted a new energy strategy: efficient combined heat and power (CHP) stations, the manufacture of solar cells, the creation of a local market for low carbon solutions that undermined the need for nuclear power. The threat was averted.

Since then, there has been remarkable consistency of policy. The planning strategy is not a 'political football', but has broad-based political commitment. Politicians and planners have worked closely with the university, businesses and civil society to transform the city. Declining traditional industries have been replaced with innovative enterprises. Public transport, cycling and walking have progressively replaced private motors as attractive options for travel. Urban renewal and urban extension schemes, worked up in partnership with residents, have improved living conditions and helped to green the city.

The centre-piece is the integrated land use/transport strategy. All major trip generators (commercial, retail, educational, etc.) have to locate close to a tram stop. More than 85 per cent of existing resi-

'The centre-piece is the integrated land use/transport strategy. All major trip generators (commercial, retail, educational, etc.) have to locate close to a tram stop.'

BEACONS OF HOPE

Network in 2013

Extensions approved
or under construction

300m and 500m radius

Travel time to terminal
stops (in 2013)

Regional rail lines
and stations

Main railway station

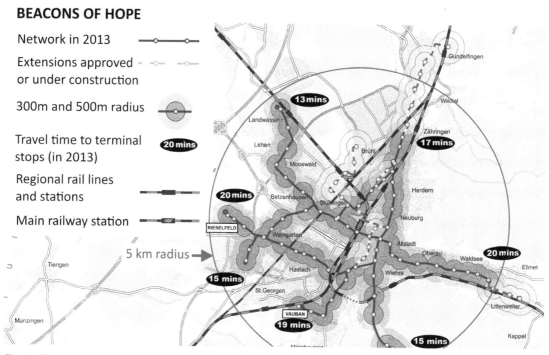

Fig 5.5 *Tram network and urban form of Freiburg*
Source: Adapted from Melia 2015 (note 14), figure 12.3.

dential developments are within 500 m of a tram stop (Figure 5.5).[14]
All new development has to match that standard. The rail and tram
networks, together with linking bus services, offer a good service to
all, including satellite settlements. There are no out-of-town retail
or business parks only easily accessible by car. Combined with the
investment in comprehensive walking and cycling networks, the
strategy means that car use in the city is unnecessary for most trips.
Tram use has soared, and the subsidy needed (after rising with initial
heavy investment) has now fallen to a historic low. By 2007, fares
accounted for 90 per cent of running costs – the highest proportion
in Europe.[15]

The acid test of an effective land use/transport strategy is *modal
split*: car trips are down to 30 per cent, half the norm in British cities;
public transport is 18 per cent, cycling 28 per cent and walking 24 per
cent.[16] Active travel (walking, cycling, including to public transport
stops) thus accounts for 70 per cent of all trips, with clear benefits to
health. In response to the quality of alternatives, car ownership levelled off in 2006, and is now falling – well below the German average.
Transport-related carbon dioxide emissions are progressively falling
despite a rising population and a buoyant economy.[17]

At the more local level the aspiration for a 'city of short distances'
is realized through close partnership between local communities
and the city authorities. The planners dedicate much time to ensuring that residents and businesses are well informed, understand the
wider strategy and able to have freedom to act within it. Community

housing initiatives, such as *Baugruppe* (co-operatives) are supported. The most exceptional neighbourhood is Vauban, mainly newbuild on a brownfield site, served by an extension of the tram system and housing 5,000 people. Every aspect of Vauban delights: it is a place designed for a diverse population, safe for children to play and cycle in the streets, very convivial, with viable local facilities (Figure 5.6).[18] The agreed design code establishes powerful conventions – three- or four-storey terraces (houses and flats) with small gardens, shared surface streets, tongues of greenspace, close allotments. Within that pattern there is maximum diversity, with each family or small-scale

Fig 5.6 Vauban tramway and humane environment: The central tramway grassed for noise reduction and next to local facilities; footpaths next to sustainable drainage systems; and play-street with mixed housing

'Every aspect of Vauban delights: it is a place designed for a diverse population, safe for children to play and cycle in the streets, very convivial, with viable local facilities.'

Up-front infrastructure provision

Freiburg has powers of land assembly and purchase, allowing facilities to be created ahead of population growth, and costs recouped from sale of plots.

'Portland shows how radical social goals can be pursued in a neo-liberal context. The 2012 Portland Plan has the four principal pillars of "health, equity, prosperity and education".'

developer able to design their own dwellings and frontage, giving a sense of visual vitality. Due to both carrot (excellent accessibility) and stick (the cost of parking), car ownership has fallen to only 150 per 1,000 people – a third of what might be expected. Households have more disposable income as a result. Vauban is a model healthy and socially inclusive neighbourhood.

How, then, has Freiburg achieved such success? German cities are fortunate in having a significant level of financial and policy autonomy. Freiburg City Council can exercise substantial control over the process and shape of development, act as a key partner in public transport management, and take a hard-headed commercial approach to development. Its powers of land assembly, physical and social infrastructure provision, development management and cross-sectoral, cross-border partnerships, all mean it can do things that cities in some other countries can only dream about. These mechanisms are explored further in Part V. It is also clear that the success of Freiburg is not just due to systems. The quality, motivation and continuity of key politicians and officials have been central. The city has pursued a consistent spatial strategy for more than 30 years. It takes time and persistence over at least a generation to turn a city around – to alter the perceptions and behaviour patterns of households and businesses through debate, education, policy and physical change. Let us hope the strategy can be sustained in the future.

Portland: breaking the neo-liberal taboo

The European examples above all benefit from being in social democracies. There is an assumption that policy-makers, democratically elected, will make decisions in the interests of all, and that private rights, including property rights, can sometimes be less important than communal rights. But the balance between public and private rights varies hugely between countries. In places such as the United States with a pioneer, ex-frontier tradition, and many countries in Eastern Europe where state communism distorted social interests, *laissez-faire* is the rule.

Portland, Oregon, shows how radical social goals can be pursued in a neo-liberal context. Portland is a mid-sized city of 590,000 in a metropolitan region of over two million. It has a long tradition of planning stemming from the early twentieth century, with utility networks, a street car system, planned civic centre, parks and conservation. But then mid-century up to the 1970s the priority was to plan for the motor car. The result was a formidable network of freeways, causing high car dependence, a sedentary population, air pollution at unhealthy levels, and a city centre gradually dying as activities suburbanized and car parking took over city blocks. In the early 1970s, a radical shift in public and political opinion occurred, challenging the planned freeways and market-led approach. The priority became public transport, cycling, gradual densification in well-served neighbourhoods, re-investment in the city centre, and the extension of natural, ecological landscapes. While the low density suburbs still sprawl, the trajectory of the city has been altered. The peak of per capita car travel was 1997, falling significantly since then. Portland is now the 'epicentre of hipness',[19] benefitting from the in-migration of well-educated young people, and the retention of older households, who support the direction of change.

Belief in the importance of the public good has been blended with a libertarian tradition. The 2012 *Portland Plan* has the four principal pillars of 'health, equity, prosperity and education'. The city assesses its success or failure by performance measures which include:

- falling levels of obesity;
- increases in active travel (walking and cycling);
- reduced carbon emissions;
- increased economic self-sufficiency;
- more residents living in accessible neighbourhoods.

These are not *primary* measures of well-being (such as 'happiness' or 'longevity') but are more directly amenable to spatial planning influence. While the direction of change is now positive, Portland still suffers from maladies in three generations: obese children, sedentary adults, lonely seniors. All three can be helped by more walking and cycling, so the creation of a walkable and convivial environment has become priority.

A key planning mechanism at the strategic scale has been the *urban growth boundary (UGB),* required by Oregon State legislation. Its purpose is to discourage longer-distance commuting by preventing estate development in the rural areas beyond the boundary. Like the British *greenbelt* policy, the UGB encourages the real estate industry to look inwards and consider urban renewal. Unlike greenbelts, it does not encourage development to 'leap-frog' the belt – because there is no outer edge until the next city UGB.

The Portland renewal strategy is to permit intensification in zones along the main public transport routes, in what they call '20-minute neighbourhoods'. These are areas within 20 minutes' walk time of a good local centre, reinforcing the viability of local facilities and public transport. Empirical evidence in Portland suggests that densities have to be more than twice the American norm of 4 dwellings per acre (10 per hectare) to support light rail transit.[20] The higher density accessible developments have attracted middle-class households to these previously poor inner city neighbourhoods. Property prices and rents have risen, with the unintended result that some poorer families have been pushed out to less accessible locations. The question of equity in the housing market has come to the fore.

The centre of the city has been progressively transformed, initially through environmental improvement and strong political intervention to trigger market interest. A critical element was an urban design code which reversed the conventional layout of car parks next to the street and buildings behind, instead requiring buildings to front the street, with direct ground-level access. The standard 200-foot (60 metre) grid of streets (inherited from the foundation of the city, and similar to Priene) has been maintained, with the amalgamation of blocks for massive redevelopments not allowed. This has ensured maximum permeability for pedestrians, and sufficient streets to allow some to be access-only for traffic.

The old industrial zones near the city centre are rejuvenating, on the same principles, increasing substantially the number and diversity of people living close in. As with many other cities in Europe and America, once the blight of derelict factories and goods yards is lifted, a new housing market is revealed – for people who value an accessible, walkable environment, and enjoy the energy that comes from a mixed use development. The Pearl District in Portland's North-West neighbourhood is now famed for its creativity and quality of urban life (Figure 5.7).[21] The grid of streets (some pedestrianized) is enlivened by squares, pocket parks and playgrounds. There is very considerable freedom for building designers and investors, but within a design code that ensures streets are directly fronted by the buildings, heights are controlled (typically four storeys), and ground floors are adaptable for a range of uses – residential, retail or office. Bribery is permitted! The planning authority can allow higher plot ratio (i.e. more cubic metres of building on a given plot) if the developer provides a new public square, perhaps over a car park. Adaptability and opportunity within a clear spatial framework are the watchwords of the plan.

Fig 5.7 *The Pearl District, Portland. A new walkable neighbourhood arising phoenix-like from an obsolete inner industrial area – with renovated and infill buildings, connected to the central business district by streetcar.*

Source: Tillett 2015 (note 21), p.582.

Portland demonstrates that, even in a country with a belief in the pre-eminence of property rights and the free market, it is possible to plan strategically and locally for greater health and sustainability, and to do this while also fostering new economic growth opportunities. Health has been a potent motivator. Portland also shows there is no quick fix. The 1973 plan took 24 years to 1997 to reverse the powerful trends set in motion by the earlier car-oriented policy choices, and still has far to go to achieve the equitable, humane and healthy urban environment desired. Like the *Titanic*, cities take time to turn around. It is not just the longevity of physical structures, but the lifestyle habits of residents, and the conventional thinking of businesses and institutions. The bad habits of one generation are foisted on their children and children's children. The hope is that, unlike the *Titanic*, cities can survive the icebergs of obesity, couch-based lifestyles and social isolation.

Lessons from inspirational cities

The four cities reviewed above – Copenhagen, Kuopio, Freiburg and Portland – share many characteristics of spatial planning policy and process. In relation to policy there is recognition that:

- The health, social opportunity and quality of life of people are linked to the health of the city in terms of air quality, environmental quality and economic success, and to the health of the planet in relation to climate change.
- The twentieth century's love affair with the motor car has taken cities down a false path, exacerbating both personal and urban health issues. Instead it is essential to plan cities that promote physical activity through active travel by foot and bike, shortening distances, improving safety, making accessible places, while encouraging longer-distance trips to be made by public transport.
- In order to achieve this, it is necessary to fully integrate transport and land use planning at local, urban and city region scales, encouraging densities that are sufficient to support local facilities and good public transport, progressively retrofitting car-based suburbs and exurbs for sustainability and well-being, and encouraging renewal of declining inner city areas.
- Redeveloped and new neighbourhoods should be planned with good street permeability and sufficient space to allow cycle/walkways, play, greenspace and access to nature; plus diversity of housing, flexibility of building use and design within a clear urban design framework.

In relation to the processes of planning, there is a surprising degree of common ground:

- Political and professional leaders need the clarity of vision to set clear long-term spatial goals and pursue them consistently.
- They need to work creatively and persuasively with different policy agencies, public and private sector investors, to achieve co-ordinated programmes.

- Cities need to have the ability to take the initiative – shaping urban form, buying up development land, investing in public transport and the public realm.
- Planners of regeneration or new community projects need to engage with civil society and existing/potential residents and businesses from the start.
- Public authorities need continuity of staff, employing people of high calibre in terms of skills, understanding, communicative abilities and management.

Further reading

Abbott, C. and McGrath, M. (2015) 'Progress and challenges in Portland, Oregon', in H. Barton, S. Thompson, S. Burgess, and M. Grant (eds) *The Routledge handbook of planning for health and well-being.* London: Routledge, pp. 566–577.

Cullingworth, B. and Caves, R. (2014) *Planning in the USA: policies, issues and processes,* fourth edn. London: Routledge. See pp. 215–219 for a succinct history of planning in Oregon.

Grant, M. and Barton, H. (2015) 'Freiburg: green capital of Europe', in H. Barton, S. Thompson, S. Burgess, and M. Grant (eds) *The Routledge handbook of planning for health and well-being.* London: Routledge, pp. 540–551.

Hall, P. (2014) *Good cities, better lives: how Europe discovered the lost art of urbanism.* London: Routledge.

Kent, J. and Thompson, S. (2015) 'Healthy planning in Australia', in H. Barton, S. Thompson, S. Burgess, and M. Grant (eds) *The Routledge handbook of planning for health and well-being.* London: Routledge, pp. 443–454.

Kosonen, L. (2015) 'The three fabrics strategy in Finland', in H. Barton, S. Thompson, S. Burgess, and M. Grant (eds) *The Routledge handbook of planning for health and well-being.* London: Routledge, pp. 521–539.

Tillett, P. (2015) 'Designing for conviviality and city vitality in Portland', in H. Barton, S. Thompson, S. Burgess, and M. Grant (eds) *The Routledge handbook of planning for health and well-being.* London: Routledge, pp. 578–586.

Notes

1 Lord Reith, Chairman of the New Towns Committee, UK,1946, as quoted in Alexander, A. (2009) *Britain's new towns: cities to sustainable communities* (London: Routledge).

2 Hancock, T. and Duhl, L. (1998) *Promoting health in the urban context.* WHO Healthy Cities Papers No. 1 (Copenhagen: FADL Publishers).

3 Barton, H. and Tsourou, C. (2000) *Healthy urban planning: a WHO guide to planning for people* (London: Spon Press).

4 Freestone, R. and Wheeler, A. (2015) 'Integrating health into town planning: a history', in H. Barton, S. Thompson, S. Burgess, and M. Grant (eds) *The Routledge handbook of planning for health and well-being* (London: Routledge), pp. 17–36.

5 Barton, H., Mitcham, C. and Tsourou, C. (2003) *Healthy urban planning in practice: experience of European cities* (Copenhagen: WHO Regional Office for Europe).

6 Barton, H. and Grant, M. (2013) 'Urban planning for healthy cities: a review of the progress of the European Healthy Cities Programme', *Journal of Urban Health,* 90(1) Suppl.: 129–141.

7 Leah, L. (2015) *National healthy cities networks in the WHO European Region* (Copenhagen: WHO Regional Office for Europe).

8 Helliwell, J., Layard, R. and Sachs, J. (2013) *The world happiness report 2013* (New York: Oxford University Press).

9 See Frey, H. (1999) *Designing the city* (London: E & FN Spon).

10 City of Copenhagen, Bicycle Account 2010, as reported in Wikipedia 'Cycling in Copenhagen', sourced 7 May 2015.

11 Kosonen, L. (2015) 'The three fabrics strategy in Finland', in H. Barton, S. Thompson, S. Burgess, and M. Grant (eds) *The Routledge handbook*

of planning for health and well-being (London: Routledge), pp. 521–539.

12 Kosonen, L. (1996) Transit city – a balancing alternative. A proposal for the city of Kuopio for the Urban Pilot Project of EU/DGXVI (City of Kuopio).

13 Hall, P. (2014) Good cities, better lives: how Europe discovered the lost art of urbanism (London: Routledge).

14 Melia, S. (2015) Urban transport without hot air (Cambridge: UIT Cambridge), Figure 12.3.

15 Hall (2014), op. cit.

16 Gregory, R. (2011) The Eco-tipping point project: Models for success in a time of crisis: our time: Germany – Freiburg – Green City. Available at: www.ecotippingpoints.org/our-stories/indepth/germany-freiburg-sustainability-transportation-energy-green-economy.html (accessed 31 December 2013).

17 Pucher, J., Buehler, R. and Seinen, M. (2011) 'Bicycling renaissance in North America? An update and re-appraisal of cycling trends and policies', Transportation Research Part A: Policy and Practice, 45(6): 451–475.

18 Source: Barton, H., Grant, M. and Guise, R. (2010) Shaping neighbourhoods: for local health and global sustainability (London: Routledge), p. 157.

19 Abbott, C. and McSharry, M. (2015) 'Progress and challenges in Portland, Oregon', in H. Barton, S. Thompson, S. Burgess, and M. Grant (eds) The Routledge handbook of planning for health and well-being (London: Routledge), pp. 566–577.

20 Paddy Tillett, pers. comm.

21 Tillett, P. (2015) 'Designing for conviviality and city vitality in Portland', in H. Barton, S. Thompson, S. Burgess, and M. Grant (eds) The Routledge handbook of planning for health and well-being (London: Routledge), pp. 578–586.

III Cognition

The science of healthy urban environments

Never lose a holy curiosity.

Albert Einstein

Part I of the book argued that planners and designers have a moral responsibility to advise their clients (investors, communities, policy-makers) about the likely impact of urban development on the health and well-being of people. Part II demonstrated the historical and contemporary power of this idea.

The problem has been that even when planners are conscious of their social role, they may not feel equipped to advise about what is, or is not, a healthy development proposal. From many personal contacts it is clear this stems partly from lack of knowledge of the planning/health field. Planners – perhaps especially those concerned with transport, economic development and conservation – sometimes feel it is not their business to worry about health, and in any case they assume that the evidence for the impact of planning policy on health is weak, deriving more from hunch and hearsay than science.

That excuse no longer holds. Since the turn of the century there has been a plethora of studies in the field.[1] The depth and breadth of research, linking environmental, social and physical variables to public health and well-being, have expanded exponentially. This effort has not been without tensions. In traditional health research (for example, on the efficacy of medicines), double-blind studies with 'controls', longitudinal studies and systematic reviews of similar projects are the norm. Research in the social sciences and urban spatial policy does not have that luxury. The context is complex, and can change unpredictably so that experiments cannot be 'controlled'. But for a while, the expectation that such studies should achieve the same 'gold standard' as medical research, with simple cause and effect, led researchers to be equivocal in their conclusions. There is widespread recognition now that different research paradigms are necessary.[2]

The main purpose of this part of the book is to review the evidence across the whole spectrum of the Settlement Health Map and to point in the direction of healthy spatial policies. The five chapters here reflect spheres of the health map, moving from lifestyle and physical health, through mental well-being, social, community

'Planners sometimes assume that the evidence for the impact of planning policy on health is weak, deriving more from hunch and hearsay than science. That no longer holds.'

and equity issues to global health threats, finishing with a human ecology perspective. While there are still areas of academic contention, the right direction is, to coin a phrase – 'bloody obvious!'[3] The research reinforces the validity of the choices made in the exemplary cities of Chapter 5.

Notes

1   Giles-Corti, B., Foster, S., Koohsari, M., Francis, J. and Hooper, P. (2015) 'The influence of urban design and planning on physical activity', in H. Barton, S. Thompson, S. Burgess, and M. Grant (eds) *The Routledge handbook of planning for health and well-being* (London: Routledge).

2   Personal communication with many researchers.

3   The phrase used by Jonathon Porritt at a conference.

CHAPTER SIX

PHYSICAL HEALTH, LIFESTYLE AND PLANNING

It is good to collect things, but it is better to go for walks.

Anatole France[1]

Choose the life that is most useful, and habit will make it the most agreeable.

Francis Bacon

Introduction: obesity and physical activity

From the perspective of spatial planning, physical health and well-being relate to two distinct aspects. In the first place, there are environmental qualities that impinge on physical health, for example, the quality of the air that we breathe (see Chapter 10). In the second place, there is the influence of the environment on behaviour, which is dealt with here (Figure 6.1). Lifestyle choices strongly influence physical health. The critical aspects of lifestyle affected by the urban environment are physical activity and diet. In terms of the Settlement Health Map, the chapter concentrates on the interaction between the built environment (sphere 6), lifestyles (sphere 2) and individual health and well-being (sphere 1).

The WHO highlights an 'epidemic of obesity' sweeping the world – a nutrition and armchair transition as nations grow more affluent. In the USA, a third of adults are obese and being overweight is the norm. In England, there has been an alarming increase in the proportion of overweight children since 1995. If present trends continue, half the UK adult population will be clinically obese by 2050.[2] Excess weight and lack of exercise substantially increase the risk of heart attack, stroke, osteo-arthritis, diabetes, and some forms of cancer. In the developed world there is an growing divergence between rich and poor, with the latter more prone to sedentary behaviour and junk food, exacerbating weight problems and health inequalities.[3]

The causes of obesity are complex, but there is the simple equation between diet and exercise: does the amount of food/drink consumed match the exercise taken? If the amount of physical activity is insufficient to burn up the food consumed, then people are liable to become overweight. In certain cases personal unhappiness and psychological trauma will be a factor, leading to compensatory eating

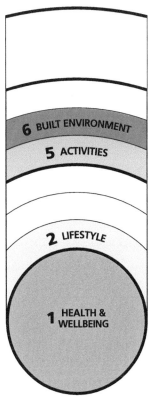

Fig 6.1 *Health Map focus: lifestyle*

Measuring obesity

The level of obesity is assessed by the Body Mass Index (BMI). BMI is calculated by dividing weight (in kg) by height (in metres squared).

- A healthy adult = 18.5–24.9 kg/m^2
- An overweight adult = 25–29.9 kg/m^2
- An obese adult = 30–40 kg/m^2
- Morbidly obese = >40 kg/m^2

'If a medicine existed which had a similar effect to physical activity, it would be regarded as a "wonder drug" or a "miracle cure".'

habits. Physical activity can help reduce feelings of depression, anxiety, and promote physiological and psychological well-being. A former Chief Medical Officer of England is reputed to have said that if a medicine existed which had a similar effect to physical activity, it would be regarded as a 'wonder drug' or a 'miracle cure'.

Physical activity is defined, rather dryly, as 'any bodily movement produced by the contraction of skeletal muscles that increase energy expenditure above a basal level'.[4] People can get useful exercise in many ways:

- Everyday activity at home, school or work: walking, carrying, making, cleaning, climbing stairs.
- 'Active travel' – walking and cycling to get somewhere.
- Children's active play: running, gamboling, skipping, skate-boarding.
- Adults' recreational activities: gardening, dancing, gym activity, energetic sex (sexercise!), walking and running for pleasure, swimming, football, rugby, tennis, cricket.

The level of physical activity taken by individuals is a matter of personal choice, but that choice is strongly conditioned by cultural norms and expectations. These vary between different social, economic and racial groups and between different places and countries. Traditional economic activities such as farming, mining, goods-handling and post delivery require physical effort, but most contemporary work is desk-bound. Lifts and escalators have replaced stairs. Children are devoted to TV, electronic games and smartphones, playing less outside. Food is collected in the car, or delivered to the door by the superstore. It is obvious that many of the activities that once gave us physical exercise without conscious decision have gone into decline. People can all too easily become lazy, while at the same time enjoying sugar-high drinks and getting pre-packaged food high in fat and sugar. There is strong evidence of weight gain and increased health risks with habitual car use.[5] Worldwide, 60 per cent of people take insufficient exercise to benefit their health.[6]

While medical advances are helping to extend life, personal lifestyle choices are reducing the period of *healthy* life. The resulting costs fall on health services and the wider economy. The UK Foresight report *Tackling Obesities* estimates that if present trends continue, NHS costs attributable to elevated BMI will more than double between 2007 and 2050, rising to 14 per cent of total NHS costs, and the wider costs to the economy (reduced productivity, disability, etc.) will be greater than the whole cost of the NHS.[7]

According to some academics at the forefront of research in this field, even a modest increase in physical activity could produce significant societal benefits, with substantial savings to global health systems.[8] Guidance on how much physical activity is necessary for health varies; for example, half an hour per day, or 150 minutes per week in 10-minute or more bouts of activity. But the intensity of activity is a key factor: gentle exercise (such as ambling) has less benefit than moderate exercise (normal walking), while vigorous exercise (running, fast walking) provides more protection from disease.

The rest of the chapter is divided into three main parts: (1) the importance of spatial planning for physical activity through walking and cycling; (2) through recreation and play; and (3) for healthy diet.

Active travel: walking and cycling

'Active travel' refers to walking and cycling journeys for practical purposes – to get to school, work, shops, bus stops, friends, etc. It does not include walking/cycling specifically for pleasure, exercise or the dog, which count as recreational. In reality, of course, the decision to walk to the shops rather than take the car may be due to mixed motives: not only the need to go shopping, but also the potential enjoyment of the route, social opportunities *en route,* the desire for exercise, and the cost or inconvenience of taking the car.

The importance of active travel for well-being is difficult to exaggerate – not only in relation to obesity but also for social inclusion, social capital, mental well-being, reduced pollution and carbon emissions. The physical act confers physiological benefits – people feel better when the endorphins kick in. Walking creates opportunities for casual meetings, building social networks. Children walking to school together build friendships. All this is positive for mental health. If there is one policy where there are multiple gains but few if any losses, then it is the promotion of walking. It is central to WHO, EU and UK strategies for sustainable communities.[9]

For some people, active travel may be the only affordable or feasible way of accessing essential services, school and work. This remains the case for many (often the majority) in developing countries and for some in developed countries. For those on very low incomes, or who are not able to drive – including children – the ability to reach places and do things without reliance on costly vehicles or lifts from others, is a fundamental aspect of freedom. If the environment deters active travel through distance, unpleasant or unsafe routes, that is an infringement on liberty. Planning settlements that enable active travel, including especially those who are less mobile, is therefore central to planning for equity and social inclusion as well as health.

Walking has declined as car ownership has spread through the population. The ownership and use of cars are for many people associated with status and self-respect – a symbol of having reached adulthood for teenagers and of being integrated with mainstream society for those already adult. As cities have evolved to suit car use, car ownership has become a necessity for those living in suburban, exurban and rural settings. The car is needed just to access the increasingly dispersed motor-dependent locations of retail, office and service functions. This is a classic vicious circle (Figure 6.2). As more people buy more vehicles, businesses find it expedient to locate where car access and parking are cheaper, and that increases the need, for purely practical purposes, for every adult to have a car.[10] If people are to walk (to public transport as well as direct to facilities) and to cycle rather than rely on the car, then it is not just a matter of private preference. It is about shaping the city and its environs so that walking and cycling are easy.

Fig 6.2 *The vicious and the virtuous circles of travel choice*

'If people are to walk and to cycle rather than rely on the car, then it is not just a matter of private preference. It is about shaping the city and its environs so that walking and cycling are easy.'

What is not so clear, however, is the degree to which people who do not walk or cycle to places compensate by getting more physical activity elsewhere. The population is divided crudely into two sets of people, whom we may typify as active and sedentary. The active people may or may not travel actively, depending on where they live, but will get sufficient recreational physical activity. If they do walk and/ or cycle for functional reasons, they are prepared to travel greater distances than the average. Conversely the sedentary people will only walk and cycle, if at all, shorter distances, and do not compensate with recreational activity. For these people their limited active travel is often the only means by which they get exercise. This is particularly so for those in traditional physical occupations who now find themselves in sedentary jobs. The culture of resting from hard physical labour persists even though the hard physical labour has gone. All this points to the potential importance of creating places where the distance and quality of routes between homes and facilities are such that both the more active and the more sedentary find it convenient to walk.

There is consensus in the research literature that urban environments influence the levels of active travel.[11] Trying to tie down individual aspects of the environment – such as density or mixed use – as determinants of active travel has proved problematic.[12] But many studies have proved what may seem obvious, that there is a powerful relationship between distance and the propensity to walk. Closeness matters.[13] When the routes between home and facilities are close, direct, safe and pleasant, then many more people walk and cycle. The distance people are willing to walk/cycle varies according to the nature of the facility. Based on data from 12 English suburbs, of those who walk or cycle to superstores, the median distance is 600 m, while for other food shops it is 1,600 m. Figure 6.3 contrasts the distribution of trips by mode for a range of 'local' facilities.[14]

The same study shows there are striking differences in the proportion of active trips in different suburbs, ranging from 20 per

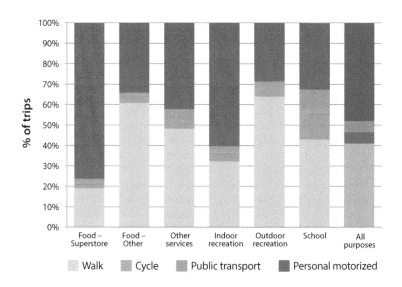

Fig 6.3 *Active travel to local facilities by purpose and mode*

Source: Adapted from Barton et al. 2012 (note 14).

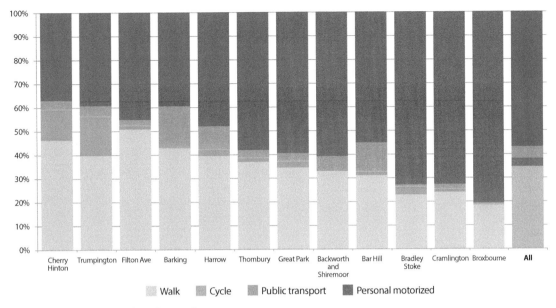

Fig 6.4 *Suburban variations in active travel*

Source: Barton 2011 (note 15).

Percentage of Walking and Cycling Trips by Distance (SOLUTIONS Project)

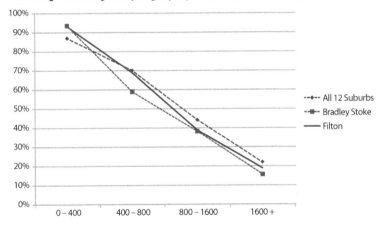

Fig 6.5 *Active travel trips to local facilities by distance*

Source: Analysis of SOLUTIONS research data reported in Barton 2011 (note 15) by Steve Melia. Within a given cultural context, behaviour is surprisingly similar. This shows the distance people are prepared to walk or cycle to reach local facilities. The average across 12 varied English suburbs is much the same as two Bristol suburbs – one with more local facilities and quite high active travel, the other with fewer accessible facilities and therefore lower active travel.

cent to 60 per cent (Figure 6.4).[15] Density variation (often suggested as a key factor) is not the explanation in this case. Social structure accounts for certain differences, but the distance to facilities is much more important. Within a given culture there is some consistency in how far people will walk (see Figure 6.5). Culture of course can evolve, but in devising spatial policy you have to work from where people are at present, and try to create the situation where it is natural for them to choose to walk or cycle. People are willing to walk more frequently and further when there are several potential reasons for doing so – such as a food shop close to a newsagents, a library or a coffee shop where one can meet friends.

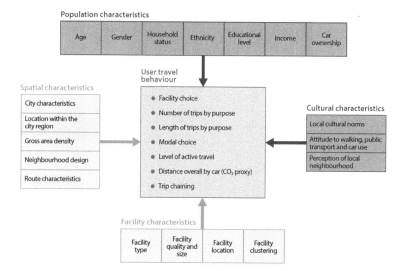

Access to Facilities: Logic Model

Fig 6.6 *Factors affecting travel mode to facilities*

Source: Adapted from Barton et al. 2012 (note 14).

It is important to have a clear view of the complex factors influencing travel behaviour. Figure 6.6 sets out the relationship between spatial and design characteristics, the nature of facilities including size, quality, location and clustering, the characteristics of the population, cultural/attitudinal factors, and the variables that are involved when users choose where to go and how to go.

Cultural differences in behaviour can be substantial, particularly in relation to cycling. However, the level of cycling is also about the provision of safe and comprehensive cycling facilities. Where cities have invested heavily, radical changes in behaviour occur. Conversely, when policy is based on trend forecasts, and cycling is a low proportion of trips, subsequent low investment perpetuates the situation.[16] By way of example, in Sydney, New York and Toronto, the cycling share of trips is around 1 per cent; in the UK, 2 per cent is typical, though Cambridgeshire achieves 10 per cent, which is the *average* level for Germany. The average in the Netherlands is 25 per cent, with some towns nearer 40 per cent.[17] The UK Department for Transport has collated studies of many cycling schemes, and found they offer very strong returns to society. The cost to benefit ratio is over 1:5.5 – far better than most road or rail schemes. The health benefits account for 60 per cent of the total.[18]

The *perception* of quality and safety of the pedestrian and cycling environment is important.[19] Parental consent for children to walk or cycle to school, a friend's house or a playground is notoriously low in the UK by comparison with much of Europe, due to real or perceived traffic and stranger danger. Children's freedom to roam has been curtailed. Physical improvement to route continuity, directness, safety, informal surveillance and aesthetic quality is part of any strategy to change perceptions and culture. Once there are more people on the streets, perceptions begin to change, and we have a virtuous circle.[20] If there are more walkable destinations, there is

'Parental consent for children to walk or cycle to school, a friend's house or playground is notoriously low in the UK by comparison with much of Europe.'

more walking *per* destination.[21] Studies in Australia suggest that when teenage girls (for example) had plenty of choice of local destinations, they had 85 minutes more physical activity per week than girls with fewer facilities.[22]

Transforming policy

Official policy for urban revival and sustainable development in Europe has for some years laid great stress on the need to rejuvenate neighbourhoods and reverse the decline of facilities within walking distance of people's homes.[23]

Accessibility standards for facilities in relation to housing aim to maximize the likelihood of walking while being practical in relation to catchment populations and urban form. Figure 6.7 gives maximum acceptable actual distances for moderate densities. Some facilities can be very local, in the street or block; others should be neighbourhood-based, within a normal maximum of 800 metres; some facilities require the population of a small town or urban district to support them, but can still be within walking, and easy cycling, distance for more active people.[25]

Distance is only one factor which influences potential walkers and cyclists. The perceived safety and attractiveness of the route are also critical. Traffic congestion, noise, fumes and accidents are deterrents to active travel. Children, frail elderly and cyclists are most at

Key policy documents[24]

In the UK, key documents were probably the remarkable Planning Policy Guidance 13 on Transport, in 1994, and Towards an Urban Renaissance in 1999. At the more practical level the 1995 Guide to Sustainable Settlements was influential with British local authorities.

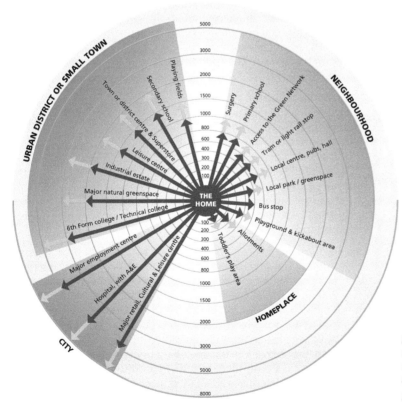

Fig 6.7 *Illustrative accessibility criteria for active travel, assuming certain catchment populations and average densities*

Source: Barton et al. 2010 (note 25).

risk from accidents. International comparisons can be shocking. For example, there are five times more pedestrian accidents per distance walked in the USA than in the Netherlands.[26] Accidents show a social class gradient.[27] In the UK, accidents to the lowest socio-economic group are four times as likely as in the highest.

The risk of traffic accidents increases progressively with traffic volumes and with speed over 40 kph (25 mph). The design of streets is a critical factor. Engineering solutions attempt to segregate traffic from walkers and cyclists with barriers and controlled crossings, while urban design solutions promote pedestrian and cycling priority, taming traffic. In terms of accidents, evidence can be used to support either strategy.[28] In terms of promoting active travel, taming traffic, slowing speeds, providing an attractive, well-connected network are critical.

A key insight is that the promotion of active travel through planning, for health reasons, complements other aims. The EU and UK policy documents above argued variously from a standpoint of urban regeneration, social cohesion, climate change and sustainable development. Economic productivity also benefits from a healthier population. There are, in other words, many potential constituencies of support for full-hearted walking and cycling strategies. Healthy travel behaviour is linked to healthy towns and to a healthy planet.

Active recreation

Physical activity through recreation brings pleasure, stress relief, refreshment and social benefits as well as improving physical health. A 'playful city' should recognize the diverse play needs of all age groups, from toddlers to the frail elderly.[29] This relies on many different kinds of spatial provision:

- private gardens for gardening and young children's play;
- allotments and community gardens;
- children's playgrounds, for a range of ages;
- play streets and cul-de-sacs with very little traffic;
- parks and informal greenspaces;
- playing fields for schools, private clubs and general public use;
- leisure centres, squash courts, swimming pools, gyms;
- hard surface provision for team sports, tennis and youth games;
- off-road walking and cycling routes through attractive landscapes.

All these require land, careful planning and appropriate mechanisms for implementation and management, and have importance for levels of physical activity. For some activities, people with access to a car are willing to travel a considerable distance to reach the club or activity of their choice. But the options that are locally accessible are important in order to give choice to everybody – especially young and old – and to combat health inequalities.

Apart from the provision for specific activities, the natural environment itself plays a significant part in facilitating physical activity: 'Evidence consistently shows that accessible and safe urban greenspace has a positive influence on levels of physical activity.'[30]

Evaluation of programmes for encouraging exercise indicates that attractive, green environments close to the home or work provide the best opportunities to encourage daily exercise, walking or cycling. People also keep exercising longer in natural surroundings.[31] One analysis of a European cross-sectional survey suggests that the likelihood of being physically active is three times greater, and the prevalence of obesity 40 per cent less, in neighbourhoods with high levels of greenspace as opposed to those with low levels.[32]

Greenspace Scotland have undertaken a comprehensive literature review, selecting 87 studies from 550 identified across the world (a third from the UK), and advise that the level of physical activity is influenced by these attributes:[33]

- distance of residence from greenspace;
- ease of access in terms of routes and entry points;
- size of greenspace in relation to levels of population use;
- connectivity to residential and commercial areas;
- the range of amenities for formal and informal activities;
- perceived safety of the greenspace;
- the quality of maintenance.

Cities that invested in parks in an earlier era (Alexandra Park in Manchester, Regent's Park in London, Central Park in New York, Parc du Boulogne in Paris) value them highly. But not all places managed this. Some high density cities – such as Milan and Barcelona – have recently been creating them as essential parts of their 'healthy city' regeneration programmes.

Children's play

Children's play is especially critical, helping to establish a pattern of healthy activity from an early age. It is defined as 'non-compulsory, driven by intrinsic motivation and undertaken for its own sake, rather than as a means to an end'.[34] Children who have easy access to safe greenspaces (parks, playgrounds, kick-about areas) are more likely to be physically active than those who are not so close, and this has a positive effect on health, particularly for those from low-income families.[35] In some countries the use of the outdoors by children has declined sharply in the last 50 years because of alternative sedentary attractions, and parental over-protection and risk aversion due to traffic danger and perceived stranger danger.[36] Only 15 per cent of British children now play in the street.[37] The same thing has happened with active travel. Whereas in 1971, 80 per cent of British 7- and 8-year-olds walked to school without an adult, in 2011 it was 11 per cent.

Children's own untutored preference is often for natural environments with an element of adventure and challenge, not the tame, risk-free environments of many playgrounds. Indeed while playgrounds are important for younger children, streets and home gardens are more frequently the locus for play. Sustrans, the campaign for sustainable transport, talks about *free range kids*: children who get out and about where they live, know their neighbourhoods – where to walk, play, chat and cycle – and have the skills and confidence to keep safe.[38] When neighbourhoods are perceived as safe, children

'The likelihood of being physically active is three times greater, and the prevalence of obesity 40 per cent less, in neighbourhoods with high levels of greenspace as opposed to those with low levels.'

get more physical activity.[39] Cul-de-sacs are natural play areas. However, connected street networks encourage more independent walking and exploration, so the ideal is traffic-free or low traffic streets which lead somewhere.

Healthy diet

In the context of the obesity epidemic, the food issue has loomed large in recent years. The title of one learned paper puts it in a nutshell: 'Global nutrition dynamics: the world is shifting rapidly toward a diet linked with non-communicable diseases'.[40] While a billion people worldwide do not have enough food, the rest of us are often eating more than we need, with diets high in sugar, salt and meat. Diet-related disease is now a leading contributor to premature mortality through coronary heart disease, type 2 diabetes and cancers. The question here is whether dietary choices are entirely a matter of culture, cost and affluence in an increasingly globalized economy, or whether spatial configurations play a part.

The debate has tended to focus on fresh food availability, fast food outlets and, to a lesser extent, local food production. The significance of spatial planning is not entirely clear from the research done so far. There has been much speculation about food deserts – neighbourhoods in relatively isolated locations lacking local access to fresh food, particularly fresh fruit and vegetables. In the ultra low-density suburbs and rural settlements of the USA, fresh food deserts exist, often associated with low income and Afro-American communities. Some 23.5 million Americans live in places that do not have supermarkets – the main source of fresh food. However, the absence of fresh food outlets does not mean there are *no* food outlets: disadvantaged neighbourhoods are often replete with low-quality, fast food options. Several US studies point to observed health benefits where supermarkets with a good range of fresh food are accessible.[41]

In most European contexts fresh food deserts are probably a myth. Densities are higher and distances less. One longitudinal study of the effect of a supermarket opening in a poor outer Glasgow estate previously lacking a fresh food outlet, found that the impact on diet was negligible – the local residents changed their habits at the same rate as the city as a whole. However, the study did find a marked effect on active travel – many more people walking to the superstore because it was now close.[42] So local provision had a beneficial lifestyle impact, but not the one anticipated.

Studies about the location of fast food outlets affecting diet are also inconclusive. While some municipalities and public health bodies are intuitively convinced that the local availability of fast food triggers demand, it seems more likely it is the other way round, with demand triggering supply. Eating habits are largely a cultural, habitual matter, and are not heavily influenced by spatial planning. The important exception is fast food outlets and sweet shops near to schools, seducing the students – especially those from poorer families – into bad habits.[43]

Local food production is dependent on space, and therefore on spatial planning. Many places that have been built at relatively high

'Eating habits are largely a cultural, habitual matter, and are not heavily influenced by spatial planning. The important exception is fast food outlets and sweet shops near to schools.'

densities with small gardens or no gardens at all, make home food growing very limited. Alternatives can take the form of local allotments and urban farms or 'leisure gardens' at the urban fringe, as in Holland. The health benefits of food growing are not simply the direct access to fresh fruit and vegetables, but the physical exercise involved, and community building with neighbours or other allotment holders (Figure 6.8). In some situations local production can also alleviate poverty. It is said that 100 m² in a suitable climate can provide all the fruit and vegetable needs of a family.[44]

Lower densities allow larger back gardens, which can be devoted to vegetable growing. However, in the absence of financial pressures, only a minority of households use the space to grow food. In terms of urban space it is more efficient to offer allotments to those who do want to grow food, and keep gardens a modest size. However, in the UK, allotments are often at an inconvenient distance from the home, making it awkward to carry compost, tools and produce without recourse to a vehicle – thereby undermining the environmental benefits. One practice guide recommends a maximum distance of 200 metres from the home.[45] Many cities have waiting lists, yet over the past few decades some allotments have been sold off as housing sites, and few recent housing developments have provided accessible allotments. There is clearly a need to review town planning policy and related research into enhancing the potential for local food production.

Fig 6.8 *Allotments: fresh food and much more! Education, exercise, community, contact with nature*

Cautions and counsels

Spatial planning can affect some aspects of lifestyle. While people make their own choices, the context of those choices is set by the environment they live in as well as economic circumstances, cultural norms of behaviour and their personal characteristics and experience. Figure 6.9 illustrates the way that planning exerts influence

The pathway from spatial planning decisions to personal health and well-being

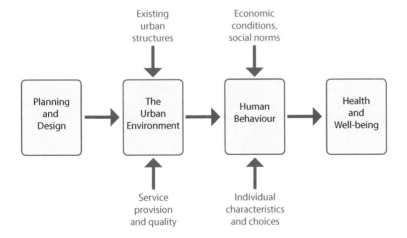

Fig 6.9 *Spatial planning: only one of many factors influencing personal health*

through a series of intermediate stages. At each of these stages there are other forces at work which affect outcomes, and often these have more importance than planning and design. So due humility is appropriate on the part of planners, while also accepting their core responsibility for ensuring a healthy environment. Equivalently public health professionals and politicians, keen to find answers to intractable problems of unhealthy lifestyles, need to recognize both the potential and the limits of spatial planning.

Having said that, it is clear from research and practice that the spatial arrangement of towns can influence active travel and recreational activity to a significant extent – and in certain situations it can influence diet. There are some policy choices that are 'no brainers'.

- *Walkable environments*: streets and places where it is convenient, safe and pleasant to walk. The benefits are multiple. Priority for pedestrian movement is fundamental to healthy and sustainable town planning.
- *Cities of short distances*: where the viability/provision of local facilities, local recreational opportunities, neighbourhood and district mixed use centres, is a top planning priority – implying restriction on car-based developments such as business parks and out-of-town shopping malls.
- *Cycling city*: safe and convenient bike networks that percolate through the urban area. The potential benefits again are multiple, including efficient use of road-space. Top priority is children being able to cycle to school. While in some (especially hilly) places, cycling starts from a very low base, the potential with electric-supplement bikes is considerable.
- *School gates temptation*: restriction on fast-food outlets and sweet-shops close to schools.
- *Home-grown food*: accessible allotments, urban farms or private gardens (depending on density) that allow people to grow fresh vegetables and fruit, and have exercise.

Further reading

Dannenberg, A., Frumpkin, H. and Jackson, R. (eds) (2011) *Making healthy places: designing and building for health, well-being and sustainability*. Washington, DC: Island Press.

Davis, A. and Parkin, J. (2015) 'Active travel: its fall and rise', in H. Barton, S. Thompson, S. Burgess, and M. Grant (eds) *The Routledge handbook of planning for health and well-being*. London: Routledge.

Giles-Corti, B., Foster, S., Koohsari, M., Francis, J. and Hooper, P. (2015) 'The influence of urban design and planning on physical activity', in H. Barton, S. Thompson, S. Burgess, and M. Grant (eds) *The Routledge handbook of planning for health and well-being*. London: Routledge.

Mahdjoubi, L. and Spencer, B. (2015) 'Healthy play for all ages in public open spaces', in H. Barton, S. Thompson, S. Burgess, and M. Grant (eds) *The Routledge handbook of planning for health and well-being*. London: Routledge.

Townshend, T., Gallo, R. and Lake, A. (2015) 'Obesogenic built environments: concepts and complexities', in H. Barton, S. Thompson, S. Burgess, and M. Grant (eds) *The Routledge handbook of planning for health and well-being*. London: Routledge.

Notes

1 As quoted in Chatwin, B. (1998) *The songlines* (London: Vintage), p. 174.

2 Butland, B. *et al.* (2007) *The Foresight report on tackling obesities: future choices* (London: Government Office for Science).

3 For comprehensive information about obesity and physical activity in England, see the Public Health England website, currently available at: www.noo.org.uk

4 CDC (2008) Centers for Disease Control and Prevention, available at: www.cdc.gov/physicalactivity (accessed 5 May 2009).

5 Davis, A. and Parkin, J. (2015) Active travel: its fall and rise', in H. Barton, S. Thompson, S. Burgess, and M. Grant (eds) *The Routledge handbook of planning for health and well-being* (London: Routledge).

6 WHO (2006) *Obesity and overweight* (Geneva: WHO).

7 Butland *et al.* (2007) op. cit., p. 40.

8 Giles-Corti, B., Foster, S., Koohsari, M., Francis, J. and Hooper, P. (2015) 'The influence of urban design and planning on physical activity', in H. Barton, S. Thompson, S. Burgess, and M. Grant (eds) *The Routledge handbook of planning for health and well-being.* (London: Routledge).

9 See, for example, Sustainable Development Commission (2010) *Sustainable development: the key to tackling health inequalities* (London: Sustainable Development Commission).

10 This issue is one of urban form, and will be discussed at length in Chapters 12 and 13.

11 See, for example, Lee, C. and Moudon, A. (2008) 'Neighbourhood design and physical activity', *Building Research and Information*, 36(5): 395–411; and Brown, A., Khattack, A. and Rodriguez, A. (2008) 'Neighbourhood types, travel and body mass: a study of new urbanist and suburban neighbourhoods in the US', *Urban Studies*, 45: 983–988.

12 Boarnet, M. and Sarmiento, S. (1998) 'Can land use policy really affect travel behaviour? A study of the link between non-work travel and land use characteristics', *Urban Studies*, 35(7): 1155–1169; and Handy, S. (2005) *Does the built environment influence physical activity? Examining the evidence* (Washington, DC: Transportation Research Board).

13 Frank, L.D., Schmid, T.L., Sallis, J.F., Chapman, J. and Saelens, B.E. (2005) 'Linking objectively measured physical activity with objectively measured urban form: findings from SMARTRAQ', *American Journal of Preventive Medicine*, 28(2): 117–125; and Lee

and Moudon (2008), op. cit.; and Giles-Corti *et al.* (2015), op. cit.

14 Barton, H., Horswell, M. and Miller, P. (2012) 'Neighbourhood accessibility and active travel', *Planning Practice and Research*, 27(2): 177–201.

15 Barton, H. (2011) *Reshaping suburbs.* A report produced as part of the EPSRC *SOLUTIONS* project. Bristol: University of the West of England. Google 'Reshaping Suburbs' or www.uwe.ac.uk/et/research/who/publications

16 Davis and Parkin (2015), op. cit.

17 Ibid.

18 Department for Transport (2014) *Value for money assessment of cycling grants* (London: DfT).

19 Pickora, T., Giles-Corti, B., Bull, F., Jamrozik, K. and Donovan, R. (2003) 'Developing a framework for assessment of the environmental determinants of walking and cycling', *Social Science and Medicine*, 56: 1693–1703.

20 Hume, C., Salmon, J. and Ball, K. (2005) 'Children's perception of their home and neighbourhood environment, and their association with objectively measured physical activity', *Health Education Research*, 20(1): 1–13.

21 McCormack, G., Giles-Corti, B. and Bulsara, M. (2008) 'The relationship between destination proximity, destination mix and physical activity behaviours', *Preventive Medicine*, 46(1): 33–40.

22 Giles-Corti *et al.* (2015), op. cit.

23 Commission of the European Communities (1990) The Green Paper on the Urban Environment, Luxembourg, CEC; and EU Expert Group on the Urban Environment (1995) *European Sustainable Cities Part II*, ESDG XI (Brussels: EU Commission).

24 Department of the Environment (1994) *PPG 13, Transport* (London: HMSO); and Urban Task Force (1999) *Towards an urban renaissance* (London: Spon/Department of Environment, Transport and the Regions); Barton, H., Davis, G. and Guise, R. (1995) *Sustainable settlements: a guide for planners, designers and developers* (Luton: Local Government Management Board, and Bristol: University of the West of England).

25 Barton, H., Grant, M. and Guise, R. (2010) *Shaping neighbourhoods: for local health and global sustainability* (London: Routledge).

26 Sleet, D., Naumann, R. and Rudd, R. (2009) 'Injuries and the built environment', in A. Dannenberg, H. Frumpkin, and R. Jackson (eds) *Making healthy places: designing and building for health, well-being and sustainability* (Washington, DC: Island Press).

27 McCarthy, M. (1999) 'Transport and health', in M. Marmot and R. Wilkinson *Social*

determinants of health: the solid facts (Copenhagen: WHO).

28 NHTSA (National Highway Traffic Safety Administration) (2008) *Countermeasures that work*, third edn (Washington, DC: US Department for Transport).

29 Mahdjoubi, L. and Spencer, B. (2015) 'Healthy play for all ages in public open spaces', in H. Barton, S. Thompson, S. Burgess, and M. Grant (eds) *The Routledge handbook of planning for health and well-being* (London: Routledge).

30 Croucher, K., Myers, L., Jones, R. and Ellaway, A. (2007) *Health and the physical characteristics of urban neighbourhoods: a critical literature review* (Glasgow: Glasgow Centre for Population Health).

31 Bird, W. (2004) *Natural fit: can greenspace and biodiversity increase levels of physical activity?* (London: Royal Society for the Protection of Birds).

32 Ellaway, A., MacIntyre, S. and Bonnefoy, X. (2005) 'Graffiti, greenery and obesity in adults: secondary analysis of European cross-sectional survey', *British Medical Journal*, 331: 611–612.

33 Croucher *et al.* (2007), op. cit.

34 UNCRC (United Nations Committee on the Rights of the Child) (2013) General comment No. 17, as quoted in Mahdjoubi and Spencer (2015), op. cit.

35 Mitchell, R. and Popham, F. (2008) 'The effect of exposure to natural environment on health

inequalities and observational population study', *Lancet*, 372: 1655–1660.

36 Mahdjoubi and Spencer (2015), op. cit.

37 Sustrans (2011) *Autumn newsletter* (Bristol: Sustrans).

38 Ibid.

39 Ibid.

40 Popkin, B. (2006) 'Global nutrition dynamics: the world is shifting rapidly toward a diet linked with non-communicable diseases', *American Journal of Clinical Nutrition*, 84(2): 289–298.

41 For a fuller analysis of the US evidence, see Cannuscio, C. and Glanz, K. (2011) 'Food environments', in Dannenburg *et al.* (2015), op. cit.

42 Cummins, S., Findley, A., Petticrew, M. and Sparks, L. (2005) 'Healthy cities: the impact of food retail led regeneration on food access, choice and retail structure', *Built Environment*, 4.

43 See review in Townshend, T., Gallo, R. and Lake, A. (2015) 'Obesogenic built environments: concepts and complexities', in H. Barton, S. Thompson, S. Burgess, and M. Grant (eds) *The Routledge handbook of planning for health and well-being*. (London: Routledge).

44 The Lancet and University College London Commission (2012) 'Shaping cities for health: complexity and the planning of urban environments in the 21st century', *The Lancet*, special edition.

45 See Barton *et al.* (2010), p. 138.

CHAPTER SEVEN

PLANNING FOR MENTAL AND SOCIAL WELL-BEING

Introduction

Physical and mental well-being are intimately connected, as are physical and mental illness. While, of course, people can be physically ill and remain happy, or depressed but physically well, our minds and bodies are conjoined. It is no accident that some of the same environmental features affect both mind and body: contact with nature and active recreational opportunities, an urban environment that encourages physical activity, accessible local facilities, safe and friendly streets. If, for example, we go for a brisk walk, play tennis or dig the garden for half-an-hour, we not only improve our physical fitness, but we *feel* better.

Being mentally well implies being positive, self-possessed and happy. Conversely, mental illness implies depression, operating below par, lacking dynamism or confidence; when colour is bleached out of daily life, lethargy and *anomie* set in. In more extreme cases, people become psychotic or paranoid, when there is a loss of contact with reality. Before homing in on the *environmental* influences on mental wellness, it is important to recognize the huge significance of *social* and *personal* factors, including:

- our role and status in society – sufficient income, and a job, particularly a satisfying job with a level of control over our own work;
- the quality of our relationships: family relationships are critical, but also wider social engagement – social networks that reinforce a sense of identity and belonging;
- personal values – being interested in others, in society, in broader issues, and caring about them, helps to avoid excessive introspection;

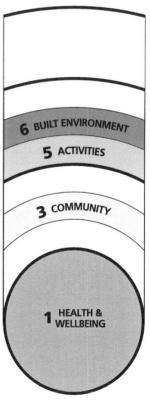

Fig 7.1 *Health Map focus: community*

- physical health – persistent illness can compromise mental well-being and relationships with others. Conversely, good physical health reinforces emotional well-being.[1]

In this context it is important not to over-egg the relevance of urban planning. But equivalently the environmental conditions people may experience – such as the stress of commuting, noise, street danger, the lack of daylight or contact with nature, the lack of physical activity– all affect mood. The spatial nature of the city also influences apparently independent issues of income and of work (see Chapter 8). Figure 7.2 expresses some aspects of this interdependence.

The book which first attempted to give a comprehensive evidence-based review of this field was David Halpern's *Mental Health and the Built Environment* (1995).[2] Halpern distinguished the direct and indirect influence of environment. The direct influences included noise levels and access to nature. The indirect influences concerned the effect of environment on social support networks and the perception of feeling at home in a place. Mental well-being is linked to concepts of *community, social cohesion* and *social capital.* These have a long history in sociological and planning thought, especially in relation to the idea of neighbourhoods. This chapter starts with the direct environmental influences on mental well-being, then moves on to the indirect influences and the discourse around community and empowerment.

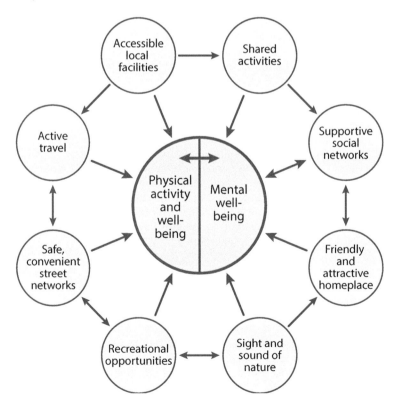

Fig 7.2 *Some influences on mental and physical well-being, illustrating mind/body interdependence and the agenda of this chapter*

Nature, greenspace, sun and sound

Intuitively we know it: contact with nature and natural light is good for us. The ancient Greeks, Chinese and Persians shared a conviction that contact with nature ameliorates stress and provides relief to the ill.[3] As noted, the Victorians created parks in industrial cities and Napoleon III did the same in Paris. Yet as approaches to health became increasingly medical in the twentieth century, the significance of nature was marginalized. Only recently has research from round the world reaffirmed its importance.

Health is linked to daylight and sunlight access, which helps to ameliorate Seasonal Affective Disorder (SAD) and improve the cognitive functions of dementia sufferers. Better light in homes, and (in the UK) more direct sunlight, also helps to reduce fuel bills and thus combat both fuel poverty and carbon emissions. Yet the principle of solar design, with correct orientation of buildings and appropriate fenestration, has not caught on. In Britain, most new houses face any way irrespective of aspect, and windows are small and mean.

Access to trees, wildlife and greenspaces, especially when well managed and safe, promotes mental well-being, social interaction and social cohesion.[4] Humans have an instinctive affinity with the natural world. It gives relief from stress and a heightened sense of well-being. People with access to nearby nature are generally healthier than those without, as contact with nature impacts positively on blood pressure, cholesterol levels, outlook on life and stress levels.[5] This is particularly true for less advantaged groups: their perceived health is positively associated with the local percentage of greenspace.[6] Residents of urban social housing who can see trees or open space from their homes demonstrate greater ability to deal with stress than those who have no such views.[7] People who are more locally based benefit especially.[8]

'Humans have an instinctive affinity with the natural world. It gives relief from stress and a heightened sense of well-being.'

In relation to children, Dutch researchers show that contact with nature enhances child development by encouraging recovery from stressful experiences and providing opportunities for exploration and play.[9] Dutch children are allowed to roam much younger and further than in Britain, where parents typically keep children on a tight leash. It may be pure coincidence that Dutch children are, according to a UN study, the happiest in Europe, while British children are the least happy.[10] The Dutch researchers demonstrate that for adults, too, contact with nature stimulates feelings of relaxation, autonomy and competence.

The benefits of nature and greenspace for well-being come at three levels, each with implications for planning and design:

- *viewing nature* – through windows, from the car, even indirectly on the television. This has value and emphasizes the need for trees and natural features to permeate the urban environment; for example, through street planting.
- *experiencing nature* – feeling a part of the natural world by sitting in gardens or pocket parks, smelling the perfume of flowers, listening to the birds, hearing the trickle, swirl or tumble of water.

- *being active in nature* – playing, walking, running, climbing, trekking, gardening, sporting activity.

Gardening is one good way of being active in nature. A survey of allotment holders in Newcastle, England, found that a substantial majority feel that there are psychological and spiritual benefits as well as physical. Allotments are described as 'havens', places to escape from the concerns of everyday life. As well as providing fresh food, exercise and contact with earthy reality, allotment societies also build a social fabric that cuts across socio-economic status.[11]

More generally, the quality and safety of open space are important. In the UK, 40 per cent of parks in the more deprived local authorities were in poor condition and most of those getting worse. If the community perceives the risk of assault or intimidation to be high, then the potential benefits of greenspace largely evaporate.[12]

Noise and the quality of the soundscape

Our sense of hearing brings both joy and pain. Health research has tended to concentrate on the pain, when sound becomes unwanted noise. Traffic is the most ubiquitous source of noise in urban areas but other sources can be a problem in particular locations: aircraft noise, trains, industrial processes, fans, construction sites, noisy neighbours. Exposure to chronic noise, such as that from a busy road junction, can affect mental well-being, especially in children, leading to negative classroom behaviour, reduced attention span and greater anxiety. Sleep deprivation can lead to weakening the immune system, hyper-tension, and serious stress related behaviours.[13] Only *some* people will be affected in this way, with the likelihood increased by poverty, low status, housing stress and neighbourhood stress. It is difficult, if not impossible, to isolate one cause and effect from others. The factors reinforce each other and increase the probability of mental and physical ill-health and premature death.

'When British people are asked what do they hear when they imagine themselves waking up in the morning in their ideal city (in a "visioning" exercise), the vast majority say "birdsong".'

But there is another side of the story. The 'soundscape' can act to boost well-being as well as compromise it. When British people are asked what do they hear when they imagine themselves waking up in the morning in their ideal city (in a 'visioning' exercise), the vast majority say 'birdsong'.[14] Natural sounds of birds, water, leaves rustling, even children playing (but not too close!) tend to relax tensions and raise the spirit.

Allowing natural sounds to be heard is therefore an aspect of place-making. The art is to ensure that the mechanical noises do not overwhelm the natural sounds in the public realm. Ideally noise should be reduced at source, but if not, through mitigation measures such as better layout, noise barriers and double glazing. Trees, bushes and hedges as barriers have a role: while they have only modest impact on noise levels, they have a greater psychological significance, reducing the perceived dominance of mechanical noise.

Social networks and community

The indirect effects of environment may be even more important. Mental well-being is closely related to social well-being. We are social creatures. We gain our sense of who we are through the communities we belong to. Social ties – especially to family and close friends – and social interactions more generally, provide the sense of identity, practical and emotional support that enable us to feel positive and happy.[15] The tangible sense of social support is particularly critical for older and more vulnerable people, combatting the danger of isolation and loneliness. Elderly people with strong social networks live longer, in better mental and physical health, and with lower fear of crime, than those without.[16]

Before examining the effect of the physical environment on social connections, I want to link these concepts of social support and social networks to that of *community*. In common parlance, community is a concept used with casual abandon. To some, it is the residents of a neighbourhood or a city. Politicians and the media hype it up as a kind of sacrosanct (though nebulous!) court of appeal. But to sociologists, it has a more precise meaning. A community is a network of people who know each other, as friends or simply associates, and who may provide mutual support to each other. Traditionally three types can be distinguished: (1) place communities – people knowing each other because they live in the same place; (2) interest communities – growing around shared activities; and (3) cultural communities – based on tribal, ethnic or religious groupings.[17]

In the modern age we often belong to many community groups. Our horizons expand as we grow. Babies and toddlers relate initially to the primary group, the nuclear family. They may rapidly adopt the more extended family: grandparents, uncles, aunts and cousins. As young children, they discover peer groups and adults acting *in loco parentis* at playgroup, nursery and school. Friendships emerge out of shared activities, whether through formal (parentally organized) activities or informal association, as in the street or playground or on the beach.

Fast forward to young adulthood, and the range and complexity of formal and informal groups an individual belongs to are of a different order. They may be connected to a local 'place community'. But if they have moved away from the parental home, local roots in their new (often temporary) locality may never grow. Instead they belong to 'interest groups' based on education, work, sport, cultural activities, etc. The concept of belonging to *one* community breaks down. Social contact and friendship occur on an increasingly individualized pattern, especially in major cities, reflecting personal networks and inclinations (Figure 7.3). Social media and professional networks link people to the 'global village', creating virtual communities with only rare face-to-face contact being possible. The whole shifting scene can appear almost random – so the question arises as to whether the spatial planner has a legitimate role in trying to support communities.

'Social media and professional networks link people to the "global village", creating virtual communities – so the question arises as to whether the spatial planner has a legitimate role in trying to support communities.'

Fig 7.3 Social networks flourishing in the public realm: a street party, women chatting, toddlers playing, people meeting casually in the market, and men at play

The importance of locality

Some influential sociologists and planning authors have suggested that planning for place communities is pointless.[18] Anthony Giddens argued that, 'The primacy of place ... has been largely destroyed by disembedding and time-place distanciation. Place has become phantasmagoric ...'[19] These views contributed to a professional belief that neighbourhoods were dead, or at least didn't matter. High mobility, free association and virtual connections were assumed to be the way forward.

However, for many people, place-based social networks remain critical to their sense of identity, social support and mental well-being. These groups include elderly people, infirm or disabled people, young parents and their children (especially single parent families), teenagers, unemployed and unskilled people, all of whom are likely to live more local lives, and some of whom are particularly vulnerable. For them, the social networks in their own neighbourhood, both the formal groups and informal associations, are essential for well-being. If they perceive their locality to be unsafe and threatening, their sense of community is undermined. Crime, or the fear of crime, can lead to feelings of isolation and low self-esteem.[20]

Policy for the physical environment can exacerbate social pressures, or create social opportunities. People's own perceptions of their neighbourhood reflect objective measures of both physical and social quality.[21] If patterns of urban change can be contrived so that schools, shops, pubs, health facilities, parks and libraries are available locally, then mental and physical well-being benefit. Such activities are important generators of community. People meet by arrangement or accident and relationships develop. Often the social groupings in one place overlap with those in another: school kids from the same school find themselves meeting up again in a sports club or nature group; parents meet neighbours, workmates or other school parents in a coffee shop, store or baby-sitting circle. The overlapping networks reinforce the sense of belonging to a community, strengthening social capital and supporting well-being.[22] The simple fact of being able to walk to facilities itself encourages casual meetings, which increase the total number of social contacts and the sense of well-being.

Social contact is also affected by traffic. Most people prefer to live in a quiet street. Households that live on main roads (typically poorer people because the rents are cheaper), experience higher levels of noise, air pollution, accidents and route severance that go with high traffic volumes. It is evident that the combination of these factors inhibits social interaction. Appleyard's classic research in the USA compared the behaviour of similar populations in three streets with low, medium and high traffic levels. He found that higher flows of traffic lead to much less social interaction among neighbours. In addition, people's perception of their own 'home' territory was drastically reduced. Instead of the street being seen as a friendly extension of the home, it was seen as foreign territory, deterring walking/cycling trips and heightening a sense of insecurity. More recent research in the UK has produced similar results.[23]

Overall, then, and contrary to earlier social science assumptions, it is clear that spatial planning is important for social networks and therefore for mental well-being. This is particularly so for poorer and less mobile groups, who are more likely to be locally based. If poor and vulnerable households are clustered together in less desirable locations, forming ghettos, that will reinforce deprivation. The structure of the housing market and the allocation of affordable housing are critical factors, and the significance for health inequalities and social exclusion is clear.

'It is clear that spatial planning is important for social networks and therefore for mental well-being. This is particularly so for poorer and less mobile groups.'

Healthy, diverse neighbourhoods

While *community* is a social concept, *neighbourhood*, in its modern usage, is spatial, implying a locality which has particular identity. The discussion above leaves no doubt that we *should* plan for neighbourhoods. However, there are profound issues around the form they should take. The 'neighbourhood unit' advocated by mid-twentieth-century designers was bounded and distinct. It suffered from presumed determinism of where people have their local connections. But in reality each person conceives their own neighbourhood, depending on where they live, what connections they have locally – to family, shops or schools, parks, pubs, clubs or friends – and which way they travel to non-local destinations. Neighbourhoods thus have something in common with *rainbows*, shifting according to the position of the viewer.[24]

It is vital that spatial patterns do not frustrate these very varied individual connections, but facilitate them. Christopher Alexander argued in his influential article 'A city is not a tree', that we should see neighbourhoods as interlinked and interdependent within a lattice, offering excellent connections to other parts of the settlement, so that people and businesses have a wide range of options easily available.[25] This image does not imply an unstructured, random scatter of people and facilities. On the contrary the relationship between different land uses and movement networks requires precise planning. We saw in Chapter 6 that distance from homes to facilities is critical for walkability. In addition, the clustering of facilities facilitating social networks and casual meetings, benefit less mobile people especially. For example, there are benefits if sheltered accommodation is located close to a surgery, local shops and a bus stop. Chapter 13 develops this theme of neighbourhood planning.

Social mix or social apartheid?

A critical aspect of making social connections is the sense of being comfortable in your surroundings, feeling at home, able to wander the streets without fear or intimidation. This raises the controversial topic of social segregation. To what extent should people from different cultures, classes and incomes live together in one locality?

There is a 'natural' tendency of the housing market towards *residential differentiation*, i.e. the separation of different groups by area. The house builders, responding to market pressures, offer rich households larger properties in more 'exclusive' neighbourhoods. Rented flats for single people and couples tend to be close to town centres. Poor households may be concentrated in social housing estates. This segregation was conspicuously the case in the mid-twentieth century, but continues with the assumption of investors and policy-makers that 'like attracts like'. Affluent neighbourhoods attract up-market investment and residents fight off developments that threaten their amenity, while social housing providers are drawn to poor neighbourhoods because land prices are cheaper.

A case for social polarization can be made through concern for mental well-being. Halpern reviewed many studies on social mix which showed – unsurprisingly – that people feel more at ease if people they meet on the street are like them, sharing similar values or lifestyles, rather than those they perceive as different. The sense of difference is particularly reinforced by ethnicity and colour, but equally could be class-based or age-based. Local social homogeneity (i.e. sameness) is an important factor in giving a sense of local friendliness and security and supporting mental well-being. A number of studies suggest there is a key threshold of 'people like me' in the locality; mental health is compromised if *less than 40 per cent* of people are of similar class or culture.[26]

But the counter-arguments are powerful. Many studies have shown that living in a socially disadvantaged area affects health, with levels of mortality, sickness, coronary heart disease and mental illness higher in poor areas. So too is unhealthy behaviour in relation to diet, smoking, alcohol and physical activity. It would seem that the spatial concentration of deprived households in particular neighbourhoods tends to reinforce bad habits. One American study reported on an experiment placing difficult families from poor estates randomly into affluent localities, and found their mental well-being improved vis-à-vis the non-movers.[27] Causality is difficult to establish, but it is clear that if poor and problem households are herded into ghettos by the way the housing system works, then that will compromise their mental well-being.

A major longitudinal study suggests that the downward spiral gets worse rather than better with time. This study was undertaken in the Glasgow city region between 1987 and 2007, and followed poorer individuals in different age groups living in localities of varied social character, some rich, some poor. The results were startling. People of similar social status experienced completely different health trajectories depending on where they lived. Those living in the more deprived areas reported ill-health on average 17 years earlier than those living in the least deprived. In all other ways apart from their place of residence, these people were categorized as similar, and the study attempted to check out possible confounding factors through sensitivity analysis.[28]

Not all cities may be as polarized as Glasgow. But the powerful conclusion of all the area studies, from the 1960s to the present, is that the concentration of poor people in specific neighbourhoods is very harmful to their well-being, and costly to society in relation to social services, health services, crime and productivity. The graphic phrase 'sink estate' expresses the problem fairly. The stigma attached to living in such places, the progressive reinforcement of mental and physical ill-health (which some people courageously resist), suggest that spatial planners should seek by all means possible to restructure existing sink estates and ensure new concentrations of poverty are not created by default. Given the natural tendency for affluent groups to seek socially exclusive neighbourhoods, that default position is all too easy to fall into. Spatial decision-makers have a major task to shape the workings of the housing market so that ghettos are avoided.

The positive arguments for socially mixed neighbourhoods are summarized below, adapted from *Shaping Neighbourhoods*:[29]

- *Choice*: to allow households of all kinds the opportunity to select locations convenient to their needs, which can reduce their travel costs/distance (and consequent pollution) and maintain family and social connections.
- *Equity*: to provide more options for poorer households, who are often heavily constrained by the market.
- *Business viability*: to ensure that all areas have sufficient spending power to support local retail outlets and commercial services.
- *Population balance*: to plan 'lifetime neighbourhoods' that attract households at different stages and ages, avoiding peaks and troughs of demand for facilities such as schools, and maintaining overall population levels.
- *Skills available*: to ensure the local availability of a wide range of skills and professions, providing local services and varied job opportunities for young people, part-time workers and carers.
- *Supportive community*: to encourage mutual understanding and respect between different social/cultural groups and thus build social cohesion.

'People of similar social status experienced completely different health trajectories depending on where they lived.'

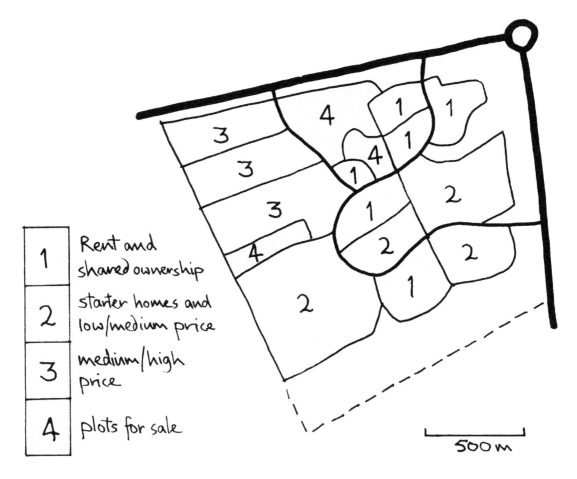

1	Rent and shared ownership
2	starter homes and low/medium price
3	medium/high price
4	plots for sale

500 m

Fig 7.4 *Socially mixed neighbourhoods in Milton Keynes: within each grid square of the city the policy has been to ensure social mix*

Source: based on Barton 2000 (note 24), p.129.

On the face of it, there seems to be an impasse between the valid need for people to feel 'at home' in their neighbourhood, and the valid need to achieve socially balanced communities. However, the conflict is more apparent than real. There is a critical distinction of scale: mental well-being is mainly affected by the people you meet outside your front door, *in your own street* – do you feel safe walking out of your home? In contrast, social mix is vital at the *neighbourhood scale* – the scale that supports local schools and shops, and avoids whole localities being stigmatized. A parallel can be drawn with pre-industrial towns, where rich and poor lived cheek by jowl, one street is of grand houses, while just round the corner are modest terraced houses. The patterns often persist to this day because of the housing size and type. Small-scale social uniformity can be combined with larger scale social diversity – see Figure 7.4.

Social capital and empowerment

The influential concept of *social capital* is broader than that of social networks, and more specific than that of community. The idea emerged in the late twentieth century, articulated by Robert Putnam in particular, as a kind of social counterweight to prevailing ideas of economic capital, intellectual capital and environmental capital. Social capital, put simply, are the features of social organization that enable people to co-operate for mutual benefit. Putnam identifies the social networks, the norms of behaviour and the degree of trust and reciprocity (mutual respect and help) which people experience.[30] A community with high social capital is able to stand up for itself, support weaker members in adversity, initiate and manage social and environmental projects. A locality with weak social capital finds such things difficult – there is not the cohesion or the culture of mutuality and creativity.

While the idea of social capital is rather instrumental, a means to an end, others – from Plato onwards – see a society of mutual support, trust and tolerance as an end in itself, helping people to a sense of social identity and belonging. The anarchist writer Colin Ward, for example, valued processes that empower the powerless in the urban jungle.[31] He cited the situation of the very poor in developing countries, where people living in unregulated, unhealthy, but self-managed shanty towns, create complex webs of economic self-help and mutual support. This web of social capital can be destroyed by a government decision to demolish informal settlements and rehouse in tower blocks, as has occurred in cities round the world. Healthier housing does not compensate for the loss of connecting networks and community support.[32]

The classic study of the destruction of community and social capital by well-meaning intervention was undertaken in East London by Young and Willmott in the 1950s.[33] It stands as an object lesson in the dangers of unthinking intervention. Young and Willmott compared two groups, one in Bethnal Green in inner London, the other in the new overspill suburb of Greenleigh in Essex, where some residents of the East End had been rehoused. In Bethnal Green, there was a rich social life built on kinship networks, providing strong mutual support, and at least partially compensating for the unhealthy physical environment. Local businesses (including many pubs) flourished in the close-knit streets. In Greenleigh, with brand new accommodation and spacious layout, the community ties were broken, families retreated into isolation and lethargy, new businesses did not flourish. A generic name was given to the experience of living in such newly created overspill settlements: new town blues.

The lesson is that interference with people's established way of life and networks of support is risky, and this applies as much within the city as in new settlements. Many regeneration schemes, despite providing improved physical conditions, result in poorer health outcomes, as a result of disruption of social and physical patterns – at least in the short term. If comprehensive renewal is necessary, it is vital to take the community with you, managing the process of change in co-operation with the local residents and businesses, using the process to empower local people rather than undermine. As part of this, it is vital to secure the future of physical facilities that help to gel the community – schools, shops, pubs, meeting rooms, parks. Spatial decision-making must facilitate, not frustrate, a convivial and supportive society. Planning a regeneration scheme, designing a new estate, building a new retail warehouse, constructing a tramway, or installing a local renewable energy system – the way it happens can either empower or alienate. Local authorities and development companies need to have a commitment to work collaboratively with local residents and businesses. The right approach to this – neither paternalistic nor manipulative – is discussed in Chapters 16 and 17.

Civil society

'A key aspect of social capital is the engagement of people in voluntary activities and decision-making processes beyond their immediate personal preoccupations.'

A key aspect of social capital is the engagement of people in voluntary activities and decision-making processes beyond their immediate personal preoccupations. This can take many forms: membership of clubs and societies, commitment to social and environmental action, political and campaign groups, village and neighbourhood plans, social entrepreneurial initiatives. Taken together, these activities constitute *civil society*, complementing state and market activity. The idea that civil society offers a valid alternative approach to community services and environmental improvement has been recognized by the powerful.[34] At a city level, the involvement of civil society in spatial planning, as a counterweight to the influence of big business, has been documented for the city of Portland.[35] In Bristol, the progressive shift of the city from conventional commercial and social priorities towards becoming European Green Capital in 2015 was in no small part due to the sustained energy of the voluntary sector.[36] An important aspect was the openness of built environment professionals and investors in public and private sectors to innovation.

At a more local level, while the strength of 'civil society' largely depends on the attitudes of the individuals and communities involved, planning in the broadest sense helps shape the opportunities. This may be by ensuring that potential meeting places and club venues are available and protected – not always easy when market rents are high. It can also be through the processes of physical development.

Spatial planning recommendations

Healthy planning and development decisions do not impinge instantly on well-being. Figure 7.5 illustrates the pathways via changes to the environment, lifestyle and experiential impacts and effects on body and mind. Nevertheless, it is possible to be very clear about the principles involved.

Mental well-being and social capital are supported by:

- Encouraging contact with nature through street trees, green private gardens (not tarmac), and a network of greenspaces including parks, playgrounds, playing fields and allotments, with every dwelling being within 300 metres of greenspace (400 m maximum actual walking distance),[37] able to experience the natural sounds and feel part of nature.
- Reducing the prevalence of unpleasant noise and smell through environmental health regulation; managing the relationship between homes and major noise sources through

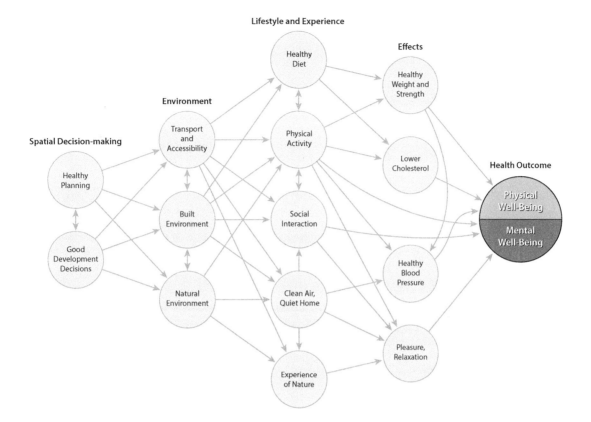

Fig 7.5 *Pathways from spatial decisions to health*

land use zoning and/or design measures; reducing traffic noise in residential, retail and cultural areas.

- Creating opportunities for recreational physical activity for all ages, including safe streets and spaces for children's play, and formal and informal recreational activities, especially in natural surroundings.
- Ensuring there are multiple opportunities and encouragement for the development of social networks and social interaction, through places to meet, socialize and/or pursue shared activities, and a safe, permeable network of pedestrian and cycling ways.
- Ensuring that every neighbourhood, urban district or small town has a wide diversity of people, with opportunities for different income groups, cultures, household types and abilities to find appropriate and affordable accommodation in suitable locations, thus helping to support a good range of local facilities, services and job opportunities.
- Planning the whole town or city so that neighbourhoods are not isolated but interconnected, so that varied social, economic and cultural opportunities are easy to access.
- Involving local people in development decisions that affect them or their sense of place-identity, especially when major regeneration or new-build projects are underway, so that

people feel empowered, not disenfranchised. Using development and social engagement as a means of contributing to social capital.

Further reading

Barton, H. (ed.) (2000) *Sustainable communities: the potential of eco-neighbourhoods.* London: Earthscan. See Chapter 1 on perceptions of neighbourhood; Chapter 6 on social capital and housing mix; Chapter 9 on the changing nature of community; Chapter 10 on community initiatives; Chapter 15 on community safety.

Barton, H., Grant, M. and Guise, R. (2010) *Shaping neighbourhoods: for local health and global sustainability.* London: Routledge. For practical policy guidance on housing mix and social capital, see pp. 91–105.

Burton, L. (2015) 'Mental well-being and the influence of place', in H. Barton, S. Thompson, S. Burgess, and M. Grant (eds) *The Routledge handbook of planning for health and well-being.* London: Routledge, pp. 150–161.

Corkery, L. (2015) 'Beyond the park: linking urban greenspace, human well-being and environmental health', in H. Barton, S. Thompson, S. Burgess, and M. Grant (eds) *The Routledge handbook of planning for health and well-being.* London: Routledge, pp. 239–253.

Cozens, P. (2015) 'Crime and community safety: challenging the design consensus', in H. Barton, S. Thompson, S. Burgess, and M. Grant (eds) *The Routledge handbook of planning for health and well-being.* London: Routledge, pp. 162–177.

Sullivan, W. and Chang, C. (2011) 'Mental health and the built environment', in A. Dannenberg, H. Frumpkin, and R. Jackson (eds) *Making healthy places: designing and building for health, well-being and sustainability.* Washington, DC: Island Press.

Notes

1   Based on Layard, R. (2005) *Happiness: lessons from a new science* (New York: Penguin Books).
2   Halpern, D. (1995) *Mental health and the built environment* (London: Taylor & Francis).
3   Townsend, M. and Weerusuriya, R. (2010) *Beyond blue to green: the benefits of contact with nature for mental health and well-being* (Melbourne: Beyond the Blue Ltd).
4   Croucher, K., Myers, L. and Bretherton, J. (2008) *The links between greenspace and health: a critical literature review* (Stirling: Greenspace Scotland).
5   Maller, C., Townsend, M., Ptyor, A., Brown, P. and St Leger, L. (2005) *Healthy nature, healthy people: contact with nature as an upstream health promotion intervention for populations* (Oxford: Oxford University Press).
6   Mitchell, R. and Popham, F. (2008) 'The effect of exposure to natural environment on health inequalities and observational population study', *Lancet*, 372: 1655–1660.
7   Kuo, F. (2001) 'Coping with poverty: impacts of environment and attention in the inner city', *Environment and Behaviour*, 33: 5–34.
8   De Vries, S., Verheeij, R. and Groenevegan, P. (2003) 'Natural environments? An exploratory analysis of the relationship between greenspace and health', *Environment and Planning A*, 15: 1717–1731.
9   Health Council of the Netherlands (2004) *Nature and health: the influence of nature on social, psychological and physical well-being* (The Hague: HCN).
10 UNICEF Innocenti Research Centre (2007) *Child poverty in perspective: an overview of child well-being in rich countries* (Florence: UNICEF). Available at: www.unicef.org.irc
11 Ferres, M. and Townsend, T. (2012) 'The social, health and well-being benefits of allotments: five societies in Newcastle', GURU Working Paper No. 47. Newcastle University, School of Architecture, Planning and Landscape.
12 Croucher *et al.* (2008) op. cit.
13 Corburn, J. (2009) *Towards the healthy city: people, places and the politics of urban planning* (Cambridge, MA: MIT Press).
14 This is based on personal experience of many visioning exercises.
15 Halpern (1995), op. cit; Sullivan, W. and Chang, C. (2011) 'Mental health and the built environment', in A. Dannenberg, H. Frumpkin, and R. Jackson (eds) *Making healthy places:*

designing and building for health, well-being and sustainability (Washington, DC: Island Press).

16 Kweon, B., Sullivan, W. and Wiley, A. (1998) 'Green common spaces and social integration of inner city older adults', Environment and Behaviour, 30(6): 832–858.

17 Barton, H., Grant, M. and Guise, R. (2010) Shaping neighbourhoods: for local health and global sustainability (London: Routledge).

18 Dennis, N. (1968) 'The popularity of the neighbourhood community idea', in R. Pahl (ed.) Readings in urban sociology (Oxford: Pergamon Press); Webber, M. (1964) 'The urban place and the non-place urban realm', in M. Webber, Explorations into urban structure (Philadelphia, PA: University of Philadelphia Press, 1964).

19 Giddens, A. (1990) The consequences of modernity (Oxford: Polity Press).

20 Whitley, R. and Prince, M. (2005) 'Fear of crime, and inner city health in London', Social Science and Medicine, 61: 1678–1688.

21 Truong, K. and Ma, S. (2006) 'A systematic review of the relationship between neighbourhood and mental health', Journal of Mental Health, Politics and Economics, 9: 137–154.

22 Lavin, T., Higgens, C., Metcalfe, O. and Jordan, A. (2006) Health effects of the built environment: a review (Dublin: The Institute of Public Health in Ireland).

23 Appleyard, D. and Lintell, M. (1970) 'The environmental quality of city streets: the resident's viewpoint', Journal of the American Institute of Planners, 38(2): 84–101; Hart, J. (2008) 'Driven to excess: impacts of motor vehicle traffic on residential quality of life in Bristol', unpublished MA dissertation, University of the West of England, Bristol.

24 Barton, H. (ed.) (2000) Sustainable communities: the potential of eco-neighbourhoods (London: Earthscan). See Chapter 1.

25 Alexander, C. (1965) 'A city is not a tree', Architectural Review, April: 58–62.

26 Halpern (1995), op. cit.

27 Leventhal, T. and Brooks-Gunn, J. (2003) 'Moving to opportunity: an experimental study of neighbourhood effects on mental health', American Journal of Public Health, 98(8): 380–386.

28 Ellaway, A., Benzeval, M., Green, M., Leyland, A. and MacIntyre, S. (2012) 'Getting sicker quicker: does living in a more deprived neighbourhood mean your health deteriorates faster?' Health and Place, 18: 132–137.

29 Barton et al. (2010), op. cit., p. 94.

30 Putnam, R. and Leonardi, R. (1993) Making democracy work (Princeton, NJ: Princeton University Press).

31 Ward, C. (1976) Housing: an anarchist approach (London: Freedom Press, 1976).

32 Hague, C. (2015) 'Rapid urbanization, health and well-being', in Barton et al. (eds) (2010), op. cit.

33 Willmott, P. and Young, M.D. (1957) Family and kinship in East London (London: Routledge & Kegan Paul, 1957).

34 For example, David Cameron, UK prime minister from 2010, talked about the Big Society, meaning much the same thing.

35 Ozawa, C. (2004) The Portland Edge: challenges and successes in growing communities (Washington, DC: Island Press).

36 Brownlie, E. (2014) Bristol's green roots (Bristol: The Schumacher Centre, 2014).

37 Barton et al. (2010), op. cit., p. 139.

CHAPTER EIGHT

PLANNING FOR PLACE EQUITY

Rise up with me against the organization of poverty.

Pablo Neruda – as quoted by the Marmot Commission

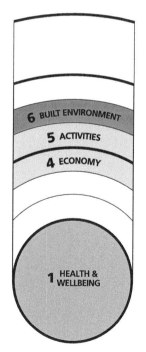

Fig 8.1 *Focus on income and place*

'There is a long-running debate about the significance of place, and the role of policy, in relation to social disadvantage.'

Social justice and health inequalities

The theme of social justice has been of concern to town planners since the new settlement entrepreneurs of the nineteenth century and early twentieth century. More recently the concepts of social inclusion and exclusion have been used to articulate the problems of disadvantage, and in the past decade a new impetus has been given by growing awareness of health inequalities (in the USA: 'health disparities').

The existence of inequality is not in dispute, but there is a long-running debate about the significance of place, and the role of policy, in relation to social disadvantage. Some on the political left believe that the structural inequities in society – the distribution of wealth and power – are so entrenched that marginal tampering with the urban environment just allows us to avoid the root cause. Others, also on the left, argue that changes to the physical form of cities bring about a significant and unjust redistribution of income and opportunity – and there is a moral obligation to act with greater awareness.[1]

Right-wing politicians may admit the reality of distributional effects, but dislike the rhetoric of social justice. They consider it is vital to let the free market operate freely, and if people suffer as a consequence, it is their own responsibility to better themselves. A more mainstream view is to recognize that the market is not perfect, and therefore it is important for governments to tackle certain facets of spatial equity – affordable housing and public transport, for example – while in general allowing private and voluntary sectors to operate freely.

Now *health inequality* has been added to traditional equity concerns, providing a powerful incentive for political and professional action. Health inequity not only severely damages the prospects of the poorest in society, but also imposes health and social care costs on society, depresses productivity and represents a waste of human potential. In 2008, the WHO published *Closing the Gap in a Generation*, reporting on global health inequities and priorities for action.[2] Subsequently there were reviews for England and for Europe.[3]

Studies reveal shocking and potentially avoidable inequalities in life and health. Internationally life expectancy in 2013 ranged from 46 years (Sierra Leone, *before* Ebola) to 84 years (Japan).[4] In England, the poorest neighbourhoods in 1999–2003 had an average disability-free life expectancy (DFLE) of 53 years, while the richest had a DFLE of 70 (see Figure 8.2). The proportion of people suffering physical or mental disability in London varies from 6 per cent for richer households to almost 40 per cent for the poorest. Whole cities can suffer short healthy life expectancy: men in Manchester in 2009–2011 had an average DFLE of 55 years.[5] The implications when the retirement age is 65+ are severe, both for individuals and society (see Figure 8.2).

Inequality is spatially organized. People living in the localities with the lowest average incomes, shortest healthy lives and highest levels of unemployment also experience the most adverse environmental conditions: poor air quality, high noise levels, traffic danger, poor and often overcrowded housing, little greenspace, unkempt places that feel intimidating and uncongenial. Typically such places also have high drug dependence, high crime levels and low social cohesion.[6] A critical realization is that the agendas of social justice and health equity, in relation to the urban environment, are the same. The question is how far the planning of the urban environment can reduce these inequalities.

This chapter cannot review all the relevant spatial issues. It looks first in more depth at social disadvantage and urban structure, then picks up the theme of *spatial opportunity for all*: concerns about equity of opportunity in relation to age, household status, race,

'The proportion of people suffering physical or mental disability in London varies from 6 per cent for richer households to almost 40 per cent for the poorest.'

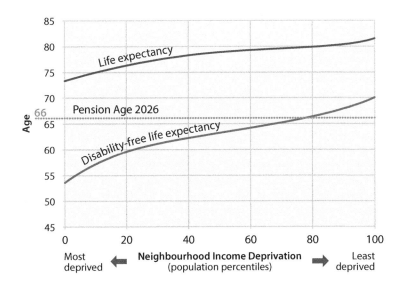

Fig 8.2 *Life expectancy and disability-free life expectancy – at birth, by neighbourhood income level, England, 1999–2003*

Source: based on Office for National Statistics, available at: www.nationalarchives.gov.uk/doc/open-government-licence

culture and disability. Later sections home in on issues of income, housing accessibility and transport. What are the problems, and how can urban planning and design help to reduce them?

The nature of social disadvantage

Given the alignment of social justice and health equity, I think it is important to learn the lessons of earlier work on the nature of disadvantage. It is not just a matter of poverty. In the 1960s and 1970s, there was a series of seminal studies in the UK. The Plowden Committee (1963), set up to examine inequalities in education, had trenchant and influential messages, many still relevant. Plowden identified a 'web of circumstances' that led to a vicious circle of cumulative deprivation from one generation to the next. The web of circumstances was spatially driven: the concentration of poor and 'problem' households in specific areas, affecting the quality of schools. The more enterprising citizens would leave, compounding the sense of powerlessness. An area-based strategy, involving positive discrimination in school investment and teacher funding, was considered essential – and has been sustained to varying degrees in the years since.

Later studies broadened the debate. In 1973, David Harvey published his influential book on *Social Justice and the City*, drawing together the evidence and arguments justifying policy to achieve what he called 'territorial distributive justice'. He articulated three criteria by which social justice can be judged – which could apply to health equity too:

- *Need* – how well are essential needs – such as housing, fresh air, facilities – being met?
- *The common good* – are there positive impacts on economic development, climate change, urban environment?
- *Merit* – do policies and initiatives 'work'?[7]

Subsequently government studies of deprivation and inner city areas observed that low income and low status were the core of the problem. They explain why people live in particular areas, which then become stigmatized. Multiple deprivations, often combined with vacant 'hard-to-let' dwellings, conspire to undermine the sense of community and sap individual initiative. The answer was a 'total' multi-agency approach, tackling all the local and national policy impacts in a concerted and systematic way.[8] A seminal study, co-ordinated by Peter Hall, showed how post-war planning policy was implicated. Greenbelt policies resulted in urban containment, escalating land and housing prices, and development leap-frogging greenbelts.[9] The unintended consequences were social exclusion and extra transport problems – which we still see today.

Social exclusion became a buzz phrase in the 1990s. People can find themselves trapped by the housing system in dysfunctional communities. Unemployment becomes the normal situation, and passed on to successive generations. Those who do get good jobs move out and up. Social landlords find themselves providing housing for the jobless, as vacancies are filled by the most disadvantaged households, reinforcing the downward spiral.[10]

Catch 22

From my own experience, what struck me most about disadvantaged communities was the *Catch 22* that people experience. This was very clearly articulated to me by a British West Indian, who was director of a local citizen's advice centre. He said that the central problem was one of demoralization: on the one hand, people absorb the materialist values of wider society, reinforced again and again by advertising, the media, and conventional political wisdom, which continually rams home their failure to compete, their low status, while at the same time the structures of wider society, the workings of job and housing markets, the dependency on state hand-outs with built-in poverty traps, actively inhibit their ability to achieve materialistic success.

Demoralization in the face of this Catch 22 (see box above) affects health. Michael Marmot's book, *The Status Syndrome*, shows how our health is closely related to our position in society – the degree to which we feel secure and empowered. Money is an important aspect of this, but not the only factor. Those who sense they have little control over their own lives are much more liable to become prematurely ill. They feel trapped in failure. Those who have more autonomy in their living situation, their work and pleasures – and a sense of self-respect reinforced by society's respect – tend to live longer, with fewer years of incapacity.[11]

The degree of social equity is a critical factor determining many of the attributes of a society. The researchers Wilkinson and Pickett show that a big gap between rich and poor in the 'developed' market democracies of the world, is associated with a wide range of health and social problems (Figure 8.3). They show it is not wealth per se that matters, but how that wealth is distributed. The least equal

'Our health is closely related to our position in society – the degree to which we feel secure and empowered. Those who sense they have little control over their own lives are much more liable to become prematurely ill.'

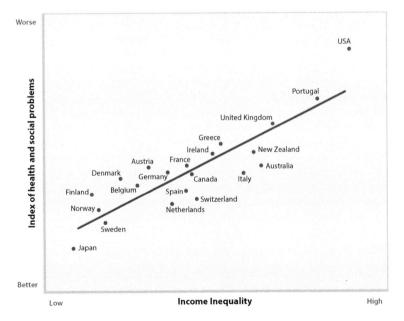

Fig 8.3 *Health and social problems in relation to income inequality*

Source: based on Wilkinson and Pickett 2009 (note 12), p.20.

societies listed are the USA, Portugal and the UK, and they are also highest on the health and social problems index. The most equal are Japan and the Scandinavian countries, with the best outcomes. Wilkinson and Pickett show that frequently all members of society benefit from greater equality, not just the poorest. Analyses across educational levels, comparing the USA and England (which is less unequal than the USA), show that rates of illness for all the major disease categories are lower in England, for *all* educational levels. From another source we discover that life expectancy in a poor but equal country, Cuba, is as good as life expectancy in the richest and most unequal country, the United States.[12] One theory is that morale is better in more equal countries, and that strengthens health, happiness and social behaviour.

Planning for *all*

The central question for planners and designers is: *in what ways do spatial and development decisions affect inequality?* This is a huge question, and there are many dimensions. I want to concentrate on a few: first, the diversity of *needs* (as highlighted by Harvey); then on *income*, given the centrality of poverty as a cause of ill-health; then on *housing* and *accessibility*.

'Urban planning is not about favouring one group of the population over another, but attempting to create places that can accommodate and provide for all the different needs that people have.'

Urban planning is not about favouring one group of the population over another, but attempting to create places that can accommodate and provide for all the different needs that people have. As policy-makers and as researchers, it is often convenient to treat the population as a whole. But people's needs and demands vary greatly by age, ability, gender, household status, class, income, educational attainment, work status, culture, religion and race. While the needs and choices of individuals cannot be predicted, the needs of generic groups *can* be anticipated. By way of example, consider the contrasting needs of 7-year-olds, 17-, 37- and 67-year-olds. Or envisage the needs of a blind person, a physically able person, and an obese person. As far as possible, the created environment should be inclusive of all these. It should provide opportunities for each person to satisfy their basic requirements and participate in the life of the community – offering challenge for the most adventurous and succour to the most constrained.

Figure 8.4 gives a typology of need groups. The breakdown provides starting points for analysis. The most basic distinctions relate to age and household status – recognition of these varying needs is fundamental to good planning. The specific needs of disabled people require sensitivity in design. Freedom for people to be able to use any mode of transport, is a central issues for planners. Subsequent chapter sections pick up some of the relevant issues in relation to income, employment, housing and transport.

Work, income and spatial policy

Income and the related variable of employment are both determinants of health, and both impact on social status, which is also a key determinant. Depression, physical illness and mortality increase

Age groups	Babies and toddlers Young children Older children Teenagers Young adults Mature adults Retired and able-bodied Frail elderly	The most basic category. Each age group has distinctive needs, which may require special places (think of recreation, for example). Groups such as teenagers should not be ignored.
Households and families	Single people Couples Adult groups Founding families Maturing families Empty-nesters	Households are commonly linked to housing needs. But beware a simplistic equation of household size with dwelling size. The market doesn't work like that.
Gender and sexuality	Female Male Heterosexual Gay and Lesbian Bisexual and transgender	Some activities are thought of as male (e.g. football) or female (e.g. childcare), but increasingly less so in most rich countries. Development per se has limited influence on sex.
Disability	Mobility impaired people Wheelchair users Blind and partially sighted Those with learning difficulties Dementia sufferers Those with emotional trauma	It is important to recognize each of these special needs in the design of the public realm. NB. Planning for wheelchairs also helps in relation to push-chairs.
Ethnicity and culture	Colour Cultural background Traveller communities Religion	It is often said that planning is colour-blind. But there are specific needs, e.g. for travellers and different faiths.
Income and employment	Low income Medium income High income Employed Self-employed Home-workers Unemployed Retired Student	Housing needs/demands vary according to income, and all groups need accommodation for a rounded community. Students (living away from home) are a particular issue. All types of employment need consideration. More home-workers implies larger units.
Movement	Pedestrians Cyclists Non-car owners One-car owners Two-plus car owners Delivery/service van and lorry users	Planning for people as pedestrians and cyclists is top priority. Non-car-owners are vulnerable in car-based societies. Car users need easy access to destinations for frail/disabled people and small children

Fig 8.4 *Social need groups*

when unemployment rises, especially long-term unemployment.[13] Poverty is associated with poor housing, limited mobility, reduced life chances and increased stress, all likely to impact on health and well-being.

Policy-makers and politicians at all levels act on the assumption that a buoyant economy is an absolutely central policy goal. Job opportunities are seen as vital for the well-being of local people. The pursuit of growth through economic regeneration and the development of new business parks is one of the main drivers of official planning policy. At one level this is absolutely right, but the evidence of the health benefits is not simple. The quality of jobs created, and who gets them, are important factors as well as simply the number of jobs. So, for example, urban regeneration schemes that are aimed at bringing jobs and a better environment to deprived populations, have often resulted in worse health outcomes than before – due to the disruption to lives and the inability of unskilled locals to get the new jobs in competition with skilled in-movers.[14] Other evidence suggests that re-employment after a period of unemployment, while sometimes beneficial, can sometimes reinforce a downward spiral if the job pays below a living wage, is temporary or insecure and does not involve retraining which can improve long-term prospects.[15]

This equivocation does not of course imply inaction. Rather it demands very careful response, not just a straightforward growth agenda, but the development of strategies that will specifically help the poor, unemployed and unskilled. Spatial planning affects the local economy through the provision of transport infrastructure, land, a high quality environment, space for essential services and retraining facilities. Regeneration programmes need not have deleterious effects on local populations if designed and managed well, with the active involvement of local residents and businesses. Commercial enterprises and public agencies share a huge responsibility to create secure, fulfilling jobs, with at least a living wage, and a pleasant, safe work environment. Where the local authority controls land or contracts, it should insist on quality and responsiveness to local needs.

'Built environment policies ameliorate or exacerbate income differentials through their impact on employment, housing and movement.'

Built environment policies cannot address the fundamental issues of wage inequality. But they do ameliorate or exacerbate income differentials through their impact on employment, housing and movement. A poor household is made poorer if it has to pay high fuel bills for an energy-inefficient dwelling. It is financially penalized if obliged to buy a car, or a second car, merely to gain access to jobs and essential services. It is very heavily penalized if the shortage of housing (and housing land) forces up rents and house prices. I have not found any *overall* calculation of the degree of financial costs imposed on poor households by poor spatial (and related) policies, or the savings that can be made by good policies. But the significance for social justice and health equity is palpable.

Local authorities, central government, businesses and institutions also have an impact through their own development decisions. There is a danger that organizations ignore the degree to which they are imposing costs on people, with distributional impacts. For example, hospitals may choose a new (spacious) site on the edge of town, ill-served by bus and inconvenient for active travel, and then add insult to injury by charging patients and visitors for car parking. The same can apply to office and retail investors. Externalizing costs onto households by choosing a car-reliant site should be considered an unhealthy act.

Housing and living conditions

Housing is normally the biggest household expense, and healthy housing is critical to health. Where the supply of housing does not match housing need, poor households will be forced into less salubrious, sometimes overcrowded conditions, exacerbating health inequalities. Healthy housing is not simply a matter of good sanitation. There is an abundance of evidence showing an association between poor housing and poor physical and mental health – even when the basics of water quality and human wastes are taken care of.[16] Indoor damp and mould are associated with chronic respiratory conditions, including asthma, Cold homes are linked to hypothermia, especially among the old. Exposure to indoor radon is related to lung cancer. The design of housing in the form of high rise flats risks social isolation, high night-time noise levels, a higher level of domestic accidents and lack of play space for children. Mental health is also compromised by overcrowding, insecurity, frequent forced moves, homelessness, threats of vandalism or burglary and perceptions of an unfriendly environment outside the front door.[17]

A particular problem in the UK in both urban and rural areas is fuel poverty. Households are defined as being in fuel poverty when at least 10 per cent of their income goes on home heating. It is ironic that the houses which are poorly insulated, draughty, with inadequate or expensive heating systems, are very frequently occupied by those least able to pay or cope with these conditions. The result is 'spatial shrink' (when old people live in their one heated room), vulnerability to illness and hypothermia. Rehabilitation and renewal programmes, aimed at bringing all houses up to an energy-efficient standard, are therefore important from the health perspective.[18]

In countries with a tropical or Mediterranean climate, keeping cool is the problem. From the viewpoint of the poor, it is vital to avoid the need for expensive air conditioning systems, instead relying on sensible building techniques. Whether the problem is cold or heat, it is not only building design that matters but also the layout of residential areas. The siting and orientation of buildings, tree planting for shade in hot climates, and reduced wind speed and heat loss in colder climes, all contribute. In high latitudes the spacing of buildings (as well as their energy efficiency) can make a significant difference to heating costs.[19]

The social segregation that can occur as a result of market and policy inequities can lead to geographical health inequalities to a shocking degree. One British study showed that the tenure of a household was a better predictor of health status than income levels. This was largely because of the poor neighbourhood characteristics of large social housing estates.[20] The social character of an estate influences the availability of services. If there is little money in an area, then shops, banks and cafés will find it harder to survive. People have to travel further to satisfy basic needs. For example, GP practices tend to be drawn to the affluent areas and eschew the very neighbourhoods where their services are most required. Secondary schools in deprived neighbourhoods have to work with poorly motivated children. Children held back by unsupportive parents and disruptive peers, with low school attainment, are likely to be held back for life – in terms of occupational status, income and health.[21]

Glasgow provides an extreme example. In 2006, average male life expectancy in one deprived suburb was 54 years, while in an affluent suburb not far away it was 82 years. These figures can be compared with the all-India life expectancy of 61.[22] The concentration of relative poverty and unemployment in large council estates in the post-war reconstruction caused individual misfortune to be magnified and reinforced. Glasgow is not unique. Many cities in Britain, France and elsewhere have resorted to mass peripheral housing projects as a means of coping with housing shortage, but with counterproductive effects.

The strategic planning of housing numbers and land requirements – a cause of continuing political conflict in the UK – has profound implications for health. If supply is unduly constrained and prices are high in relation to incomes, then social exclusion in the housing market increases.[23] Health inequalities are exacerbated as poorer households have difficulty in finding adequate accommodation at a price they can afford in a convenient location. A recent report cites evidence from Oxford to show how greenbelt and housing policies are compromising the options for poorer households, and increasing the backlog of affordable units.[24] Housing stress, as noted earlier, is a physical and mental health risk.

Movement and accessibility

Movement is not normally undertaken for its own sake (though of course you may choose just to 'go for a walk' or 'go for a spin'). It is usually undertaken to *go* somewhere. It is about getting to places where activities occur – working, schooling, shopping, meeting friends, going to the park, going to the dentist. So it is about *access*, it is about trying to ensure a good level of *accessibility*.

This point may seem obvious, but has potentially radical implications. The dominant tradition in many city regions has been to design for *vehicle mobility* not *accessibility*. The problem is that planning for high mobility for vehicle users has meant progressive increases in road capacity, aiming for (though never achieving) free-flow conditions. In practice, this has meant curtailing the mobility of other road users. Buses get caught up in traffic congestion. Cyclists are intimidated by high traffic levels. Pedestrians are forced into inconvenient detours and in places subject to excessive noise and fumes. At the same time, as car use has increased, commercial, retail and institutional developers have chosen sites that suit car access,

'The strategic planning of housing has profound implications for health. Health inequalities are exacerbated as poorer households have difficulty in finding adequate accommodation at a price they can afford in a convenient location.'

Housing issues in other chapters

- Chapter 7: housing and social mix
- Chapter 12: housing location
- Chapter 14: strategic housing policy

'The dominant tradition in many city regions has been to design for vehicle mobility not accessibility. This fashion disenfranchises the transport poor (those without access to a vehicle).'

but are too dispersed for effective public transport and too distant for most walkers and cyclists. So our transport and land use investment has ironically meant a *decline* in accessibility for many travellers. This fashion disenfranchises the transport poor (those without access to a vehicle).[25]

It gets worse yet, because the new large-scale facilities, often on the edge of town, mean the decline of local facilities, and consequent loss of local social contact in shops and on the street. Households find that they cannot survive without a car, or a second car. Car dependence increases, and active travel (walking and cycling) decreases. Lack of exercise compounds health problems. Those who cannot drive become more isolated. This particularly affects older people who are unable to afford a car on a pension, or lose their driving licence through infirmity. Equivalently, children become more dependent on adults to take them anywhere.

This is a gloomy picture. In many cities, the inadequacy of public transport and cycling provision, and the failure to tie new development to mesh with existing infrastructure, cause social exclusion and exacerbate health issues. It is evident that settlement planning has an absolutely central role to play in trying to ensure that all people, whatever their personal movement options, have good levels of accessibility. Not only is this central to a fair and equitable society. It is also good for health and well-being, good for the sense of community and belonging, good for the environment if local pollution and greenhouse gas emissions are cut as a result; potentially good for the economy in terms of reduced health service costs and higher productivity. As we have seen in the exemplary cities in Chapter 5, an equitable strategy can achieve conspicuous success.

Afterword

This chapter has shown the close alignment of concerns about social justice and concerns about health equity. The same issues are important, and spatial planning may exacerbate or mitigate inequality to a significant degree. In order to make progress:

- It is vital to spread the recognition that spatial and design decisions affect health, and health/social care costs.
- A comprehensive review of the financial costs and benefits imposed on poorer households by development decisions in transport, housing, employment and services would help to galvanize support for policy change.
- Major public sector bodies and private companies should include the social/health cost externalities of their development decisions in their calculus – as good practice and a requirement for planning permission.
- Spatial plan-makers should strengthen the evaluation of alternative policies and locations in respect of the following:
  - access to employment for poorer, less mobile households;
  - impacts on the price and affordability of housing;
  - accessibility to facilities by foot, bike and public transport.

Further reading

Allen, M. and Allen, J. (2015) 'Health inequalities and the role of the physical and social environment', in H. Barton, S. Thompson, S. Burgess, and M. Grant (eds) *The Routledge handbook of planning for health and well-being*. London: Routledge, pp. 89–107.

Boardman, B. (2015) 'Housing, energy efficiency and fuel poverty', in H. Barton, S. Thompson, S. Burgess, and M. Grant (eds) *The Routledge handbook of planning for health and well-being*. London: Routledge, pp. 271–282.

Corburn, J. (2009) *Towards the healthy city*. Cambridge, MA: MIT Press.

Corburn, J. (2015) 'Urban inequities, population health and spatial planning', in H. Barton, S. Thompson, S. Burgess, and M. Grant (eds) *The Routledge handbook of planning for health and well-being*. London: Routledge, pp. 37–47.

Kochtitzky, C. (2011) 'Vulnerable populations and the built environment', in A. Dannenberg, H. Frumpkin, and R. Jackson (eds) *Making healthy places: designing and building for health, well-being and sustainability*. Washington, DC: Island Press.

Marmot Commission (2010) *Fair society, healthy lives*. London: The Department of Health.

Notes

1 Harvey, D. (1973) *Social justice and the city* (London: Verso); Fainstein, S. (2010) *The just city* (Ithaca, NY: Cornell University Press).
2 Commission on the Social Determinants of Health (2008) *Closing the gap in a generation: health equity through action on the social determinants of health* (Geneva: WHO).
3 Marmot Commission (2010) *Fair society, healthy lives* (London: The Department of Health); Institute of Health Equity (2013) *Review of the social determinants and the health divide in the WHO European Region* (Copenhagen: WHO Office for Europe).
4 WHO (2015) Global Health Observatory data. Available at; www.who.int/gho/mortality_burden_disease (accessed 15 Sept. 2015).
5 Office for National Statistics (2013) *Annual report* (London: HMSO, 2013).
6 Allen, M. and Allen, J. (2015) 'Health inequalities and the role of the physical and social environment', in H. Barton, S. Thompson, S. Burgess, and M. Grant (eds) *The Routledge handbook of planning for health and well-being* (London: Routledge), pp. 89–107.
7 Harvey (1973), op. cit.
8 Department of the Environment (1977) *Inner Area Studies of Liverpool, Birmingham and Lambeth: summaries of consultants' final reports* (London: HMSO).
9 Hall, P., Thomas, R., Gracey, H. and Drewett, R. (1973) *The containment of urban England*, vol. 2: *The planning system, objectives, operations, impacts* (London: George Allen & Unwin).
10 Social Exclusion Unit (2004) *Jobs and enterprise in deprived areas* (London: SEU).
11 Marmot, M. (2004) *The status syndrome: how social standing affects our health and longevity* (London: Times Books).
12 Wilkinson, R. and Pickett, K. (2009) *The spirit level: why equality is better for everyone* (London: Penguin Books).
13 A useful and brief (though depressing) review of literature in Cave, B., Molyneux, P. and Coutts, A. (2004) *Healthy sustainable communities: what works?* (Brighton: Milton Keynes and South Midlands Sub-region NHS and BCA).
14 Glenn, L., Beck, R. *et al.* (1998) 'The effect of transient, geographically localised economic recovery on community health and income, studied with the longitudinal household cohort method', *Journal of Epidemiology and Community Health*, 52(11): 749–757.
15 Corburn, J. (2009) *Towards the healthy city* (Cambridge, MA: MIT Press).
16 Braubach, M., Jacobs, D. and Ormandy, D. (2011) *The environmental burden of disease associated with inadequate housing: a method guide to the quantification of health effects of selected housing risks in the WHO European Region* (Copenhagen: WHO).
17 Cave *et al.* (2004), op. cit.
18 DETR (2001) *Fuel poverty strategy* (London: HMSO).
19 For a practical introduction to this subject, see Barton, H., Grant, M. and Guise, R. (2010)

Shaping neighbourhoods: for local health and global sustainability (London: Routledge).

20 Ellaway, A. and MacIntyre, S. (1998) 'Does housing tenure predict health in the UK because it exposes people to different levels of housing related hazards in the home and its surroundings?' *Home and Place*, 4(2): 141–150.

21 Whitty, G., Aggleton, P. *et al.* (1999) 'Education and health inequalities', in G. Gordon, M. Shaw *et al. Inequalities in health: evidence presented to the Independent Inquiry into Inequalities in Health, chaired by Sir Donald Acheson* (Bristol: Policy Press), pp. 138–147.

22 Hanlon, P., Walsh, D. and White, B. (2006) *World health report: let Glasgow flourish* (Geneva: WHO).

23 Barker, K. (2007) *Review of housing supply: final report and recommendations* (London: HMSO); Bramley, G. (2009) 'Meeting demand', in P. Malpass and R. Rowlands (eds) *Housing, markets and policy* (London: Routledge).

24 Frank Knight (2009) *The future of residential development: unlocking the housing market* (London: Frank Knight).

25 National Heart Foundation *et al.* (2007) *Building health: creating and enhancing places for healthy active lives* (London: National Heart Foundation, Living Streets and CABE).

CHAPTER NINE

CLIMATE CHANGE AND SETTLEMENT PLANNING

We do not inherit the Earth from our ancestors, we borrow it from our children.

Proverb

What does prosperity mean in a world living under the threat of climate change and resource scarcity? One thing is absolutely clear. It cannot mean business as usual. It cannot mean more of the same. The idea that the economic systems and policies we have today can solve the problems of tomorrow does not seem plausible.

Mary Robinson[1]

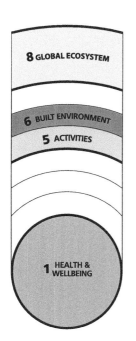

Fig 9.1 *Focus on global ecosystem*

Introduction

It is all too easy to imagine, with the pretensions of the internet age, that we know more than our ancestors. In some ways, of course, this is absolutely true: knowledge has expanded exponentially since the Enlightenment, and our access to it is, almost literally, fabulous. But knowledge and understanding are not the same. The study of human ecology – the relationship of humans to the environment – is recent as a distinct area of scientific knowledge, but peoples of the past, living closer to the earth, had an intuitive, traditional understanding, honed by experience. Some could articulate the human/environment relationship with precision. Here is Plato, writing in Greece in the early fourth century BC, looking back to a (supposed) golden age, observing the unsustainable changes wrought by his society on the landscape and climate. It makes salutary reading:

> At that time the country was unimpaired, and for its bare mountains it had high arable hills, and in place of swamps it contained plains full of rich soil; and it had much forest land in its mountains, of which there are visible signs even to this day. Moreover, it was enriched by the yearly rains from Zeus, which were not lost to it, as now, by flowing from the bare land into the sea; but the soil was deep, and therein it received the water, storing it up in the retentive loamy soil ... providing all the various districts with abundant supplies of spring-water and streams, where shrines still remain even now, at the spots where fountains formerly existed. Such then was the natural condition of the land ... and above the land, a climate of most happily tempered seasons.[2]

Plato may have been seeing the heroic Greek past through rose-tinted spectacles, to suit his dialectical purpose, but his analysis of the fourth-century BC Greece was remarkable. He understood how the natural environment had been affected by unwise human exploitation, leading to critical problems of soil erosion, water supply, food production, climate change and cultural identity. He had a holistic, ecological awareness.

The purpose of Chapters 9 and 10 is to provide a realistic understanding of the relationship between human activity, human settlements and the natural environment, drawing out the implications for spatial planning. This chapter examines the significance of climate change, identified by the WHO as the biggest threat to global health. I review the science of climate change and related predictions, to counteract the arguments of the small but vocal sceptical minority. That leads into a review of the role of settlement and energy planning, then a final section broadening the debate to other facets of global ecology.

The threat of climate change

The threat of climate change has become a central international political issue since the Earth Summit in Rio in 1992. The predicted results of climate change – in terms of temperature, rising sea levels, fiercer storms, floods, desertification, shifting biological and agricultural patterns – demand effective coping strategies, both to *adapt* to the changes and to *mitigate* (i.e. reduce) the threat. A series of summits have been held (Copenhagen, Paris) to try to reach international agreement between rich and poor nations, high and low greenhouse gas emitters. Spatial planning has a key role to play in attempting to mitigate climate change and create resilient settlements.

The scientific understanding of climate change

Arguments still persist about the truth of climate change. The argument between believers and agnostics is not about the *existence* of climate change. It is about the degree to which human activity is the cause, and if the current trends are likely to continue. In order to separate myth from reality, we must examine the evidence. The following commentary draws on the 2013 report of the IPCC – the Intergovernmental Panel on Climate Change.[3] This authoritative international body is not made up of eco-freaks but sober scientists from a wide range of earth and climate sciences with many cultural backgrounds. Figure 9.2 shows the trends of global warming since 1850. The warming of the climate system is unequivocal, and many of the observed changes, such as the speed of warming since 1980, are unprecedented over millennia. Both the ocean and the atmosphere have warmed, the amounts of snow and ice have diminished, sea levels have risen, and extreme climatic events have become more common in parts of the globe.

The IPCC used a variety of models to assess the likely causes of the observed climate change. The scenarios which included anthropogenic (human) factors as well as natural factors mirrored reality far better than those which relied purely on natural forces. The science of atmosphere is well advanced. Carbon dioxide, methane,

'The warming of the climate system is unequivocal, and many of the observed changes, such as the speed of warming since 1980, are unprecedented over millennia.'

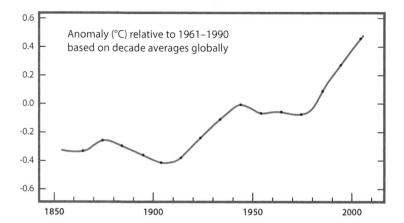

Fig 9.2 *Observed changes in global average surface temperature, 1850–2010*

Source: based on IPCC 2013 (note 3).

nitrous oxides and water vapour have critical greenhouse effects, maintaining the warmth of the planet. The atmospheric concentrations of the first three have exceeded pre-industrial levels by 40 per cent, 150 per cent and 20 per cent respectively, and now are substantially greater than levels recorded in ice cores over the last 800,000 years.

Carbon levels in the sea have increased at the same time, leading to greater acidification which alters the ocean habitat significantly. Global mean sea level has risen by about 200 mm (8 inches) since 1900, due largely to thermal expansion and the melting of glaciers. Looking back to the peak of the last interglacial (around 120,000 years ago) provides a cautious comparison with what we may experience in the next hundred years: the temperature was probably at least 2 degrees centigrade warmer than now, and sea levels were 5–10 metres higher, with the biggest contribution coming from the melting of the Greenland ice cap.

The IPCC have attempted to calculate the anthropogenic sources of carbon dioxide emissions over the industrial age since 1750. Increased emissions from fossil fuel combustion and cement production has probably accounted for two-thirds of the effect, and land use changes (mainly deforestation) one third. The extra carbon has accumulated in the 'carbon sinks' of land and ocean as well as the atmosphere. While human action has emitted unprecedented amounts of carbon dioxide into the atmosphere, it has at the same time progressively reduced the global forest cover that helps maintain carbon equilibrium. The huge increase in the second most significant greenhouse gas, methane, is due to the increased number of beef cattle, satisfying the growing worldwide desire for meat – one of the reasons for land use change. Overall, the case that climate is being affected by human activity is overwhelming. The real uncertainties concern what happens in the future.

Forecasting the uncertain future

The inertia in earth ecology is great. The checks and balances in the system mean that there can be relative stability for millennia, even for millions of years – until some fundamental natural or artificial forcing agent shifts the basic dynamics. The end of the last ice age was a case in point. The current pace of change is such that we risk a tipping point taking us into a new warmer era. The possible melting of the Greenland ice cap and of the Siberian permafrost (releasing methane), as well as the likely complete summer melting of the polar sea ice (reducing the albedo of the Earth) are three of the uncertainties that forecasters wrestle with. Conversely the ability of the deeper ocean waters to absorb heat and carbon, reducing the pace of atmospheric warming, is also uncertain.

The IPCC has attempted to model both natural and anthropogenic factors. They have made a wide range of assumptions about the degree to which international policies will succeed in moderating greenhouse gas emissions. The globe will have peaks and troughs of average temperature, but the trend is remorseless. Because of the delay factors, there is only a small variation between scenarios for 2050. But by 2100 the forecasts range from 1 degree C for the most optimistic scenario to 4 degrees C for the most pessimistic. All the scenarios except the *most* optimistic predict that warming will continue beyond 2100, and fundamentally alter the distribution of population, agricultural production, and life on Earth.

'All the scenarios except the most optimistic predict that warming will continue beyond 2100, and fundamentally alter the distribution of population, agricultural production, and life on Earth.'

At present, there is little indication that the alarming upward trend of anthropogenic carbon emissions can be halted. While some developed countries (including the UK) have achieved modest reduction in emissions, they remain at unsustainably high levels. Meanwhile the rapidly growing economies of Asia, Africa and South America are, from a very low base, increasing emissions very quickly. There are issues of global fairness at stake. Developing countries aspire to the same high energy-use lifestyles seen in the West. Carbon trading has yet to adequately incentivize carbon saving. Both richer and poorer countries may be unwilling to risk economic growth and competitive edge *now* for the benefit of *future* generations. However, the IPCC suggest it is not yet too late. If we were able to agree a low carbon strategy (including an 80 per cent cut in emissions from rich countries), then it could be possible to avoid what is considered the critical tipping point of 2 degrees C global temperature increase.

The economic argument can be turned on its head. The influential *Stern Review* in 2006 made the case that economically we cannot afford *not* to combat climate change. The potential costs of coping with more extreme weather events, flood protection, settlement relocation, water wars and global population migration to escape inundation (e.g. from Bangladesh), are crippling. By comparison, the costs of moving to a low carbon economy, while considerable, are a matter of speeding up a process that began with the energy crises of the 1970s. There is every reason for rich countries to embark on serious mitigation strategies, leading by example. There can even be economic benefits for those countries that foster new technologies – as Denmark has on wind power, and Germany on solar. However, the *Stern Review* concluded: 'Adaptation is the only response available for the impacts that will occur over the next several decades before mitigation measures can have an effect.'[4]

The health impacts could be severe. A systematic review of the available evidence confirms climate change is the biggest global health threat, with the likelihood of changing disease patterns, food insecurity, contaminated water, sanitation problems, extreme events that damage the built environment, and severe migration pressures.[5] Conversely tackling climate change with real dynamism could provide an unexpected health bonus. The 'co-benefits' could include healthier indoor and outdoor air quality and healthier life-styles as cooking, heating, electricity and travel cut use of fossil fuels through greater efficiency and substitution (e.g. by renewables and active travel). A study of cities in India suggested these health service savings would largely offset the cost of greenhouse gas mitigation.[6]

While the climate change benefits of effective mitigation policies are long term, the health and social benefits are both more immediate *and* long term. The same goes for adaptation. We can adapt the environment *now* to new and predicted conditions. For example, in the face of more severe storms and consequent flooding, we could invest in more holding ponds and up-stream afforestation to slow run-off, with the extra trees also acting as carbon sinks, and enhancing biodiversity. Resilience is, in addition, about building in the capacity to respond quickly to unanticipated threats and changes. It might be about contingency plans, keeping open potentially desirable options for the future. It might be about developing collaborative working practices that ensure we are in a position to recognize threats early and deliver a coordinated, inter-agency response.

Greenhouse gases, energy and planning

Anthropogenic greenhouse gasses (GHGs) occur largely through the burning of fossil fuels for electricity, heat, transport and industrial processes. Spatial planning affects both energy generation and energy use quite profoundly, and thereby affects carbon emissions. In this section we examine these relationships, using the UK as an example, drawing mainly on the *UK Greenhouse Gas Inventory Factsheets* produced by the Department of Energy and Climate Change.[7] The carbon intensity of different countries is sharply varied. In 2009, the UK's emissions per capita were less than Russia, and less than half the United States, but significantly more than France, normally considered a comparable country. China was surprisingly high, but most developing countries emitted less than a quarter of the UK. The differences can mainly be accounted for by the nature of industrial production, the sources of electricity (coal dependence in China), and of course the level of wealth – giving lifestyle choices.

Carbon dioxide is the preponderant GHG – UK 83 per cent in 2011. The relationship between carbon dioxide and energy varies according to the source of energy. The UK has substantially reduced its GHG emissions in recent years – from 760 million tons of carbon dioxide equivalence in 1990 to 540 in 2011, down 29 per cent, in part by phasing out inefficient coal-based power stations. Reductions between 2007 and 2011 were affected by the recession. Nevertheless the trend is positive. The European Union agreed in 2014 to achieve

Carbon intensity

- USA – 17.3 metric tons per person (tpp)
- Russia – 11.1 tpp
- UK – 7.7 tpp
- France – 5.6 tpp
- Most developing countries – <2.0 tpp

27 per cent of renewable electricity by 2030. The EU target of a 40 per cent cut in emissions by 2030, agreed in January 2014, looks achievable. Subsequently, the Paris Summit in December 2015 has strengthened international commitment.

Figure 9.3 illustrates the relative importance of different sectors' energy use in the UK in 2012. While the total amount of energy used in 2012 is similar to that in 1970, the balance of use has changed. The industrial sector was the largest in 1970, but has achieved very substantial savings of nearly 60 per cent, and its energy efficiency has improved even more, by 70 per cent, as production has risen. It now accounts for only 18 per cent of total use. By contrast, the domestic sector's share has increased from 24 per cent to 29 per cent, driven by more housing, with little overall gain in efficiency, reflecting the absence of a comprehensive retrofit insulation pro-gramme. The principal component of domestic energy use is still space heating. The biggest sector now is transport, accounting for 38 per cent, by comparison with 19 per cent in 1970. This doubling of energy use is accounted for by more motorized travel, including air travel. The gains from more efficient vehicle engines and design have been swallowed up by the use of larger vehicles, often with just one person in them.

If we cut the cake according to carbon production rather than energy use, we get a rather different picture. The energy supply industries account for 35 per cent of carbon dioxide emissions. Over three-quarters of that is from the electricity power stations, with the remaining from refining fuels, upstream combustion and flaring in the oil and gas fields. Transport then accounts for 21 per cent, busi-ness 16 per cent and households 13 per cent – the latter referring simply to the heating fuels burnt in the home. Agriculture accounts for 9 per cent, though other calculations, including not just agricul-tural production but subsequent processing, transport and selling, give a figure for food-related carbon around 20 per cent – a fifth of all carbon emitted. The apparent discrepancies are confusing, but the important lessons emerging from analysis of the figures are now: the critical areas for action are electricity production, heating and cooling of buildings, transport, and – cutting across those sectors – food.

The role of settlement planning in mitigation and adaptation is pivotal. Figure 9.4 illustrates how broad is the influence of spatial

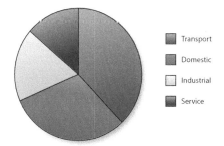

Final energy consumption in the UK, 2012

- Transport
- Domestic
- Industrial
- Service

Fig 9.3 *Final energy consumption in the UK in 2012*

Source: based on the Department of Energy and Climate Change (2013) Energy consumption in the UK 2013. Available at: www.gov.uk/DECC/ publications

Fig 9.4 *The interplay of planning policy and carbon emissions*

Source: developed from Barton 1990 (note 8).

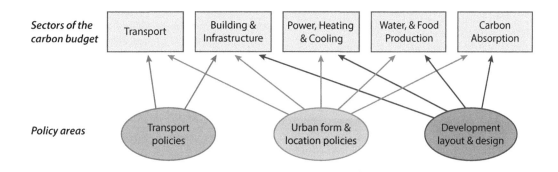

Average number of kilometres travelled by personal motorized means per household, per week

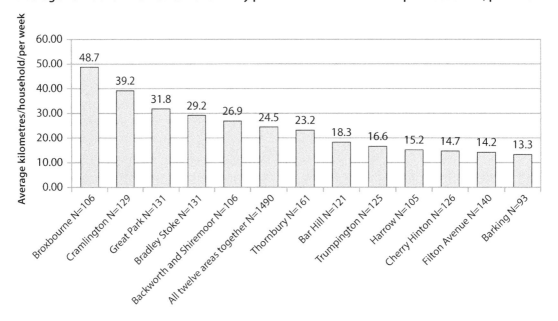

Fig 9.5 Variations in local car dependent behaviour – the distance travelled by car to access local facilities, in this study of English suburban neighbourhoods, varies greatly – depending in the main on accessibility. This distance is a proxy for local transport carbon emissions.

Source: based on Barton et al. 2012 (note 9).

policy on energy use and the resulting carbon emissions.[8] At some point, and to some degree, the planning and design of the human habitat influence at least 70 per cent of energy use.

- Transport energy use is influenced by transport and urban form policies – that could reduce the need for motorized travel, and promote alternatives (Figure 9.5).[9]
- Building and infrastructure *embodied energy* costs (i.e. for materials and construction) are influenced by mineral extraction and reuse, urban form, design and layout policies that could promote low-energy solutions.
- Heating, cooling and electricity fuel use are influenced by building design and rehabilitation, by layout, siting and urban form policies – which could include effective promotion of renewable energy and combined heat and power. (Some also suggest nuclear.)
- Food production energy costs are influenced by the design of neighbourhoods encouraging local production, exchange and composting. Water energy costs, critical in some parts of the world, could be tackled by much greater efficiency in use.
- Carbon absorption is influenced by green infrastructure and urban policies that increase tree cover.

Thus, a low carbon strategy is about the whole character of cities, towns and rural areas – about the way people use places, the options they have open to them, and the lifestyles they adopt. A low carbon city is likely to be a healthy city, with comfortable homes, good air quality, excellent accessibility, daily physical activity and accessible greenspace.

Apart from carbon, the other main greenhouse gases are methane and nitrogen dioxide. In the UK, the planning of waste and minerals is central to the level of methane emissions: landfill waste used to account for the biggest share, but has been reduced by seeing waste as a resource, and the move to reuse and recycling. The move from coal to gas electricity generation is another cause of methane reduction. All these sources and processes use land. Spatial planning is therefore a key part of implementing a sound methane strategy. However, planning has much less influence on the other main source of methane emission, and the predominant source of nitrogen dioxide: agriculture. Agricultural practice in relation to these two gases has changed little over the years, and DECC expects little change in the future unless societal attitudes to diet alter radically.

'A low carbon strategy is about the whole character of cities, towns and rural areas — about the way people use places, the options they have open to them, and the lifestyles they adopt.'

Sustainable energy strategy

A sustainable energy strategy is not simply about reducing carbon emissions. Environmentally, it aims also to reduce air pollution and the exploitation of non-renewable resources. Socially, it aims to solve the problem of fuel poverty, thereby reducing health inequalities. Economically, it aims to create jobs and release household and company income for non-energy purposes, thus fostering further job creation.

Given the interplay between energy use, energy supply and spatial/design practice, it is essential to link the agencies responsible. Some countries have given a lead in a new direction, integrating energy supply with spatial planning and waste strategy. In Denmark, for example, each settlement has an obligation to plan its own energy supply, and make itself as self-sufficient as is practicable. The local authority may create its own subsidiary company to supply electricity and heat, or forge a partnership with an energy supplier, while still being connected to the national grid to even out peaks and troughs of supply and demand. The result is true localism. The people of the town or city accept responsibility for their own future supply and their own environment. Rather than having energy developments imposed on them by government or an energy company, they have to plan them themselves. So communities *choose* to have wind turbines or combined heat and power stations (CHP) on their doorstep. They also plan urban development to minimize energy demand and energy waste.

CHP has become increasingly common in much of North-West Europe, notably Denmark, Sweden, Finland and Germany. Odense in Denmark (population 200,000) has a centralized CHP station, with dispersed mini stations across the city as back-up when the main station is temporarily shut down. Heat mains reach across the city supplying all areas with hot water for their central heating systems, and the vast majority of consumers plug in, saving themselves both capital and running costs. A small town in an agricultural district has a CHP plant relying on straw bales as its main fuel, supplying electricity and heating. Another town part-owns (with a private company) a bank of wind turbines and a gas-fired district heating

'A small town in an agricultural district has a CHP plant relying on straw bales as its main fuel, supplying electricity and heating.'

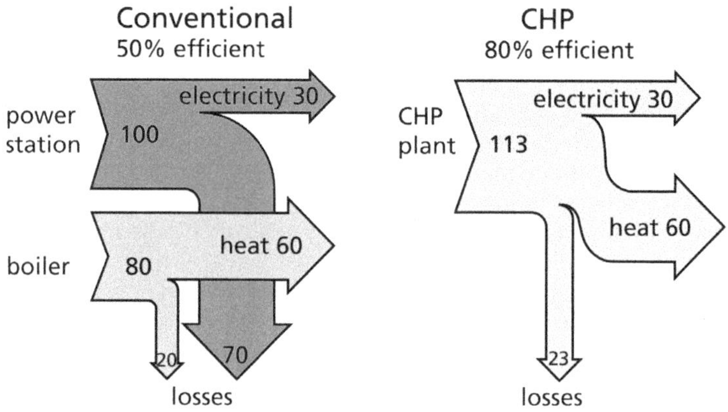

Conventional
50% efficient

electricity 30

power
station   100

boiler   80   heat 60

20   70

losses

CHP
80% efficient

CHP
plant   113   electricity 30

heat 60

23

losses

Fig 9.6 *The efficiency benefits
of combining power and
heat production: CHP versus
conventional methods*

*Source: based on Barton et al. 2010
(further reading), p.181.*

Fig 9.7 *BEDZED low carbon
housing. The first residential
development in London to claim
zero net carbon emissions, and
managed jointly by all residents.*

plant. Figure 9.6 shows the efficiency benefits of combining power and heat production, while Figure 9.7 shows an example of the BEDZED project.

Spatial planning makes a major contribution to the viability of such systems. Not only is there the matter of identifying and safe-guarding well-located sites for CHP plants and renewable energy development, but the structure of the town needs to evolve so that it supports district heating systems – so that the lengths of heat main are kept to an minimum (reducing embodied energy needs and heat loss) and heat demand is balanced out across the town. Balanced heat demand means major all-year users such as swimming pools and hospitals are well distributed, and day users such as schools and offices are balanced with evening and weekend users such as homes. A medium-to-high density and a structured mix of uses (rather than extensive single use zones) are needed for the district heating to be economic.

Energy efficiency and solar design

The central plank of any sustainable energy strategy is efficiency: pro-gressively improving the level of energy services that can be provided by a unit of energy. A significant investment in energy efficiency – insulating buildings, reducing waste from power stations, etc. – can postpone the need to reinvest in supply systems. It is often more economic to save a megawatt of electricity than it is to generate it.

Every development needs an explicit energy demand manage-ment strategy that works to reduce heat loss (or unwanted heat gain) from buildings, and open up possibilities for renewable energy and/or distributed heat linked to CHP plants. Very well-insulated buildings, with heat recovery ventilation systems to ensure healthy inside air, can reduce heating costs to a fraction of the prevailing British level. The cost of solar-electric is increasingly competitive as the market develops. In Germany, large numbers of photovoltaic systems have been installed by developers and households, sup-ported by central government through a subsidized 'feed-in tariff', in anticipation that the subsidy will soon become unnecessary. Siting, estate layout, planting and building design can facilitate or undermine the technology.

The list below includes both energy in use and in construction, emphasizing those matters within the remit of planners and urban designers. The goal is to move towards 'carbon-neutral' development that provides for the needs of users, while reducing to a minimum the global warming impact.

- In older and poorer neighbourhoods, retrofit homes with high quality insulation, draught-proofing and solar panels, thereby cutting energy use and bills, reducing fuel poverty and creating jobs.
- Choose building forms, where possible, that have low embodied energy – e.g. terraced housing, not detached or high rise – and use low energy materials in construction (e.g. wood and brick, not concrete and steel).
- Adopt building conservation policies that prioritize energy efficiency (including double-glazing) over historic rectitude.
- Understand and manage micro-climatic conditions, and site developments accordingly – e.g. avoiding exposed sites and growing shelter belts, in cooler, windier climates.
- Reduce the effect of urban 'heat islands', especially in warmer climates, by increasing tree cover and the amount of greenspace within the city.
- In cooler climes, plan the distribution of activities, and clustering development, so as to facilitate combined heat and power and district heating schemes.
- Passive solar design: in cooler places, orientate buildings and arrange windows to maximize the free heat gains from the sun; where possible, arrange back gardens and balconies that catch the sun.
- In warmer places, orientate main windows away from the sun, use sunshades as appropriate, and natural 'passive stack' ventilation; provide shady external spaces.
- Site buildings, design orientation and roof angle to maximize solar power potential – allowing some buildings to be net exporters of electricity to the grid.
- Where new or rehabilitated schemes occur, require incentives and information that encourages user awareness of energy efficiency behaviours and technologies.

Heat islands

Heat islands are caused by heat lost from buildings, by traffic and industrial processes and by the prevalence of heat absorbent materials such as brick, concrete and tarmac. In warmer climates and seasons, especially with climate warming, they lead to high cooling costs.

California's energy strategy

Since the oil crises of the 1970s, California has pursued an increasingly effective energy-efficiency strategy. Regulatory programmes have forced improvements in buildings, utilities and manufacturing, so that California is now using 40 per cent less energy per capita than the US average. This has brought economic benefits: households are estimated to have saved $56 billion in 1972–2006, redirecting their expenditure so that about 1.5 million new jobs were created.[10] The Californian Global Warming Solutions Act of 2006, with an enforceable cap on GHG emissions and the target of 80 per cent reduction by 2050, is expected to generate a further 400,000 jobs, mainly in energy efficiency programmes. There are four 'Big Bold Strategies':

- All eligible low-income homes will be energy-efficient by 2020.
- All new residential construction will be zero net energy by 2020.
- All new commercial construction will be zero net energy by 2020.
- The building services industry will be regulated to ensure optimum equipment performance.[11]

The focus of California's programme is buildings and the equipment within buildings. The concept of zero net energy allows buildings (separately or in groups) to balance export of energy with imports. For example, exporting solar electricity while importing some gas for heating or cooling. Building policies and urban design facilitate such a strategy.

Conclusion: human ecology

Mediaeval philosophers believed the world was made up of four elements: earth, air, fire and water. All four of these are now being subjected to serious human impact. The atmosphere is warming and the climate changing; the ocean is expanding and absorbing carbon, while the ice is melting; the earth is losing its forests and there is increased desertification. But the cause of all this is *fire*: the way we are producing and using energy, including food energy, transforming the ancient subterranean stored energy of the sun into heat, light and motive power in a few profligate generations.

Fossil fuel use has opened a Pandora's box of evils:

- Urban air pollution because of industrial production and vehicle use.
- High energy-input, land hungry diets, rich in meat.
- Deforestation of the rain forests, half already lost, another 25 per cent at risk.
- Mass extinction of plant and animal species – 50–100 each day.
- Soil erosion and desertification affecting a third of the land area.
- Water consumption up 500 per cent since 1960, shortages becoming frequent.

The growing human population is not living in balance with natural ecosystems, but is parasitic on the Earth. One way of expressing the degree to which we are exceeding global carrying capacity is to calculate our *ecological footprint*. This assesses the amount of land needed to support the food consumption, resource use and the absorption of wastes of an individual, city or nation. According to Professor William Rees, one of the originators of the eco-footprint concept, the productive land available per head of the world's population is 1.8 hectares – falling as the population grows.[12] London's eco-footprint per head is over three times that, the USA's footprint around 10 hectares.

Most lower- and middle-income countries are substantially below the world allowance, but most also have rapidly increasing footprints. As countries grow wealthier and adopt affluent lifestyles, there is a series of energy transitions which impact on global climate. One eminent academic expressed it in terms of the dominant means of getting around: when at subsistence level you rely on shoes, walking everywhere; a small increment above subsistence and you get a bike; a few more increments and a motor-bike is possible, then with growing affluence a car, and, finally, people travel by plane: the sequence *shoes > bike > motor-bike > car > plane* represents the transition to the energy-intensive lifestyle already enjoyed by many people in rich countries.[13] There is a completely natural feeling on the part of the poorer countries that they are not willing to make sacrifices in the interest of global stability unless the rich countries reduce their resource intensity first. If everyone in the world lived like Londoners, then we would require three Earths rather than the one we actually have; if like Americans, then we would need over five.

The exponential growth of population has been part of the problem. In the middle of the twentieth century the population was doubling every 30 years. World population has now reached seven billion: 7,000,000,000. But the doubling time is no longer the issue. Almost unnoticed, we have actually begun to conquer the problem of rapid population growth. The current estimate is that it will stabilize at around 11 billion.[14] The explanation is disarmingly simple. When child mortality is high, families have lots of children as insurance against their death. When child mortality is low, the incentive works quite the opposite way: it is cheaper to pay for two children than four, so fertility (the number of children per mother) is low too. There is a delay factor, as ingrained cultural habits change, but now, across the world families of two children are the norm, not the exception. Statistically there is a relationship between growing wealth and declining fertility.

While the 'population bomb' is thus gradually being defused (though not as yet in all parts of the world), the same cannot be said for the climate time-bomb. The last spirit to escape from Pandora's box was *hope:* 2014 was the first year when the world economy grew while total carbon emissions fell. That gives grounds for hope. Governments, businesses and communities are beginning to react to the threat. In the case of China, change is being driven by health issues: appalling levels of urban pollution has persuaded the country to cut coal burning and boost solar investment. China is also beginning (just beginning) to consider low carbon cities. Beyond doubt the spatial planning of human settlements is a crucial part of the way forward. The good news is that the same strategy that helps to keep a cap on climate change also makes for a more humane and equitable human habitat. Healthy lifestyles, healthy cities and healthy planet are mutually dependent. Microcosm and macrocosm are connected.

'If everyone in the world lived like Londoners, then we would require three Earths rather than the one we actually have; if like Americans, then we would need over five.'

Further reading

Barton, H., Grant, M. and Guise, R. (2010) *Shaping neighbourhoods: for local health and global sustainability.* London: Routledge. A practical guide, with health and climate change as key issues throughout, and a particular section on energy.

Griffiths, J., Rao, M., Adshead, F. and Thorpe, A. (2009) *The health practitioner's guide to climate change: diagnosis and cure.* London: Earthscan. Not just for health practitioners. A review of all the issues, and starting points for action.

IPCC (2013) *Climate Change 2013: the physical science basis – Summary for policy-makers.* Intergovernmental Panel on Climate Change. Available at: www.ipcc.ch

Stern, N. (2006) *Stern review on the economics of climate change: executive summary.* London: HM Treasury.

Notes

1   Mary Robinson (2009) in her commentary on Tim Jackson's *Prosperity without growth* (London: Earthscan), p. 272. Robinson is President of the Ethical Globalization Initiative, a former President of Ireland and UN Commissioner for Human Rights.

2   Plato, *Critias,* fifth century BC, translated by Bury (1929), as recorded in H. Barton and N. Bruder (1995) *A guide to local environmental auditing* (London: Earthscan), p. 6.

3   IPCC (2013) *Climate Change 2013: the physical science basis – Summary for policy-makers.* Intergovernmental Panel on Climate Change. Available at: www.ipcc.ch

4   Stern, N.H. (2006) *Stern review: the economics of climate change* (vol. 30). (London: HM Treasury).

5   Costello, A., Abbas, M., Allen, A. *et al.* (2009) 'Managing the health effects of climate change', *Lancet, 373,* 1693–1733.

6   *Lancet* (2009) *Public health benefits of strategies to reduce greenhouse gas emissions.* Five reports published online by the *Lancet,* November 2009. DOI:10.1016/S0140-61715-3 (accessed 24 Jan. 2014).

7   DECC (2013) *UK greenhouse gas inventory factsheets.* See www.gov.uk/DECC/publications (accessed 24 Jan. 2014).

8   Barton, H. (1990) 'Local global planning', *The Planner,* 26 October 1990, pp. 12–15.

9   Based on Barton, H., Horswell, M. and Miller, P. (2012) 'Neighbourhood accessibility and active travel', *Planning Practice and Research,* 27(2): 177–201.

10 Girardet, H. and Mendonca, M. (2009) *A renewable world: energy, ecology, equality* (Totnes: Green Books).

11 California's 'Long term energy efficiency strategic plan', www.californiaenergyefficiency. com as reported in ibid.

12 Rees, W. E. (2012) 'Ecological footprint analysis and the vulnerability of modern cities', lecture given to the Leverhulme International Research Network seminar in November 2012, at the University of Westminster.

13 Rosling, H. (2013) 'This world: don't panic! The truth about population', BBC2 broadcast, 9.00 p.m., 7 November 2013.

14 United Nations Population Division (2013) *World population prospect: the 2012 revision* (New York: The United Nations).

CHAPTER TEN

THE LOCAL ECOLOGY OF CITIES

Ecological resilience

Resilience in the face of climate change and other ecological threats implies the ability to survive and bounce back after a crisis. At the scale of the city, it is about the ability to cope with challenge and adapt without sacrificing the population's health. Basic life support depends on the purity of the air, the availability and quality of water, the careful management of climatic extremes and flood risk, the quality of soils for food growing, adequate shelter and – in many poorer countries – local access to fuel. Beyond the basics, people's health and well-being benefit, as we have seen, from access to natural environments, active recreational opportunities, and a convivial pedestrian environment that encourages daily physical activity and promotes social contact. The quality of the environment, both natural and constructed, is also a key factor in attracting and keeping footloose entrepreneurs, and thereby work opportunities.

All this points to the critical importance of seeing settlements not simply as human artifacts but as part of the natural world, affecting it and depending on it. The Settlement Health Map expresses this: people, place and nature. The focus is on the city and the bioregion from which it draws sustenance. Urban metabolism can drastically affect the quality of the natural stock of air, water and land: we may poison air and water to the extent that they become health hazards; redirect rivers into irrigation or hydro schemes that reduce flows downstream so that habitats are lost and human livelihoods undermined; denude the landscape of trees that store water and hold soils in place, leading to flooding, erosion, reduced food production and loss of wildlife habitats. Or we may re-orientate cities around healthy, low carbon behaviour, breathing fresh air; replant

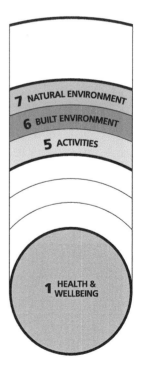

Fig 10.1 *Focus on the natural environment*

the marginal land and recover agricultural productivity; create new 'natural' habitats as part of human settlements.

Settlement Planning can be conceived as applied urban ecology. Michael Hough, in his important book, *Cities and Natural Processes*, points out that people in developed countries are estranged from the systems that support them, and therefore do not normally feel responsible for them. 'You simply turn on the light or the tap and light and water are there. You buy your food in a shop ... and put your garbage outdoors and it will be removed.'[1] It is vital that the ecological systems that underpin urban life are visible and understood by households, businesses and politicians.

Those systems – or *ecosystem services*[2] – are normally conceived as the free offerings of nature, but their economic significance is huge. One estimate puts their worldwide value at $125 trillion p.a.[3] Ecosystem services embrace the multiple ecological functions that the global and local natural environment performs for humankind, ranging from the rainforests, which act as the lungs of Earth, to the local stream which provides surface water drainage. Many of these services are under-appreciated and undervalued, and therefore degraded.

The cultural ecologist Herbert Girardet expresses the contrast between old and new thinking in terms of urban metabolism.[4] *Petropolis* is highly dependent on external inputs of energy, water, food and goods, encouraged by economic globalization, and outputs wastes, including noxious emissions, poisoning its own environment and exporting poison. *Ecopolis*, by comparison, integrates the city with its surrounding environment, reducing consumption, reusing, and recycling, relying on renewable and local sources of water, food, energy and goods.

Green infrastructure

At the city scale, the current term to convey the significance of ecosystem services is *green infrastructure*. The functions of green infrastructure (GI) are social and economic as well as environmental, including recreation, mental well-being, air quality, micro-climate, water, food, energy and wildlife. The list of functions is formidable, and they all demand space in and around the city. Unfortunately 'green infrastructure' has become something of a bandwagon phrase. There is a strong commercial temptation to use it superficially as a badge of environmental respectability – simply meaning green open space. But its implications are profound. Val Kirby of the Landscape Institute introduces the concept thus:

'Green infrastructure is the latest answer to an old question: how to convince policy and decision-makers of the need for joined-up, long-term planning.'

> Green infrastructure is the latest answer to an old question: how to convince policy and decision-makers of the need for joined-up, long-term planning, in a way that benefits people and the environment. Green infrastructure works at a variety of scales, from city region to site, always accepting the principles that the world is a system of networks and that everything connects to everything else. It ... requires an insight into system dynamics, so that we understand how wildlife, water and people move through landscapes, and how environmental networks change over time.[5]

The traditional approach, by contrast, took a disaggregated view of city open space functions, each separately provided for: a park here, playing fields there, allotments somewhere else. Playgrounds for new neighbourhoods were often located on SLOAP ('space left over after planning'); streams were hidden in culverts; areas of special ecological interest treated as discreet enclaves. This approach stems from a mechanical view of the world that looks for separate solutions to each problem. It also reflects the separate remits of different agencies, each pursuing their own agenda. Gradually there has been the recognition that functions and places are *connected* – particularly from the viewpoint of water and wildlife. In Britain, cities such as Leicester and Milton Keynes were early exemplars, planning linear parks around streams, rivers and lakes which simultaneously provide wildlife corridors and refuges, robust water systems with reduced flood risk, and recreational walkways/cycleways through beautiful environments.

GI is about a direct response to the nature of place. This is obvious when considering a riverside park, which has drainage, wildlife, climatic and recreational functions, as well as often being part of the cultural tradition of a community. The ecological approach to development takes the natural features of an area as a starting point, using them to help shape the way settlements grow, and ensuring nature percolates through the urban environment. Ridge lines, water courses, wildlife corridors, and recreational walking and cycling routes are all linear, so multi-functional open spaces are part of a connected network. Figure 10.2 illustrates a pattern of linked spaces and corridors.

GI is also understood to go beyond that – recognizing that the built environment plays a part as well as greenspace. Features such as green roofs and street trees perform many functions simultaneously. Street trees, for example, 'add aesthetic quality to an urban area, but also reduce airborne pollution, provide shade, reduce urban heat island effects, mitigate wind-chill and turbulence and increase biodiversity'.[6]

The strategy for the Central Scotland Green Network is explicit in stressing economic and social values. It sees GI as creating an environment for sustainable economic growth, for healthy lifestyles and mental well-being, for enjoyment and community identity, as well as an environment for nature and resilience in relation to climate change.[7] In the rest of this chapter, I concentrate on key environmental media and processes: first, air, then water, wildlife and food production – each of them vital for health and well-being.

Air quality, health and planning

We focus on poor air quality as the most significant environmental health risk in rich countries and cities in intermediate countries such as China and India. It is caused by urban activity – particularly industry, transport and energy used by buildings – and mitigated by green environments. For some reason, it is often omitted from discussion of green infrastructure.

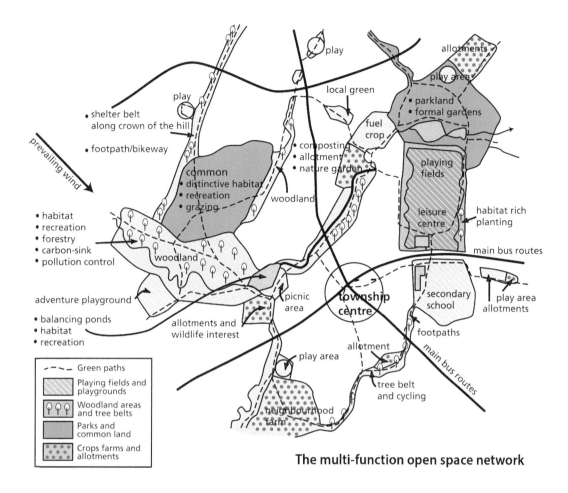

The multi-function open space network

Fig 10.2 *The multi-functional greenspace network*

Source: Barton et al. *2010 (further reading), p.253.*

Environmental pollutants, including particulate matter, ozone, carbon monoxide, nitrogen oxides, sulphur dioxide and benzene, cause respiratory problems, heart disease and cancer; conversely, breathing fresh, uncontaminated air contributes to a sense of well-being. The WHO estimate that seven million people across the world die prematurely per annum as a result of air pollution.[8] Official estimates for the UK suggest that 29,000 people die prematurely p.a.[9] The cost to UK society is huge, around £16 billion p.a., a similar level to estimates for obesity and smoking.[10]

The effect of air pollution varies according to the characteristics of the person exposed. Overweight children, for example, are more affected than normal weight children. Traffic pollution is often the most critical factor. The Royal Commission on Environmental Pollution cites several studies that show that children living close to busy roads have approximately a 50 per cent increased risk of experiencing respiratory illness, including asthma. When road traffic is reduced through policy interventions, there is a commensurate reduction in children's asthmatic reactions.[11] Air pollution exacerbates health inequalities: a study of England found that the most deprived wards were also those with highest pollutant concentrations.[12] There are large clusters of such wards in the major cities.

Pollution from industrial processes, energy generation and the heating of buildings is subject to regulation. Pollution can be tackled at source, through better engines, changed power sources, cleaner industrial processes, energy-efficient buildings and more efficient heating/cooling systems. Land use zoning remains an important tool for separating noxious industry from housing. In England, the Environment Agency sets standards for gaseous emissions – as well as industrial effluents and sewage – to safeguard air quality, often adopting EU standards. Environmental Health departments in local authorities implement controls, negotiating with the pollution producers and if necessary fining those who do not conform. Smoke-free zones have been established in many cities to limit the burning of smoke-producing fuels, reducing the risk of smog and its unhealthy impacts.

Traffic is now the main cause of poor air quality in many cities. The unhealthy impacts of air pollution are greater in urban areas with high traffic levels, high built densities and lower air dispersal characteristics. There is a complicated balance of conflicting parameters: more compact urban areas reduce the amount of per capita travel but at the same time tend to increase the density of traffic and the level of congestion which in turn increases pollution.[13]

The concentration of foul air tends to be worst in heavily trafficked 'canyon streets', where the solid phalanx of buildings on either side does not allow rapid dispersal of vehicle exhaust. Oxford Street in London is a classic example. Ironically it is both the main linking east–west bus route and the principal shopping street in the city, full of people. The only realistic solution in the case of Oxford Street is to change the motive force of the bus fleet and the taxis – which are the users – to electricity. In new developments, canyon traffic streets can be avoided by effective urban design.

'The concentration of foul air tends to be worst in heavily trafficked "canyon streets", where the solid phalanx of buildings on either side does not allow rapid dispersal of vehicle exhaust. Oxford Street in London is a classic example.'

Reducing local air pollution from traffic goes hand in hand with strategies for promoting active travel and reducing carbon emissions. Where cities have successfully created urban environments that encourage people to travel by low energy means, then traffic levels are moderated and the frequency of congestion reduced. Traffic flowing smoothly at a moderate speed is less polluting than constant start/stop. The move towards electric vehicles could also cut local pollution and should be promoted, with implications for the location of charging points. But of course the effect on carbon emissions depends on the source of the electricity.

Green infrastructure has a key role in mitigating air pollution. There are natural processes that purify the air, given the chance. Urban vegetation acts to reduce ozone pollution, absorb sulphur dioxide and remove dust, including heavy-metal particles, from the atmosphere. Soil micro-organisms reduce the amount of carbon monoxide. While plant and tree species vary in their tolerance of pollution, there are very valid reasons for reforestation of the urban environment.[14] The whole shape and character of the city affect the ability of nature to work effectively.

A green urban environment brings other benefits to which earlier chapters have alluded: moderating temperature extremes, improving the sense of well-being. We observe heat islands in cities where the ambient air temperature is several degrees higher than in the surrounding countryside. Increasing the percentage of urban areas covered by vegetation and water permits excess heat and pollution domes to be ameliorated. Cities need to breathe. Linear parkways, green lungs and water bodies that break up the continuity of hard urban development promote climatic moderation and purer air. In addition, tree planting and living green surfaces throughout the urban area, creating a fine green mesh, assist the dispersal of pollutants and heat.[15]

Sustainable urban water systems

The hydrological cycle – precipitation from cloud to land, collected by streams, rivers and aquifers, down to the sea, returned to the sky by evaporation – is like the life-blood of the Earth (Figure 10.3).[16] There are ecologically sustainable ways of intervening in this cycle to provide our water needs, and there are naïve ways of doing it that threaten the health of both people and the wider ecosystem. A memorable slogan is to avoid 'end-of-pipe' solutions that simply push problems downstream – and out of user consciousness. Instead water management should be handled as close to source as possible, so that the natural water cycle is not much interrupted, local streams and groundwater resources are maintained and flooding problems are not exacerbated.

Water problems are likely to be exacerbated by climate change, with some areas suffering water shortage, others subject to more

Fig 10.3 *Typical natural and urban hydrological patterns*

Sources: derived from Hough 1995 (note 14), p.40, and Barton et al. 1995 (note 16), p.34.

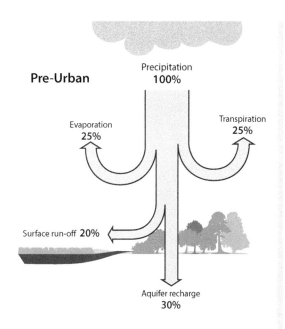

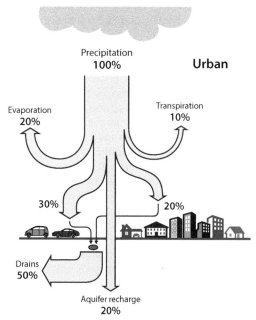

violent storms and increased flood threat. Water management is not simply an engineering issue, but a matter for planners, urban designers, landscape architects – and the users. Urban surface water drainage illustrates this point. In the natural water cycle, rain is absorbed by vegetation, percolates into the ground to recharge the underground aquifers, or runs down streams and rivers at a rate moderated by vegetated banks and flood plains. In the standard urban situation, vegetation and earth have been replaced by the impermeable surfaces of roofs, roads and car parks. The speed of run-off is far faster. Surface water is piped away to streams and rivers, which are then much more liable to flood at times of storm – a problem further exacerbated if the water courses themselves have been canalized, speeding the water downstream. At the same time the local ground water supplies are contaminated by vehicle oils, pesticides, fertilizers and urban detritus, and may not be fully replenished, threatening the longevity of wells. This is foolish planning, increasing risks and distorting a natural process on which we all depend.

Water-sensitive planning

Water is no respecter of boundaries. The water catchment area that a city relies on can be very extensive, often shared with many other settlements. Security of supply, water quality and the reduction of flood risk require sustainable strategies for agriculture and afforestation throughout the catchment area. The storage of water in reservoirs, the management of rivers and storm water, and changes in land use cover, all have health and resilience implications. The effect of land use change on the speed of run-off, turbidity, soil loss, water supply reliability and quality, is particularly critical. Figures from Canada, for example, suggest that the change from forest to agriculture to urban development can result in soil being lost 10 to 100 times faster than before.[17] There are implications not only for water supply but food production, micro-climatic conditions and biodiversity. Water-sensitive planning within settlements needs to address all stages of the water cycle.

- *Demand management:* activities should be designed or retrofitted to minimize the demand for drinking water ('white' water), so as to avoid over-exploiting supply systems and reduce the costs of treatment. This applies to industry, agriculture, parks and offices as well as homes. It is most easily achieved if pricing mechanisms incentivize saving and penalize heavy use (quite the opposite of common practice). Techniques described below can allow discrimination by use: white water should only be used when necessary, normally when associated with human consumption.
- *Rain water and grey water:* for many purposes rain water and/or reused water are quite adequate. Toilet flushing uses a substantial proportion of water (c.30 per cent) in homes, schools and offices, but does not require drinking water quality. In some countries (such as Bermuda), water supply is decentralized and rain water from the roof, after passing through sand

'Village-scale natural systems can take the form of sewage parks. Only the top pond, where solids are deposited, requires protection; the rest can be features in a public landscape, and provide wildlife havens.'

and gravel, is used for drinking, washing *and* flushing. There are ramifications for the design and structure of buildings which need to be incorporated from the outset.

- *Sewage treatment:* within urban areas, where space is at a premium, foul or 'black' water is often most easily dealt with by piping it to be treated by conventional sewage farms, using non-chemical dispersal and filtration methods. There are examples of other, less centralized, techniques; for example, the sewage pyramid in a Kolding renewal scheme.[18] In more suburban areas, on-site methods avoid long and energy-costly pipe runs; tried and tested techniques include cesspits and composting loos, which need only occasional clearance (e.g. every seven years). Village-scale natural systems, requiring no artificial assistance, can take the form of *sewage parks:* a series of gravity-fed ponds progressively purifying the water. Only the top pond, where solids are deposited, requires protection; the rest can be features in a public landscape, and provide wildlife havens.

- *Slowing run-off and recharging aquifers:* whereas conventional urban development speeds surface water away, sometimes causing problems downstream, sustainable drainage systems (SUDS) are about mirroring natural drainage systems *in situ*. The aspiration for all new schemes should be water discharge neutrality. In other words, the water run-off should be the same in quantity and quality as in a naturally vegetated state. Soakaways, permeable surfaces, swales, holding ponds and lakes allow replenishment of local aquifers and managed release downstream (Figure 10.4). Well-designed SUDS achieve diverse objectives: not just water management, but visual amenity, recreational opportunities (Figure 10.5) and wildlife habitats. SUDS increase resilience by reducing the threat of flooding downstream, and shape the relationship of development to landscape. In regeneration sites (often having extensive impermeable surfaces) or agricultural fields where compaction may have speeded run-off, the application of SUDS can be an environmentally healing process.

- *Water courses and flood plains:* within urban areas the tendency to treat streams and rivers as mechanisms rather than ecosystems leads to increased risk and loss of habitat. The sins to be avoided are the restriction of flowing water by culverts and canals, which lead to increased speed of

Water-Sensitive Planning
(avoiding end-of-pipe solutions)

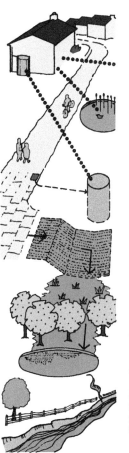

White water
reduce consumption of water of drinking quality

Black water
on-site/local treatment of foul water

Grey water
recycling of waste water, collection and storage of rainwater (for irrigation, car-washing, etc.)

Surface water
to soakaways

paving: minimum area, absorbent

Swales and filter strips
earthworks for improved filtration

choosing planting not needing irrigation in summer and increasing transpiration

wildlife habitat conserved

Detention and holding basins

Natural drainage
Land Use Planning to reduce point/non-point source pollution

10.4 *Water-sensitive design*

Source: adapted from Barton et al. 1995 (note 16), p.34.

flow and flood risk. Instead the aim should be to maintain the natural character of water courses, with vegetated banks slowing water speeds, providing opportunities for wildlife and an attractive environment for people. The network of streams and rivers, with their associated flood plains, give essential structure to greenspace in the town, and form the core of the green infrastructure, influencing the overall shape of settlements.

Fig 10.5 *Water-balancing pond designed for play – look, no fences!*

Source: Barton et al. 2010 (further reading), p.188.

Biodiversity

Our innate affinity with nature runs deep, and as seen in Chapter 7, we need nature for mental well-being. Plants are the basis of all life on Earth – producing oxygen, sequestrating carbon, through photosynthesis providing the food and habitat that all animals depend on. Plants, especially trees, help regulate the flows of water in streams and rivers, purify the air of pollutants, and moderate local climatic extremes. Humans and all creatures live in symbiotic relationship with the plant world. Yet our actions too often belie our interdependence and our affinity.

Biodiversity is the concept that links nature locally and globally. It refers to 'all aspects of biological diversity, especially including species richness, ecosystem complexity and genetic variation'.[19] Biodiversity was recognized internationally at the 1992 Earth Summit as essential to maintain the gene stock for medical research and application. European wildlife directives (and equivalents elsewhere) safeguard particular rare species. At the local level, biodiversity is usefully interpreted in terms of preserving and enhancing a diversity of habitats, capable of supporting a wide range of flora and fauna. The urban green network can provide habitats that partially compensate for their loss in rural areas dominated by agri-business and mono-culture forestry.

Nature conservation is often a very popular cause where mature trees, furry animals or raptors are concerned. But nature is all too easily marginalized in practice when development pressures are on. Particular protected species (such as bats and badgers in Britain) can start dominating decisions while the bigger picture is sidelined. It is vital not to see wildlife policies as fixed in aspic, or just for specific sites. Nature reaches into unexpected places and is forever evolving, and will do so more in the future as climate changes. From the biodiversity perspective the green infrastructure permeates the city. At the strategic level, there is the need for major natural refuges and linking wildlife corridors. At the design level, there is the possibility for a finer network of threads and micro-habitats. Every new development is an opportunity. We need to promote the idea of the ecologically sensitive city in which humans recognize that they cohabit with nature.

10.6 *Town centre trees, the Promenade, Cheltenham, England, a people-dominated environment offering shade, relaxation, contact with nature, supporting trading*

Source: Barton et al. (2010), p.2.

The miracle of urban trees

Street, garden and park trees are a critical part of the green infrastructure (Figure 10.6). They provide ecosystem services and contribute to health and well-being:

- providing pleasurable sounds, smells, sights and sense of the seasons;
- supporting mental well-being, assisting recovery from illness;
- increasing life expectancy and fewer low weight births;[20]
- increasing the value of dwellings (and related taxes) in tree-lined streets;[21]
- absorbing air pollution and storing carbon;
- reducing over-heating and air conditioning costs in summer;
- moderating cold in winter, and reducing heating costs;
- allowing natural evaporation and slowing run-off, reducing flood risk;
- growing food (apple trees are the commonest trees in London);
- providing leaf mould for urban composting and allotment productivity.

Strategic biodiversity infrastructure

- *Major reserves*: the city can plan, extend and manage its extensive semi-natural parks, woodlands, commons and coastal zones for biodiversity *and* recreation. This means not attempting (at great expense) to keep everywhere artificially tidy, in the tradition of formal gardens, but managing discreetly for diverse biological processes. For example: maintaining occasional clearings in woods, where different species prevail; leaving undergrowth for wildlife (and children's dens), rather than cleared for aesthetic or safety reasons; judicious tree clearance (and use for furniture, sculpture or firewood) where heathland species are valued; seeding and replanting with indigenous species where necessary.

- *Other wildlife refuges*: remnant woodlands, wildflower meadows, lakes and ponds, marshland, old quarry cliffs, can provide locally rare habitats. New developments offer an opportunity for safeguarding such places, following an ecological survey (required in many countries), and/or creating new habitats as part of an overall landscape scheme. This is particularly relevant where derelict sites have been colonized by hardy indigenous plants and animals.

- *Wildlife corridors*: connectivity between reserves and refuges is vital in order to allow wildlife movement and colonization – and to provide continuity between town and country. Isolated refuges are vulnerable to change and may not be of sufficient size for some species and habitats to be self-perpetuating. Green corridors and networks of indigenous vegetation can be along natural features such as streams and rivers, ridges and escarpments; they can also be along transport corridors like railway embankments, or narrow open spaces planted for shelter belts or biomass coppice, linking between assets such as parks, playing fields, allotments and cemeteries.

'Connectivity between reserves and refuges is vital in order to allow wildlife movement and colonization – and to provide continuity between town and country.'

Local wildlife opportunities

- *Street trees* create habitats while also providing shade and supporting human well-being. In lower density areas, street trees may combine with front gardens to offer rich habitats – so long as those front gardens are not concreted over for car parking.

- *Back gardens*, especially when planted with trees and linked by hedgerows, provide green threads on a finer scale than corridors, creating permeability for wildlife.

- *New developments* can make good use of remnant countryside hedgerows, and mature trees, to give natural interest and sense of place, as well as wildlife havens.

- *Buildings* can be designed with green roofs (with urban cooling and water retention as well as habitat benefits), and nesting opportunities as part of the building structure.

- *Open spaces and roadside verges* can be managed so as to upgrade habitat quality, with maintenance regimes designed to encourage wild flowers, and planting of native shrubs and trees.

Local food production

At least 800 million people across the globe are undernourished, and many more suffer from nutrient deficiencies. At the same time nearly one and a half billion people are overweight and obese. The traditional pattern of food grown around settlements and thence direct to households has been replaced in richer countries by industrialized agriculture, international trade, and pre-packaged meals. People are estranged from the earthy reality of food production.

In reaction, there has been an explosion of interest in independent and community food ventures. Local food systems not only give easy access to fresh food and encourage recycling of organic waste, they give participants physical exercise, contact with growing things and, in many situations, convivial human contacts. Local food-producing activity takes many forms. Back gardens remain vital, speeding the composting and harvesting processes because of their accessibility to the home; brilliant training for young children. But many urban areas, where flats and close-knit housing predominate, do not offer more than token growing space. Allotments, city farms, community orchards and food hubs provide alternatives – but often are under threat from development.

The implications for spatial planning are significant and radical. Past practice has tended to see provision of allotments (for example) on land left over after planning – awkward sites, slopes, fringe locations. Often allotment holders have to travel a considerable distance to reach their vegetable plot. The distance inhibits daily use, and frequently requires motorized transport to move gardening equipment, composting materials, and produce. The planning principle should be allotments close to the home. One neighbourhood guide recommends 200 or 300 metres maximum, as being the kind of distance people are prepared to wheel barrows and carry tools on foot.[22] Some cities have pursued such a policy: in Odense, Denmark, allotments provide an attractive area adjacent to blocks of flats, offering an important outdoor social focus for residents; in Vancouver, housing co-operatives have been surrounded by gardens and horticulture with great effect.[23] Key to such initiatives is community control and responsibility.

'In Odense, Denmark, allotments provide an attractive area adjacent to blocks of flats, offering an important outdoor social focus for residents.'

Conclusion

A GI approach to the relationship of human settlements to their landscape enables the simultaneous achievement of diverse goals, increasing local resilience and autonomy: retaining and reinvigorating the soils which grow local food, regulating air quality, moderating climatic extremes, managing the supply of fresh water and the treatment of used water, reducing the threat of flooding, controlling erosion, promoting biodiversity. Human well-being is further supported by opportunities for active travel and recreation, contact with nature, strengthened community engagement and cultural identity (Figures 10.7). Economic benefits stem not only from a healthier population and reduced ecological risks, but also the social business opportunities opened up by energy crops, food hubs, woodcrafts and tourist attractions.

The history of the world provides many cautionary tales about societies that destroyed their own natural inheritance. The loss of the sophisticated culture on Easter Island – due largely to over-

Fig 10.7 Play and leisure activity
in green environments

population, deforestation and resource exhaustion – is a classic case. The decline of classical Greece as documented by Plato in the quote at the start of Chapter 9 is another. Sustaining the ecology of cities, as indeed the ecology of rural areas, depends on finding an equable and sustainable balance between satisfying human need and maintaining the viability of natural systems locally and globally. It is essential to treat climate, air, water, land and biodiversity as environmental assets which need to be treasured, safeguarded and replenished if depleted. We must do this not simply out of love of nature, but for our own long-term health and well-being.

Further reading

Barton, H., Grant, M. and Guise, R. (2010) *Shaping neighbourhoods: for local health and global sustainability.* London: Routledge. Practical guidance.

Barton, H., Thompson, S., Burgess, S. and Grant, M. (eds) (2015) *Routledge handbook of planning for health and well-being.* London: Routledge.

Hayes, E. (2015) 'The spatial determinants of air quality', in H. Barton, S. Thompson, S. Burgess, and M. Grant (eds) *Routledge handbook of planning for health and well-being.* London: Routledge, pp. 283–292.

Hough, M. (1995) *Cities and natural processes.* London: Routledge.

Kirby, V. (2015) 'A strategic approach to green infrastructure planning', in H. Barton, S. Thompson, S. Burgess, and M. Grant (eds) *Routledge handbook of planning for health and well-being.* London: Routledge, pp. 386–402.

Lamond, J.(2015) 'Water management, urban development and health', in H. Barton, S. Thompson, S. Burgess, and M. Grant (eds) *Routledge handbook of planning for health and well-being.* London: Routledge, pp. 293–314.

Sinnett, D., Smith, N. and Burgess, S. (eds) (2015) *Handbook on green infrastructure: planning, design and implementation.* Cheltenham: Elgar. Many useful chapters, for example: Sinnett, D. on green infrastructure and biodiversity; Short, M. on green infrastructure and the sense of place.

Notes

1   Quote from Tjeerd Deelstra, 'Enforcing environmental urban management – new strategies and approaches', conference material for the UN Conference on Environment and Development (UNCED), Berlin, Feb. 1992, as reported in Hough, M. (1995) *Cities and natural processes* (London: Routledge).

2   MEA (Millennium Ecosystem Assessment) (2005) *Ecosystems and human well-being: synthesis* (Washington, DC: Island Press).

3   Costanza, R., de Groot, R., Sutton, P. *et al.* (2014) 'Changes in global value of eco-system services', *Global Environmental Change,* 26: 152–158.

4   Girardet, H. (2015) 'Healthy cities, healthy planet', in H. Barton, S. Thompson, S. Burgess, and M. Grant (eds) *The Routledge handbook of planning for health and well-being* (London: Routledge).

5   Kirby, V. (2015) 'A strategic approach to green infrastructure planning', in H. Barton, S. Thompson, S. Burgess, and M. Grant (eds) *The Routledge handbook of planning for health and well-being* (London: Routledge), p. 386.

6   Landscape Institute (2013) *Green infrastructure: an integrated approach to land use.* Position Statement (London: Landscape Institute).

7   Kirby (2015), op. cit.

8   WHO (2014) 'Seven million premature deaths annually linked to air pollution' available at: www.who.int/mediacentre/news/releases

9   COMEAP (Committee on the Medical Effects of Air Pollution) (2010) *The mortality effects of long-term exposure to particulate air pollution in the UK* (London: HMSO).

10 House of Commons Environmental Audit Committee (2011) *Air quality: a follow-up report.* Ninth report of session 2010–12, HC 1024 (London: HC).

11 Royal Commission on Environmental Pollution (2007) *The urban environment,* Cm 7009 (London: HMSO), p. 36.

12 Walker, G., Fairburn, J., Smith, G. and Mitchell, G. (2003) *Environmental quality and social deprivation,* R & D project record E2-067/1/TR (London: Environment Agency).

13 Frank, L., Schmit, T., Sallis, J. *et al.* (2005) 'Linking objectively measured physical activity with objectively measured urban form: findings from SMARTRAQ', *American Journal of Preventative Medicine,* 28: 117–125.

14 Hough, M. (1995) *Cities and natural processes* (London: Routledge).

15 Ibid.

16 Barton, H., Davis, G. and Guise, R. (1995) *Sustainable Settlements: a guide for planners,*

designers and developers (Luton: Local Government Management Board, and Bristol: University of the West of England).

17 See Hough (1995), op. cit., p. 42.

18 Barton, H. (ed.) (2000) *Sustainable communities: the potential for eco-neighbourhoods* (London: Earthscan).

19 Definition of biodiversity, according to the *Concise Oxford Dictionary of Ecology* (1994) ed. M. Allaby (Oxford: Oxford University Press).

20 In Toronto, researchers found that people living on tree-lined streets reported health benefits equivalent to being seven years younger. US scientists have identified a correlation between tree-lined streets and fewer low-weight births – reported in the *Guardian*, 15 August 2015.

21 Evidence from Portland, Oregon, reported in the *Guardian*, 15 August 2015.

22 Barton, H., Grant, M. and Guise, R. (2010) *Shaping neighbourhoods: for local health and global sustainability* (London: Routledge), p. 138.

23 Hopkins, R. (2000) 'The food-producing neighbourhood', in Barton (ed.) (2000), op. cit.

IV   Navigation

A route map for healthy planning

A city is more than a place in space – it is a drama in time.

Patrick Geddes

N ow we come to the crux! All the carefully acquired knowledge about health, social and ecological issues can tell us sound planning principles, but not *how* to plan cities for the enjoyment and well-being of the inhabitants. Geddes (above) elegantly captures a central truth: towns and cities are spatial dramas in time. A city is not like a sculpture, a finished creation. It is not even like a building: constructed then with little change for long periods of time. It is continuously evolving, shifting, adjusting. The Settlement Health Map emphasizes that the city is the people and their behaviour, the communities, the economy, the activities, buildings, streets and places, the flora, fauna and the landscape within which they all sit. The art of city planning is to see all the elements dancing together in harmony.

The chapters in this part can do no more than introduce some key ideas and principles. The emphasis is on understanding the spatial drama and how to navigate towards our goal in terms of policy and design. The starting point is the development process – how does urban change happen? It is essential to understand the market in land and buildings in order to make realistic policies for healthy environments. That leads into consideration of overall urban form – how cities evolve, what spatial options there are and how they impact on health and sustainability. Then we come down in scale and examine neighbourhood planning and the design of the public realm. The final chapter grapples with broad city region strategies for future population, economic development and infrastructure provision.

Criteria for judging healthy urban policy

So what direction should we be heading in? What makes a healthy place? The following paragraphs summarize the evidence gained from the preceding five chapters, and provide headline criteria that assist later evaluation of urban form theories.

Chapter 6 on planning for physical well-being stressed the importance of active travel, active recreation and access to healthy food.

Active travel relies on having places to travel to – close enough to homes and each other to mean that people find it not only healthy but convenient to walk or cycle. If schools, shops and other local facilities are to thrive, then density, social mix, layout and environmental quality have to support them. Active recreation and local food growing are also encouraged by propinquity – the greenspace needs to be accessible, attractive, well managed for many activities.

Chapter 7 shows that the sense of mental well-being is enhanced by supportive social networks, feeling part of the community, at ease in the locality, and having experience of nature. All these are promoted by the same spatial characteristics as foster physical activity. In addition, mental health is strongly related to employment, income and status.

Chapter 8 highlights the degree to which spatial planning influences the economic status of households, and thereby the level of social and health equity. It shows the importance of job creation; the critical significance of housing availability and affordability; the relevance of being able to move around freely, able to access a full range of facilities, irrespective of income, ability and car ownership.

Chapter 9, on climate change, reinforces all the messages stemming from the consideration of health. The reduction of transport carbon emissions, given the current dominant technologies, relies on the substitution of walking, cycling, public transport and train freight for motor vehicles. Sustainable energy use and generation require an integrated approach with economic and spatial planning. The sequestration of carbon and adaptation to climate extremes are increased by extensive tree planting.

Chapter 10 turns to the necessity of living in harmony with land, air and water at a more local level. The emphasis is on a greenspace system performing many linked functions – water management, wildlife habitats, pollution reduction, urban agriculture, recreational opportunities as well as urban resilience. The landscape character, in terms of the hills, woods and valleys, streams, rivers and their flood plains, helps to define the form of the city.

So, five headline criteria for healthy urban form – not exceptional in themselves, but rarely given sufficient priority:

- Is active travel practical, convenient and safe for everybody, reinforcing the viability of local facilities and supporting local social networks?
- Are active recreation and mental well-being promoted through the availability of accessible greenspace and natural environments?
- Is suitable housing available and affordable in convenient locations for all sectors of the population?
- Are diverse job opportunities, commercial and public services viable/available – and accessible to all by efficient public transport and/or active travel, reducing the necessity for car use?
- Is there a resilient spatial strategy for the city, especially in relation to flood risk, water security, air quality, wildlife and local food production (the green infrastructure)?

CHAPTER ELEVEN

REALITY CHECK

The economics of land and development

Introduction

It is easy to pontificate on what kind of city we would like. But unless we understand the mechanisms – primarily economic mechanisms – that influence developments in the built environment, our hopes will not be realized. Spatial planners and designers advise private, public and community *investors* in the built environment. It is all too easy to assume that intentional planning, given good insight and evidence, can *deliver* a healthy environment. But reality is not that simple! So putting wishful thinking to one side, this chapter examines how the investment happens, the factors that determine the way the physical fabric of a settlement change.

The literature on the development process, drawn on by surveyors, project managers and planners, tends to assume a free market situation. Land and buildings are considered as *commodities*, to be bought and sold, subject to the laws of supply and demand. But, as I have argued, the dominant economic and institutional forces are in many places delivering unhealthy environments. The issue is: how do we re-orientate those forces? This chapter is designed to provide a corrective to economic orthodoxy. The chapter starts by looking at urban change at the level of the individual plot, and gradually works up in scale, recognizing the interests of the companies and agencies that make change happen, aspects where the market fails, and the role of public authorities in guiding the market.

The life-cycle of a plot

Plans of themselves do not create the physical fabric of cities: investment does. So let us for the moment study the dominant process of physical urban change – through the market. How do urban

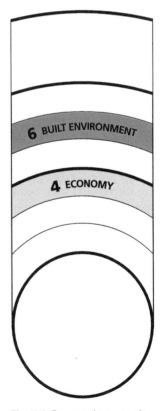

Fig 11.1 *Focus on the economic drivers of change*

development and renewal happen? Plots of land are bought and sold and built upon, buildings grow old, renewal occurs ... Plots come in many different sizes, from the narrow plots of individual terrace properties in a mediaeval town, to large sites bought by developers for commercial exploitation, or by public authorities for schools or hospitals. While plots may on occasion be amalgamated or divided, and buildings will come and go, for the most part plots, like streets, are very stable elements in the urban structure.

Consider the life history of a plot of land. We may imagine it is on the edge of an urban area. There is an extensive literature from the late twentieth century that examined the process of development, some listed in the Further reading section. The idea of a *cycle of development* is taken from the 'development pipeline' model devised by Susan Barrett *et al.*[1] Figure 11.2 extends the cycle to include the building in use and feedback mechanisms that help keep it in use.

At the outset, the plot might be non-urban ('greenfield') land or vacant land previously in urban use ('brownfield'). An investor (private, public or community) undertakes a development feasibility study. If that is positive, the investor proceeds to consider finance, design, necessary consultations and works towards achieving planning permission. Once permission is obtained, then the site can be purchased, contracts let, and work on infrastructure, building construction, fitting out and marketing can proceed. At completion, the building and its curtilage are sold, leased or let and occupied by users for whom the building was designed. Over the years the building gradually deteriorates and becomes dated – it no longer offers all the features or style that clients want. But through the 'feed-back' loop' of judicious up-dating and good maintenance, it might remain fashionable for many decades. Conversely it may become occupied

Fig 11.2 *The life-cycle of a plot*

Source: Author, developing a concept in Barrett et al. 1978 (note 1).

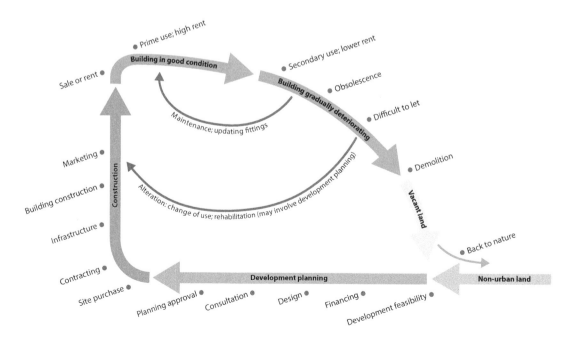

at a lower rent and continue to deteriorate until eventually it is inappropriate for its original use. Then there are two possibilities: rehabilitation could occur, substantially altering the building, maybe changing its use altogether; or the building could become redundant and hard-to-let, left empty and eventually demolished. The resulting vacant land is then available again as a brownfield site, or if there is no demand, goes back to nature, becoming a wilderness.

In order to highlight basic dynamics this is a highly simplified model. In reality, some of the processes marked sequentially may occur in parallel, or differently ordered. The model does not specify land use – albeit timescales and funding mechanisms vary widely between uses. While most housing tends in developed countries to be long-lived, and may be paid for by a 25-year mortgage, commercial property, particularly of the 'large shed' variety, tends to have a much shorter lifespan, and payback is expected within 10 years. Also note that for reasons of clarity, Figure 11.2 distinguishes graphically between the rehabilitation and redevelopment route, with the former assumed to involve a less fundamental re-appraisal. In practice, they may raise quite similar funding and planning issues.

There are some critical transitions within a plot's life-cycle which can cause delay or decay – such as difficulties in initial plot purchase because of unrealistic 'hope value', planning permission requirements and/or the financial risks involved; subsequently in use, the need for regular investment in maintenance and updating to avoid obsolescence, and sometimes uncertainties about the future of surrounding areas, reducing the incentive to invest. Given the range of potential hiccups in the life-cycle, it is likely that some buildings and plots will be underused, under-maintained, fall derelict or vacant.

Settlement planners, advising public or private sector clients, need to be aware of the whole life-cycle of a plot and the way plots, taken together, affect the broader life-cycle of neighbourhoods. Their task is not only to facilitate the development process, but also to foster the conditions in which feedback loops of continuous maintenance and renewal occur, so that the environmental capital represented by buildings is adapted to match the changing needs of the population.

'Settlement planners need to be aware of the whole life-cycle of a plot and the way plots, taken together, affect the broader life-cycle of neighbourhoods.'

Players in the development game

Over the years plots are developed, change, occasionally amalgamate or separate. Who is playing the development game, and how does planning operate in the game? The process of development is made complex because of the number of interests involved. Figure 11.3 (repeating Figure 1.6) is a reminder of the diversity of stakeholders. But the stakeholders are not equal. The investors and policy-makers are the key decision-makers. Other influences on decisions are in some cases the operators, service providers and voluntary groups ('civil society'). The individual users or consumers of the urban environment normally have little direct influence. Below, some of the key players in the development game are listed.

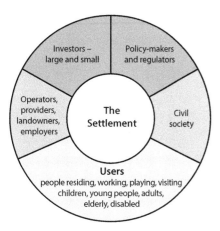

Fig 11.3 *Stakeholders in the development process*

Investors and their helpers

- *Developer/investor* – the key decision-maker: private, public or community; if a private company, the investor is primarily looking for a return on investment; if public or community sector, the need for good returns and viable projects may be combined with community benefit.
- *Landowner* – without the landowner the developer can do nothing; they may be one and the same; landowners some-times hoard land, waiting for the price they want.
- *Land or estate agent* – oils the wheels of exchange, matching buyers with sellers, interpreting market conditions.
- *Financier* – a mortgage company, a bank or pension fund; they lend to the investor, and recoup interest; tend to be very risk averse; like predictable markets and planning policy context.
- *Professionals advising investor* – not just architects and plan-ners, but a wide range of experts; their first duty is to their client, but also have a responsibility to be true to their profes-sional ethics.
- *Builders* – may be the developer or hired in; co-ordinate the contribution of all the building trades; aim to make significant profit to cover unforeseen circumstances.

Policy-makers

- *Spatial policy advisors* – transport, housing, environmen-tal, conservation and land use planners employed by local authorities and government agencies who set the frame for decisions.
- *Regulators* – development managers and other professionals safeguarding building, environmental and social standards; tend to be reactive.
- *Politicians* – democratically elected decision-makers; gate-keepers for the community; attitudes may be geared more to party allegiance and vociferous minorities than the overall community.

Operators

- *Operators and providers* – rather a catch-all category embrac-ing agencies and businesses which provide services and employ people (manufacturers, retailers, public transport companies, education and health departments, housing pro-viders, social services): the organizations that keep the settle-ment going, and which, on occasion, become developers in their own right; they represent the demand side of the equa-tion, needing space for their operation.
- *Building and property managers* – manage buildings and their curtilage, often having a significant influence on, for example, energy efficiency, wildlife habitats and cycling provision; normally driven by the 'bottom line' rather than social and environmental goals.

Voluntary organizations, users

- *Civil society* – includes all the varied voluntary groups who try to influence the outcomes of decisions through political engagement, and who take community initiatives which can alter the use of land and buildings: residents management groups, neighbourhood fora, civic societies, chambers of trade, environmental pressure groups, allotment societies, local anti-development groups, community and social project groups. Typically community campaigns are triggered by frustration or fear, such as the threatened loss of green fields. They sometimes have a hotline to elected representatives or the press.
- *Residents, workers, visitors and other users* – the ultimate beneficiaries of the development, but often with no direct influence on the process, unless they join or form a group.

The developer or investor

This is the key player, the agent who initiates, pursues and realizes development. While the term 'developer' is conventional, it implies the normal market approach, with private profit the motive. I prefer the term 'investor' because it is more inclusive, can encompass public and voluntary sector agencies and firms building for their own use as well as speculative developers, and could include households whose main motive is not profit but their own housing. *Investor* also emphasizes that from the community's perspective their role is investment in the quality of the urban environment. Occasionally a community group can itself become a major investor, as in the case of Coin Street on London's South Bank.[2] An ethical stance on the part of any investor can also be enlightened self interest, maintaining good relations with clients and the wider community.

Typical development companies aim for a good return on investment (e.g. 20 per cent), and tend to specialize in particular kinds of development: residential, retail, leisure, commercial office, or industrial. They will search for sites that have the right locational characteristics for their prospective clients. They tend to be risk averse, conservative in their judgement, reproducing built products that they know from past experience will sell. The development appraisal will estimate the supply and demand situation, potential profit and risks.[3]

It is important to recognize the difficulties which investors sometimes face, blocking the development process and impinging on the on-going process of urban renewal (Figure 11.4). Simply getting hold of the site can be awkward:

'Typical development companies aim for a good return on investment (e.g. 20 per cent), and tend to be risk averse, conservative in their judgement, reproducing built products that they know from past experience will sell.'

- Uncertain attitude of funding organizations and the future level of interest rates, affecting the availability of funds.
- Landowner inertia – due to bankruptcy, incapacity or death – especially when the owner dies intestate (without a will) – so the investor cannot proceed.
- Hope value – where the owner fondly anticipates being able to sell for much more than the current value, and waits for the market to come up to his hopes, which it may not.

Risks and the Development Process (adapted from Carmona *et al.* 2003)

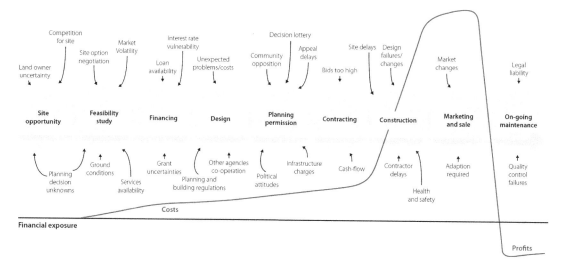

Fig 11.4 *Risks in the development process*

Source: Based on Carmona et al. *2003 (note 3).*

- Multiple land ownership – small plots, often in town centres, awkward to develop individually, and making development on a larger commercial scale impracticable unless all the owners are willing to sell.
- Ransom strips – one person owning a narrow strip of land that is vital for access to a much more extensive area, demands an unreasonable proportion of the total profits of the scheme (in the UK, this is typically one third of the value).

Site conditions are critical:

- Ground conditions and contamination – flood risks, land slippage, decayed infrastructure or contaminated land can all increase costs prohibitively; for example, on old industrial sites.
- Access problems – the difficulty of achieving direct access up to modern engineering standards.
- Obsolescent but valued (Listed) buildings requiring refurbishment and adaptation, often at great cost.

Policy, finance and market risks:

- Unexpected extra costs and delay associated with biodiversity and heritage regulations: for example, protected species on site, or the discovery of Roman remains.
- Uncertainty of the attitudes and decisions of the local authority, including required financial contributions for associated infrastructure and/or social housing.
- Perverse incentives for not developing the site – when its value as collateral for bank loans, or as an investment to await rising property prices, is greater than its development value.
- Development risk in relation to future market conditions, which can change unexpectedly – as in the financial crisis of 2008–2013 – threatening company profits or even survival.

Given the risks, it is all too easy for investors to adopt blinkered attitudes. House-builders, for example, tend to reproduce the same kind of dwellings in the same kind of locations that have made a safe profit in the past – missing out on new market opportunities. In Britain, in the late twentieth century, it took huge efforts on the part of local authorities to persuade builders to invest in city centre housing, but when they did so, it was immediately more profitable than expected, and other developers piled in.

In and around urban areas, investors may become speculative land-holding companies, holding onto land to increase its scarcity and therefore its price. They may take an *option* on land in the hope of one day winning planning permission – making a binding agreement with the farmer to buy the land in certain situations and on certain terms. When a public authority owns land, motives can often be similar to the private sector – the city valuer's job is to get the best value for the land, in order to reduce pressure on the public purse.

The range of experts involved in major development projects is huge, both advisors to the investor, and to public authorities. They include investment analysts, lawyers, planners, land and/or building surveyors, environmental, arboreal and ecology consultants, market analysts, architects, urban and landscape designers, transport consultants, building engineers, project managers ... the list is endless! They have a prime duty to their client or authority – their paymaster – but they also have professional standards. When a building collapses despite being built according to plan, the building engineer is held responsible. Equivalently planning and design professionals have a duty to ensure that as far as possible their scheme enhances the health and quality of life of future users. The professional values and instincts of the advisors are likely to be at odds with each other, unless a very effective team is put together.

When the players in the development game are identified, it becomes obvious why it is difficult to deliver coordinated, health-giving, human environments. Each group of actors has its own remit, priorities and vested interests. The planning advisors may find themselves in a weak and invidious position, obliged to accept compromises that they know undermine fundamental objectives. To achieve towns and cities of well-being the most powerful players need to co-operate, and they need to accept that, as well as their own ambitions, the long-term well-being of the population is paramount. Collaboration is essential. This book is designed to give players stronger well-being arguments in the negotiation process.

'When the players in the development game are identified, it becomes obvious why it is difficult to deliver coordinated, health-giving, human environments. Each group of actors has its own remit, priorities and vested interests.'

Land and housing markets

Now we move from individual plots and the actors involved to the wider picture. Urban planners need to be able to understand land and housing markets, and anticipate the way they will change, given certain conditions, so that their advice can be sound. The language of economists is tied to financial transactions and analysis of supply and demand. The concept of 'perfect competition' remains hugely influential. Figure 11.5 illustrates its application to the housing

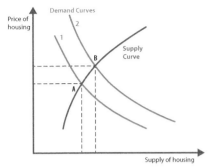

Supply and demand curves given perfect competition

Fig 11.5 *Housing supply and demand curves given perfect competition*

'*In both Britain and the USA official planning policies have the effect of reducing the supply of development land, pushing up its price.*'

market. When the demand for housing, and therefore the price, go up, then the supply will rise as house-builders seek to maximize the opportunity for profits. Conversely if demand and price go down, then supply will fall too. Thus, after the crash of 2008 mortgage availability fell, house building reduced and the UK government sought to increase supply by re-stimulating demand.

However, this logic is often flawed. Figure 11.5 assumes that both demand and supply are *elastic* – i.e. they are able to respond easily to changes in price. In Britain, post 2010, demand was stimulated (particularly affecting the 'buy-to-let' market), prices rose, but supply did not follow. There was *inelasticity* in the supply side. The causes of this inelasticity are contentious. The planning system can act to ration the amount of land available for housing development. In both Britain and the USA official planning policies have the effect of reducing the supply of development land, pushing up its price.[4] Supply in Britain is also dominated by a limited number of large firms, and also land speculators who tend to tie up much of the available land, so that small builders and self-builders become excluded from the market. Once the land is in their hands, speculators hoard the land, without building houses. By not matching demand they 'dramatically inflate the price' so the profits of onward sale or subsequent house-building will be greater.[5]

At the same time the banks and building societies act as gatekeepers on the *demand* side. The gate's position is critical to well-being. Open it too wide, as in the years leading up to the sub-prime crisis in America, and households take on debts that they cannot afford, with family stress and bank failure resulting. Open it not enough, as in the subsequent years of recession, and households struggle to find accommodation to meet their needs. Demand is about ability to pay. When the price rises, affordability is sacrificed and needs are not met. What we have in this situation is far from the ideal of perfect competition – yet that remains an economic myth believed by many.

The impact of planning policy on land values

There are many sub-markets for land, powerfully influenced by planning policies. Figure 11.6 showing comparative land values offers an extraordinary range. Potential sellers will normally seek the highest value use that the market and policy allow. Land with 'hope value' for housing can fetch 10 times the price of farmland. Land which is designated for future residential use in development plans can fetch 100+ times that of farmland. Planners intervene in the market to ensure that the full range of urban needs is met. In areas of growth, this not only includes essential infrastructure but allocations for parks, playing fields, allotments, schools, industrial enterprises and local retail services that cannot compete in the open market with the highest value activities – often housing or superstores. Planning authorities have a huge responsibility to ensure that all the land-based needs of populations are satisfied, 'low rent' and 'no rent' uses are protected, and land prices generally are not inflated by land scarcity.

Type of land	Price per hectare
Average for farmland	£18,000
Land for horses, with stable, SE England	£60,000
Land with long-term hope value	£160,000
for residential....	
Land with permission for housing, SW England	£2,000,000
Housing land in prime locations, Bristol	£6,000,000

Fig 11.6 *Typical land values in England, based on various sources in 2015*

How land values shape the city

Commercial locational needs

Despite the ubiquitous effect of telecommunications, location remains a key market concern. Retailers are fond of declaring that there are three factors that influence their viability: location, location and location. With the growth of online shopping this may not always be the case. But the prime sites at the heart of cities or motorway junctions on the urban edge can command large premiums. Each land-based activity has its own distinctive locational requirements. Some may be quite flexible and footloose. Others may be very particular. Some can afford prime sites. Others are economically marginal or dependent on tax revenues.

Identifying the different needs is not too difficult (see sidebar list). The problems come for the enterprise when trying to convert needs into reality, i.e. the ability to pay for what is needed within the constraints of what is available. The hospital, for example, needs a large site, and easy access for a large number of employees, patients and their relatives. The city centre is the obvious location. But central sites are often physically constrained and almost invariably expensive. So the hospital board decides on a greenfield site on the urban fringe with plenty of space, much lower cost and few physical problems. The disadvantage is its poor accessibility for employees and patients by bus, bike and foot. The predictable result: high car-dependence, inconvenience and frustration for non-car owners and non-drivers, including many vulnerable hospital users. So the location chosen for the institution which is officially dedicated to promoting health becomes a cause of ill-health: increasing accidents, air pollution and carbon emissions from traffic, preventing active travel, exacerbating the problems of the transport poor, and reducing visitor support for patients (especially if car parking is charged for).

The city planners have a role in trying to ensure that a suitable site is available for the hospital. More generally there is a series of questions which any enterprise seeking a new site must ask, and city planners should be mindful of:

1. *Scale of operation*: what area does the activity serve? The locality, the city, the wider sub-region, the country as a whole, international interests?
2. *Site requirements*: what are the essential site needs – in terms of size, flatness, stability, aspect, access, neighbouring uses?

In imagination, contrast the typical needs of the following:
- a financial services head office
- a regional distribution centre
- a large clothing store
- a craft workshop
- a superstore, mainly selling food
- a trendy coffee-shop
- a city hospital
- a primary school

3. *Access for people*: who is most critical to the activity in terms of ease of access? Employees, local clients/customers, business people in other cities? For the primary school, access for children is critical. For the coffee shop, the superstore and the clothes store, it is access to customers. For the head office it is access to a large, qualified employment pool and to branch offices in other cities.

4. *Access for materials*: is access for raw materials or other goods important? Where do they come from? Do products need to be transported to retail outlets, or distributed to firms and households? If so, where?

5. *Transport mode*: How will most people and/or goods reach, or travel from, the business? What site maximizes active travel and minimizes total transport energy use (therefore both costs and carbon emissions)?

6. *Association*: does proximity to similar firms or other activities matter to the success of the business, and, if so, which activities? Shoe shops benefit from clustering, making comparison shopping easier. Financial services and legal services are activities that like to cluster in easy walking distance. Libraries benefit from being in centres where people come to shop.

7. *Subjective values*: what locational preferences do the enterprise leaders and key workers have in respect of accessibility, the quality of the environment, cultural opportunities, social character?

Returning to the list of uses, there can be conflict between operator and community priorities. The superstore, for example, requires a very large and ideally flat site with excellent vehicle access for their potential customers in an uncongested location; the community priority is that the superstore – if it has to happen – should be part of a district or town centre, helping to reinforce its attractiveness. The coffee shop, by comparison, requires an in-centre retail unit with good visibility and high pedestrian footfall, and this coincides with the perspective of the community.

The competition for urban land

Land values are related to accessibility. Traditionally locations in a city centre are highly accessible and the price per hectare high, while the countryside around is the reverse. There is a price gradient from centre to periphery. So households and firms trade off space for accessibility. This is observed in current land use patterns. For similar cost, offices can choose a city centre building on a small site, with basement parking, or a business park location on the urban fringe with ample space for parking and a landscape setting.

The question arises, how do different uses compete and sort out the best location available? Traditional economic theories for land allocation through the market compare the *bid-rent curves* (the amount investors are willing to pay) for the retail/office sector, manufacturing industry, housing and agriculture (Figure 11.7).

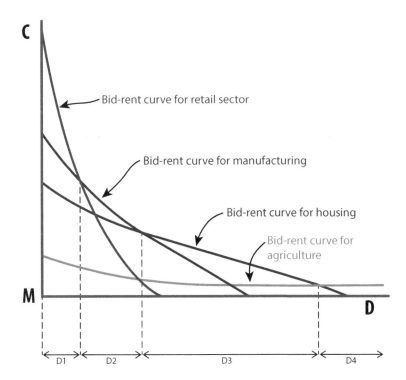

Fig 11.7 *Traditional urban land use market patterns*

Source: Based upon McCann 2013 (note 7).

Shops selling durable goods relied on 'comparison' shopping, and needed accessible central locations as close as they could afford to the 'peak value intersection' at the heart of the central business district (CBD). Manufacturing needed access to rail goods yards and port/canal facilities. Housing surrounded these facilities. So we get the sequence from the centre of retailing (D1), manufacturing (D2), housing (D3) and, beyond that, agriculture (D4). The city was structured according to rent-paying ability. Socially beneficial but low rent paying uses tended to be squeezed out of the more accessible locations, unless there was municipal action.

Turning to more contemporary conditions, Figure 11.8 illustrates a bid-rent curves for commercial and residential development in a polycentric city. Figure 11.9 shows the residential pattern in a conurbation where rapid gentrification and escalating apartment prices are taking place in the city centre, but there is market failure in certain obsolete suburbs, with a high level of vacancy and dereliction. Further out, the high income groups predominate in more spacious suburbs close to open country.

Planners in a market economy cannot determine the future use of an area unless they take careful account of land value differentials and the locational requirements of different users. The market in land is driven by relative profitability and by the willingness of landowners to sell. High-rent-paying uses dominate the most accessible locations, and more marginal activities are pushed to less desirable sites. It has been said: 'You cannot buck the market.' I would express

'Planners in a market economy cannot determine the future use of an area unless they take careful account of land value differentials and the locational requirements of different users.'

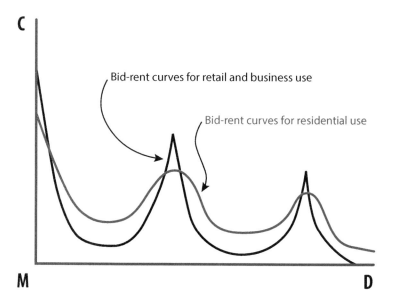

Fig 11.8 *Land values in a polycentric city*

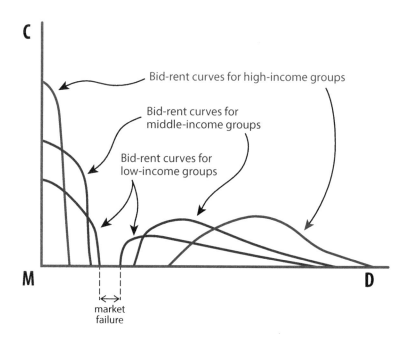

Fig 11.9 *Gentrification and market failure in a modern city*

it differently: you cannot ignore market signals. However, the market is far from a perfect mechanism for allocating the scarce resource of urban land. Plans aimed at health and well-being, equity and environmental sustainability need to be fashioned in partnership with market interests, not in opposition, capturing the power of the market for social ends.

Urban renewal and managing the market

The life-cycle of a neighbourhood

Individual development proposals gain their attributes from context. For the community, each development is welcomed (or not) as part of the trajectory of the surrounding neighbourhood. The planner's job is to note that trajectory and assess how new developments can best contribute to the area's economic, social and environmental qualities. Property prices and rent levels are useful indicators. While across the city a range of prices and rents allows diversity of market niche, it is important to avoid the critical situation of market failure, which is bad for people, business and the public purse.

Figure 11.10 illustrates the basic process of neighbourhood change. The development phase occurs in many ways. Older places may have grown up haphazardly over generations or centuries, gaps being gradually filled as populations expanded, resulting in a mixed age locality. Recent places have normally been constructed over a much shorter timescale, using all available space, leaving less flexibility for subsequent infill. Either way the desirable state is one of *dynamic equilibrium*, whereby continuous gradual renewal occurs, refreshing the physical fabric of the neighbourhood so as to maintain and upgrade its quality as fashions change. Gradual renewal includes a variety of 'feedback loops': investment in maintenance, building alterations, extensions, use-change adaptation and small-scale infill or redevelopment. These indicate confidence in the future as populations, lifestyles and businesses evolve. Local authorities play a part in the process: encouraging good quality developments that up-grade expectations and become local exemplars, investing positively in local facilities, parks and the public realm.

Modest changes to the urban environment add up. Residents are often very aware of this, fearful of change and argue that new developments injure the *amenity* of the area. Over time, the form and function of areas within the city alter. For example, an area of grand Victorian houses would start as the abode of the rich, then might be split into flats, go progressively down-market, until expanding businesses take it over for trendy offices. Each micro decision by investors, designers, public bodies, even families moving home, contributes to the macro processes of urban change, conservation and renewal, infrastructure efficiency, environmental quality, health and sustainability.

In older areas with a relatively poor and ageing population, where the municipality has tacitly ignored increasing obsolescence, gradual decline in the quality of place is almost inevitable. The market may bounce back. If the overall level of demand in the city is strong, then areas with low prices can invite non-premium users and investors – such as young workers, landlords specializing in poorer clients, social housing providers. Small-scale marginally profitable workshops and industrial services become viable because of low rents. This can be positive, allowing the area to serve parts of the market that other

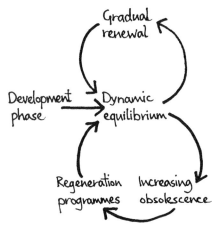

Fig 11.10 *Neighbourhood change: gradual renewal or crisis renewal?*

localities price out. But there is a downside: the problems of social polarization persist, with consequent underspend on maintenance and renewal, and declining services. The area might be termed 'pre-critical', and could go either way.

> ## Conservation as part of gradual renewal
>
> Localities that are valued for their historic and aesthetic qualities have particular problems due to age. Renewal is vital to keep buildings and environment from obsolescence, the two options being **preservation** and **conservation**. Preservation – meaning restoration to the original character – is only feasible is quite specific cases, such as a building funded by tourism. A policy of 'no change' can lead to long-term vacancy and blight. Area conservation implies change which safeguards the essential aesthetic values while encouraging re-investment and reuse by the market in a sustainable way. The test is not about keeping places in aspic, but enhancing them. Official policies – say for grants, sub-division, parking and public realm renewal – can act to block or facilitate effective conservation.

Depending on the location and physical attributes, gentrification may occur. Initially poor but articulate artists and radicals give the area a new buzz. Then young middle-class 'colonists' arrive, drawn by the low prices, trailblazing for the speculators, estate agents and builders, who suddenly spot advantage. This will tend to happen in accessible inner city areas with a distinctive visual character. Re-investment in buildings and the social fabric follows. Dwellings are sold for increasingly high prices, forcing social change. In this situation, when house prices and rents have rocketed, poorer households increasingly depend on state-supported housing provision.

Market failure

In some places the revival never occurs. Market-based investors develop a nose for declining neighbourhoods and tend to shy away. What they smell is *reputation*, which in turn affects price. Banks increase the deposits needed, to safeguard themselves against loss – or may 'red-line' the area altogether, refusing to lend. Accommodation becomes unsaleable and hard-to-let. Those with initiative leave the area, leaving a residual population of elderly people and 'problem' families. Vacancy levels and dereliction increase and begin to dominate the impression of the area. People applying for jobs find themselves tainted by the place they live. There is gradual and then catastrophic decline of population, accompanied by vandalism and increasing fear of crime. Local facilities – schools, shops, medical services, public transport – decline in quality or close down as local spending power falls. Earlier chapters have highlighted the impact on people's health and well-being. The neighbourhood is, in effect, critically ill. The market has failed.

The dying neighbourhood is in need of drastic state intervention. Where overall demand is low, this could take the form of a holding

'Market-based investors develop a nose for declining neighbourhoods and tend to shy away. What they smell is reputation, which in turn affects price.'

action – demolition and grassing over the vacant plots; alternatively new investment (working through development partnerships) to create new/rehabilitated buildings, transform the public realm, and transform market perceptions. Comprehensive reshaping of the area could give it a new start – as in the Gorbals, Glasgow, and the Pearl District, Portland (see Chapter 5).

Research suggests that housing market failure is not a significant issue in Germany and France, where the housing market and governance structures differ from both Britain and the USA.[6]

Conclusion: managing change

We have explored the way in which investors operate in the context of the market in land and buildings. The incentive to invest is profit, but the wide range of potential risks to investment helps to explain why the process of development is disjointed, and many plans do not happen in the way envisaged. This is particularly the case in inner urban areas, where land ownership is often fragmented, infrastructure obsolescent and contamination common. Major developers often prefer greenfield sites, where the conditions are more predictable, and comprehensive masterplans can co-ordinate development. Whether an investment company, a business, a university or a householder, investors hate a vacuum. Effective plans reduce the uncertainties, and give confidence to the market.[7]

Spatial planners – those working for developers as well as for the local authority – face a difficult balancing act: on the one hand, they want investment to create new jobs, accommodation and facilities; on the other, they want to achieve healthy, equitable urban environments and a well-functioning city. Planners need to have a sophisticated understanding of the land, and the commercial and housing markets so that their advice is economically realistic, while working with public and private investors to ensure that realism is not the enemy of the good.

A crucial dimension is the gradual renewal of every part of the urban area, so that re-investment in buildings and infrastructure compensates for the ageing process. In dying neighbourhoods re-investment by the authority itself (new school buildings, greenspace or improved transport infrastructure, for example) can both assist the residents and give greater confidence to the market. Gradual re-investment is as essential in historic areas as mundane estates, but the art is to ensure the distinctive heritage is enhanced by change, not destroyed. At the same time areas that have a poor environment cannot be left to fester, with new developments reinforcing the drab image. Quality is important everywhere. Private sector surveyors, planners, designers and builders have a prime responsibility.

Further reading

Adams, D. and Tiesdell, S. (2014) *Shaping places: urban planning, design and development*. London: Routledge.
   A persuasive review of actors, markets and regulation in the development process, in the context of good place-making.

Carmona, M., Carmona, S. and Gallent, N. (2003) *Delivering new homes: processes, planners, providers.* London: Routledge.

De Havilland, J. and Burgess, S. (2015) 'Delivering healthy places: the role of the private sector', in H. Barton, S. Thompson, S. Burgess, and M. Grant (eds) *The Routledge handbook of planning for health and well-being.* London: Routledge.

Squires, G. (2013) *Urban and environmental economics.* London: Routledge. A useful introductory textbook to the subject, clearly written, taking a conventional economic perspective but including review of contemporary issues such as climate change. Deals briefly with spatial forms and influences.

Notes

1   Barrett, S., Stewart, M., and Underwood, J. (1978) *The land market and development process: a review of research and policy* (Bristol: University of Bristol, School for Advanced Urban Studies).

2   See the review of the Coin Street initiative in Brindley, T., Rydin, Y. and Stoker, G. (1989) *Remaking planning* (London: Unwin Hyman).

3   Carmona, M., Carmona, S. and Gallent, N. (2003) *Delivering new homes: processes, planners, providers* (London: Routledge).

4   White, M. and Allmendinger, P. (2003) 'Land use planning and the housing market: a comparative review of the UK and the USA', *Urban Studies,* 40(5–6): 953–972.

5   Cahill, K. (2001) *Who owns Britain?* (Edinburgh: Canongate).

6   Couch, C. and Sykes, O. (2008) 'Thirty years of regeneration in France, Germany and Britain', *Town and Country Planning,* April.

7   McCann, P. (2013) *Modern urban and regional economics: second edition* (Oxford: Oxford University Press).

CHAPTER TWELVE

SUSTAINABLE URBAN FORM

I have it on good authority that they are not making any more land.

Mark Twain

Introduction

The distinctive remit of planners is to guide the spatial evolution of settlements so that they 'work' in the interests of all. It is futile to expect the vested interests of private and public investors – in the absence of an overarching strategy – to deliver this. Beauty, said Palladio, will proceed from the form, the relationship of all the parts to the whole.[1] We need to understand how the whole works, how it changes, and fashion a place that is economically efficient, ecologically sustainable, socially just and healthy.

This chapter provides starting points for systematic analysis of settlement form and function. It does not pretend to give easy answers – but rather offers concepts and evidence that can aid understanding. It is about the geography of urban space, and the relationship of space to human activity: spheres 4, 5, 6 and 7 on the Settlement Health Map.

Urban form is a term extensively used by researchers into sustainable development, but is in some ways a misnomer. Urban functions do not stop at the edge of the built-up area. The critical spatial scale for strategic planning is the *city region*: the city together with its commuting and service hinterland. The villages and exurbs within that hinterland are mainly urban in their function, tributary to the main settlement. The same principles apply to towns and their hinterlands, and conurbations. In higher density regions (such as the Ruhr in Germany and West Yorkshire in England), the city regions overlap and are interdependent.

It is essential to realize the interlocking nature of decisions at different scales. Figure 1.5 on p. 13 shows scales from plot level up to international, and their relationship to planning issues. If we are to plan urban form, we must understand the whole sequence of scales

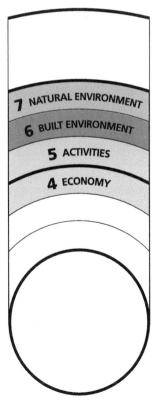

Fig 12.1 *Focus on the whole city*

and how they interact over time. The layout of streets and blocks, the process of incremental change, the shape of neighbourhoods, the structure of whole urban areas, and the wider pattern of settlements in the bioregion are all interdependent, reinforcing or undermining well-being.

Understanding urban form

There are three distinct strands of urban form thinking: normative, empirical and modelling. The normative strand starts from the kind of place we want to create and is essentially design-led. The city design tradition from Hippodamus to the planners of the British and Dutch new/expanded towns fall into this tradition. Designers start with clear goals and devise a spatial concept to achieve them. For example, the 'compact city' principles advocated by the Urban Task Force in Britain, was inspired by the goals of environmental sustainability and urban regeneration.[2]

The empirical strand is research-led: finding out what is really happening and theorizing about the significance of the findings. In the twentieth century human geographers have pursued this course, from a variety of angles. In the 1980s one important angle was energy-efficient urban form. In the last 20 years there has been an explosion of empirical research under the general heading of *sustainable urban form*, particularly debating the merits or otherwise of the 'compact city' ideal.

The mathematical model-building strand draws on empirical evidence, testing normative theories by trying to mirror reality and forecast the future. The biggest model builders have been the transport planners, devising ever more complex land use and transport models as computing power has increased – with the prime aim of testing alternative strategies: private vehicles versus public transport, dispersal versus concentration (see Chapter 14).

Classic theories of urban form and change

We start with the early empiricists. They asked, what urban forms do we observe? How do they change over time? What factors lead to those changes? According to the Chicago School of 'urban ecologists'[3] between the wars, there are parallels between the process of city growth and natural ecology. Competition for urban space through market mechanisms mirrors competition for ecological space. In a heathland area where grazing has reduced, grassland gradually gives way to scrub, which is then suppressed as woodland becomes established, and new undergrowth develops in the woodland shade. This process of ecological 'succession' leads ultimately to the 'climax' vegetation, which provides for a diverse ecology, in dynamic equilibrium, with evolving habitat 'niches' for many different flora and fauna.

The Chicago ecologists observed population groups and land uses competing for space in the same kind of way, with one group 'invading' the territory of another group (as, for example, in the process of gentrification), until succession occurred and they become the dominant land user. Some uses and groups, as in nature, develop symbiotic relationships – as when retail centres flourish in affluent suburbs, benefitting from the local spending power. Other uses tend to repel – as industrial zones repel richer households.

The urban ecology terminology has value, in that it links human activity to nature, and recognizes the unequal competition for urban land. In nature, competition and symbiosis go hand in hand. A wide range of flora and fauna can occupy different niches in the same ecosystem, and climax culture is rich and diverse. City land markets can have the effect of squeezing out marginal uses – for example, small business workshops – but often can also offer diverse niches in older buildings and spaces.

The principal theorist of the early urban ecologists was Burgess. On the basis of observation of Chicago in the early twentieth century Burgess devised his *concentric ring theory* of urban form, trying to capture the dynamic of change as the city expanded (Figure 12.2).[4] Essentially he saw outward-shifting rings of social privilege and deprivation, reflecting a free market in land and buildings, with the richest and most mobile households choosing the new spacious homes on the outskirts, while poor (often immigrant) households moved into the oldest, most cramped environments in the inner city. He observed a fractured environment immediately around the central business district, which he called the *zone of transition*, as old housing decayed, industrial buildings became obsolescent, city centre commerce expanded and pushed outwards, land speculation and market uncertainties led to blight. Often the housing in such areas suffered from appalling environmental conditions, and was occupied by transient and marginalized populations, trapped by poverty.

Others later criticized the concentric model as not representing reality. Hoyt (1939) observed that many cities were organized in

Fig 12.2 Early models of the structure of cities

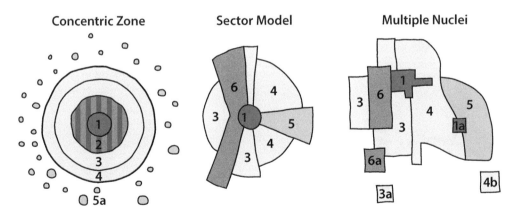

1.	Central business district (CBD)	
1a.	Suburban business district	
2.	Zone of transition: transient and excluded population; industry and warehousing	
3.	Low-income suburbs	
3a.	Low-income exurb	
4.	Middle-income suburbs	
4b.	Middle-income exurbs	
5.	High-income suburbs	
5a.	High-income commuter zone	
6.	Industry and warehousing	
6a.	Heavy Industry	

sectors, not circles. Industry would often lie across the city along-side the railway, the canal or the docks. Poorer households live in the sectors accessible on foot to the ugly and polluting industrial areas. The rich live further away, in pleasant surroundings.[5] Hoyt elaborated on the mechanisms of social change: as new high-rent houses are occupied by the most affluent, they release their original properties for occupation by less affluent groups – a process (not always observed) known as *filtering.* His model does not replace the concentric picture, but adds a new dimension.

The elegant simplicity of these dynamic models is of course belied by complex reality: the natural geography of rivers, flat land and hills, mineral deposits and bogs; the whims of early investors; the historic routes of canals, railways and highways; the progressive absorption of smaller settlements by larger; the locations chosen for social housing estates – all shape each city in unique ways. Harris and Ullman observed this diverse pattern of cities – how in many cases there were 'multiple nuclei' serving the city – and gave us the third classic model of urban form, as shown in the Figure 12.2.[6]

Centrifugal and centripetal forces

The concepts of the early theorists remain helpful in understanding more recent trends. The effect of motorization on urban form since the later twentieth century has been dramatic. The first example in the Prologue, based on Birmingham, Alabama, illustrates the unfortunate combination of suburban sprawl and central decay. Figure 12.3 illustrates the concept of the 'doughnut' city, with the hole in the middle, and the 'edge' city, with all the principal retail, office, and leisure functions having moved to car-based sites in affluent suburbs or the urban periphery. The arrows indicate the

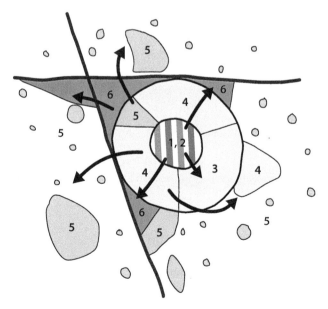

Doughnut City, Edge City

1, 2. Residual CBD and hollowed-out zone of transition
3. Low-income suburbs
4. Medium-income suburbs
5. High-income commuter villages and suburbs
6. Edge city: retail and leisure centres, office parks, distribution centres and industry

Fig 12.3 *Doughnut city, edge city and sprawl*

centrifugal movement of population into sprawling suburbs. The form is anathema to equity and health.

The force which creates this 'counter-urban' city is a combination of private aspiration and state investment. Increasing affluence, rising car ownership and the desire for family space have led in the USA, Australia and elsewhere to the quarter or half acre plot being a symbol of success. At the same time huge public investment in freeways facilitated the suburbanization of the city and surrounding country areas. It was no doubt politically expedient to do so, responding to public demand and allying with dominant commercial interests. In the 1930s and 1940s, the General Motors (GM) subsidiary, National City Lines, bought up and then closed down electric street-car and trolleybus networks in 45 cities in America. The demand for bigger, better roads became irresistible. Los Angeles was an extreme case where an unholy alliance of commercial and political interests condemned the city to become a byword in profligate use of the key resources of land and energy.[7]

In Western Europe the same trends were manifest, but modified by a more social version of capitalism. In Britain, the suburban densities were typically 10 to the acre (25 per hectare), not four – at a level that was initially sufficient to support local shops and good bus services. But as car ownership rose, motorways and ring roads multiplied, there were waves of decentralization. First, the warehousing and distribution centres, then industry, followed by supermarkets and other major retail outlets, then offices and leisure centres. The provision of low density, peripheral business parks and science parks became an essential symbol of civic aspiration, encouraging job creation. The 'edge city' phenomenon thus colonized Europe. Ten years ago (2006) most European cities were still tending to decentralize.[8] The same pattern is happening in many of the developing cities of the world where a newly affluent middle class has demanded to escape the common crush.

It is a classic error to assume that processes of decentralization and suburban sprawl are inevitable. Nothing could be more misleading. City and state authorities have chosen to invest in infrastructure which fosters sprawl – progressively excluding less mobile people from enjoying the fruits of affluence, compromising their well-being. The low density of quarter-acre plots is also the direct result of land ordinances enforced by city authorities. Both transport investments and plot size rules are aspects of spatial planning.

Britain in the late twentieth century reacted to centrifugal forces in contradictory ways. On the one hand, Britain protected open country from urban development, with strong rural restraint policies and greenbelts around many cities. Powerful conservation lobbies sought to maintain the sanctity of the countryside even while government was investing in ring roads and bypasses, promoting exactly the dispersal that countryside policies were intended to halt.[9]

The containment of the city led to planned and unplanned decentralization into commuter towns and exurbs. London, with its powerful greenbelt policy and its ring of planned new towns, is an

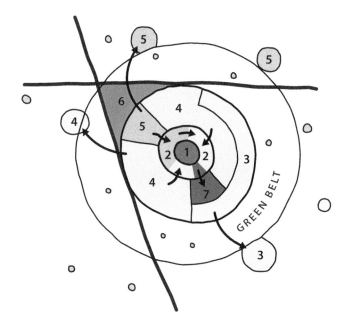

Rural restraint, overspill and regeneration

1. Diversifying CBD
2. Zone of transition: progressive gentrification
3. Low-income outer and overspill estates
4. Middle-income suburbs and commuter town
5. High-income suburbs and commuter town
6. 'Edge city' development
7. Transient and marginalized populations

Fig 12.4 *Rural restraint, regeneration and overspill*

extreme case. Smaller cities relied on private enterprise initiatives in the context of a strategic plan, together with the progressive sub-urbanization of hinterland settlements. At the same time the constraint on available development land put up prices within the cities to the point where redevelopment occurred in the transition zone (on derelict industrial and utility land); the old housing areas, long the preserve of the poor, were invaded by the rich. In other words, the rural restraint fostered regeneration and gentrification. Figure 12.4 shows the combination of centrifugal forces and centripetal forces.[10]

Government and local authority policies helped to trigger and shape this process of regeneration. For example, Urban Development Corporations (UDCs) led new investment in the fracture zones of London and Newcastle; forward-thinking local authorities changed the climate of conventional market thinking in Birmingham and Bristol. In continental Europe, re-investment in inner areas occurred in many cities, without the need for draconian rural restraint. There was, then, a wider social move, valuing the character of inner areas and the vitality of urban life.

Urban regeneration is a necessary and welcome corrective to inner urban decline, but the impacts on well-being are complex. Re-investment and gentrification may increase housing stress. Hoyt's process of filtering does not work well. The options for lower-income groups are progressively squeezed as the rich occupy their territory, forcing up rents and house values. The rich simply occupy more space, including on occasion second homes, empty for much of the year. Unless an increased supply of social and affordable housing in suitable locations is facilitated by the state, people will be forced to live in overcrowded conditions, or in remote locations, or in the worst case made homeless.

Decentralization versus the compact city

So if many twentieth-century trends have been undesirable, what direction *should* we be taking? Idealists and analysts have been at work. The overarching debate is between those who believe in a more decentralized settlement pattern and those who believe in a more concentrated one. Below we explore the competing images of sustainability: decentralized autonomy, compact cities, polycentric cities and linear structures.

But, first, a brief reflection on the research in this field. It has not been able to provide unequivocal answers. Much of the early research was drawn together by Susan Owens in her book, *Energy, Planning and Urban Form* in 1986.[11] Subsequently there have been a useful series of academic compendiums on the subject edited by Mike Breheny, Mike Jenks, Elizabeth Burton and Katie Williams.[12] Academic papers continue to proliferate, now with health a more explicit theme. This is valuable, and the chapter draws on them, but there is an inevitable limitation. Most urban form research (empirical and modelling-based) necessarily examines past or current situations, and then may try to reach conclusions about the future. Owens makes a critical point. She says that current behaviour – such as the propensity to drive or walk, shop in the superstore or the local store – cannot simply be extrapolated into the future. Current behaviours derive from particular conditions: the price of fuel; learnt behaviour; social attitudes; physical constraints. Values can and do change. What we need are spatial forms that create the *opportunity* for sustainable behaviour and potential energy saving, and are therefore robust. Good urban form is a *necessary* though not *sufficient* condition for improvement.[13]

Decentralized autonomy: a false hope[14]

Deep green environmentalists have often promoted an idealized picture of rural sustainability: small-scale, low-density, self-sufficient communities harvesting their own food, managing their own water and wastes, catching natural energy, and living a healthy outdoor life, while at the same time teleworking and participating in the global internet village. Radical publications in the 1970s inspired a generation with the belief that only by decentralization can we create a humane social system and minimize the burden of human society on the ecological systems we depend on.[15]

The Eco-village movement, launched at that time, tried to implement the ideal. Occasionally 'low-impact development', as articulated and lived by Simon Fairlie in Somerset, England, could be achieved.[16] If work is truly 'rural' – based on agriculture, forestry, countryside recreation, etc. – then there is logic to village growth tied to those jobs. But for the most part eco-villages have been compromised by their dependence on the urban economy and services.[17] Over time, people's behaviour tends towards societal norms.

Ironically the image of this supposed rural idyll also reflects the aspirations of the consumer society. Many people want to live in the countryside. The cost of rural housing within commuting distance of a city reflects the high demand, and the result is the reverse of the ecological dream. A review of British and overseas experience shows that rural settlements are substantially car dependent, with much greater vehicle distance travelled than more urban settlements.[18] Working from home is no panacea – there is still need for social contact, activities and services which require travel – it simply means people travel at different times, often much further distances. The cost of mobile services (post, deliveries, repairs) is affected in the same way.

Advocates of population dispersal point to the need to disperse employment at the same time. However, the dispersal of urban employment into small settlements does not mean that local people get the local jobs. In an era of increasing job specialization, employees may come from far afield. The dispersal of employment into locations that are very poorly, or not at all, served by public transport, is a recipe for very high car dependence.

The argument becomes even stronger when we consider the options that poorer people have open to them. Living in small settlements within commuting distance of major towns, there is no choice but to travel out of the village for many purposes. Car ownership is necessary, putting pressure on household finances. Those who are no longer able, or cannot afford, to drive, are penalized, potentially exacerbating health inequalities. We can conclude: decentralization of urban-dependent populations is no solution.

The compact city debate

At the opposite end of the spectrum are the urban revivalists who advocate the 'compact city'. We are not talking here about the lunatic fringe of architectural mega-structures, but the principle of urban reinvestment and intensification promoted as a reaction to urban sprawl and the hollowing out of the city. The European Commission's *Green Paper on the urban environment* (1990) pointed to the problems of economic decline, social polarization and deprivation in the inner city areas. Environmentalists highlighted the issues of unsustainability – land-hungry, carbon-intensive development.[19] The Urban Task Force, reporting in 1999, advocated a higher density, mixed use pattern of building to create a sustainable, vibrant and enriching urban environment.[20] Researchers in the transport field lent weight to the energy argument, particularly the seminal work of Newman and Kenworthy. In their book, *Cities and Automobile Dependence* (1990),[21] they looked at the relationship between modal choice, trip generation, density, centralization and transport systems. If density is taken as a proxy for degree of compactness, then they demonstrated a very strong relationship between average city densities across the world and transport energy use (Figure 12.5). When they assessed intra-regional variation they also found surprising contrasts; for example, a *five-fold* variation in transport energy use per person between central New York and the outer commuting hinterland.

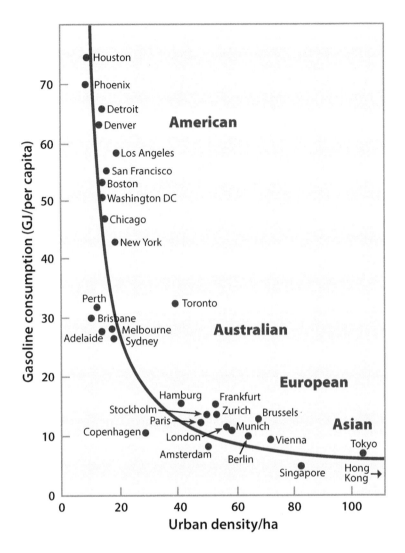

Fig 12.5 *The relationship between urban density and transport energy consumption*

Source: Based on Newman and Kenworthy 1990 (note 21).

Car use and trip length both play into the variations. Studies have found that households in commuter exurbs generate two and a half times the car travel of similar households in towns.[22] This does not mean that people were travelling less often, quite the reverse, but their trips were shorter, and more often on foot. This is not just about commuting. A study comparing suburban neighbourhoods in England found a threefold+ variation (18–62 per cent) in the percentage of walking/cycling trips for 'local' purposes, excluding work.[23] The variation reflected not so much density, or car ownership levels, as locational, urban form and cultural characteristics. The lessons for spatial planning are clear. Other things being equal, the bulk of new development should be located in and close to urban centres offering a wide range of jobs and services.

Other things, though, are rarely equal. The compact development of larger towns and cities implies urban intensification. More

Density ranges wide!

- 5 dpha (dwellings per hectare) in some US suburbs
- 25 dpha in leafy interwar UK suburbs
- 40 dpha in UK estates post 2000
- 100 dpha in Victorian terraces
- 400 dpha in central Paris
- 960 dpha in Hong Kong

people living and working in urban areas, though, is a mixed blessing. According to those living in such areas, intensification brings improved public transport, better services and more walkable distances, but also more congestion, poorer air quality and loss of greenspace.[24] This has been called the *paradox of intensification*.[25] The effectiveness of any such policy depends on avoiding the downsides of intensification by transforming the quality of place – creating a pedestrian-friendly environment, reducing the dominance of vehicles, enhancing open space – not simply providing more housing.

The European Commission has been at pains to ground the debate. One study (which examined the problems of urban sprawl) cites Munich as a rare example of a city which has overall, including satellite settlements, become more compact in recent decades. The total population has risen faster than the built-up area, and new residential areas are contiguous and integrated. Regional co-operation and stakeholder involvement have been critical in pursuing:

- an integrated city plan, across departments;
- development areas inside the urban structure through brownfield development, supported by economic incentives, rather than peripheral expansion;
- a strong emphasis on public transport, with little road building;
- the preservation of large green recreational areas throughout the city.[26]

Another European study concluded it was vital that urban policy should be developed and evaluated as a whole: land use, transport, environment, social infrastructure and economic development together. It recommended demand management through pricing policies for car and public transport, reflecting the external costs (of congestion, pollution, etc.), investment in better public transport speed and service quality, and a land use plan supporting people to live close to service centres and along public transport routes.[27]

The compact city strategy has been adopted – at least in theory – by many rich cities. The revival of the city centres and inner areas this century, after generations of decline, has been a notable success. But at the same time growing affluence (and often growing populations) has triggered longer commuting distances and greater dispersal: urbanizing the countryside yet further, exacerbating social polarization. So we have the ironic combination of urban concentration combined with rural suburbanization.

The compact city approach can be made to work, where there is good regional co-operation and well-funded programmes of urban transport and environmental improvement with supportive fiscal and regulatory systems. But these conditions are difficult to fulfil.

Polycentricity and linearity

According to Susan Owens, there is an optimum size for cities – when they are large enough to offer a full range of services, but not so large as to generate diseconomies of scale (including very long commuting distances). She put this threshold at around 2–300,000 population, and argued for a pattern of what she called *dispersed concentrations.* This concept does not deny the benefits of compactness, but discourages the continued growth of over-inflated cities. This means infrastructure investment and the encouragement of commercial development in several centres rather than one, creating counter-magnets to the dominant centre, providing a focus for the decentralizing tendencies of the market. Promoting a new major centre within the conurbation is one option (Canary Wharf in London, for example). Boosting the growth of suburban towns or 'garden cities' in the hinterland is another.

Many urbanized regions already exhibit a polycentric pattern, which provide logical starting points for 'dispersed concentrations'. The social advantages of polycentric structures are, in theory, reduced traffic congestion and related pollution, and better accessibility for all inhabitants. One practice guide suggests that 5 kilometres is a critical distance for accessibility – the maximum that people should be expected to have to travel from their homes to reach town services, diverse job opportunities, and major greenspace or countryside. This is based on analysis of cycling distances, bus travel times and population thresholds, and could match the 2–300,000 population figure above.[28]

Each of the compact concentrations needs to be large enough to support a good range of jobs, services and diverse housing opportunities, so that it becomes equivalent to a compact city in its own right. One study for the UK government suggested the *minimum* viable size for a free-standing town is around 25,000 people.[29] This accords with analysis of population thresholds for superstores, durable goods retailing, secondary schools and technical college, library and leisure centre. It equates to the scale envisaged by Ebenezer Howard. His original 'garden cities' were high density compact settlements set within the productive countryside (see Chapter 4). However, in urbanized regions, significantly higher populations are needed, because towns are far from self-sufficient. Larger centres cream off trade and services, which may induce high car dependence, as people travel between settlements. The quality of the public transport network – its accessibility and level of service – is critical. The strength of polycentricity is resilience: if the friction of distance increases, deterring travel, then people are close to existing services, and those services can grow.

Linear patterns

The *linear* concept normally works at a less strategic scale. It is about the internal structure of the city. We saw in Copenhagen (Chapter 5) how linearity was a key principle enabling efficient public transport services and good access to greenspace for all. In the Netherlands the linear principle was articulated by Sybrand Tjallingii in his book, *Ecopolis*[30] – the result of a study into ecologically sound urban development for the Dutch National Physical Planning Agency. The essence of this twin track model is the shaping of urban areas by the two networks of public transport and green infrastructure (Figure 12.6). In Britain, the historic city of Oxford illustrates this pattern. The new town of Runcorn famously involved a figure of eight

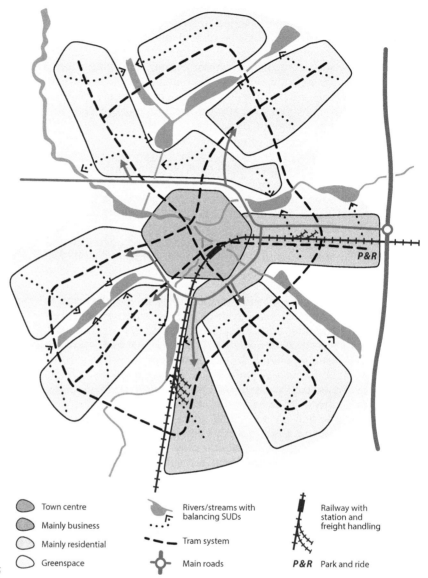

Fig 12.6 *The twin-track linear approach to urban form*

Source: Based on Tjallingii 1995 (note 30), p.96.

Town centre		Rivers/streams with balancing SUDs		Railway with station and freight handling
Mainly business		Tram system		
Mainly residential		Main roads		*P&R* Park and ride
Greenspace				

Note: The centre includes high density housing. Local facilities are along tram routes. Bikeways thread throughout.

linear form, with a segregated busway serving a string of neighbourhoods, industrial areas and the town centre, all surrounded by parks and playing fields.

The first track is about identifying the key elements of the natural environment that give logic to the green infrastructure. Rivers, streams, canals and flood plains provide the starting point. 'Blue-space' is then supplemented by analysis of greenspace: designated wildlife habitats, woodland reserves, high quality farmland and allotments, culturally valued commons and parklands. Continuity of greenspace is desirable for wildlife, recreational walking and cycling.

Plans can identify possible new links to enhance the existing greens-pace network. The second track is about facilitating the diurnal patterns of human life. The public transport system provides the spine of linear townships, offering potentially excellent quality of service at minimum cost. Good pedestrian access to the spine high street services gives the opportunity for healthy physical activity and social contact. In older cities this pattern is often still evident along radials. The problem is that those radials can be badly congested, which impedes bus efficiency and is unpleasant for pedestrians and cyclists. Comprehensive transport and environmental plans are needed to reduce vehicle use to acceptable levels. Extensive bus/tram priority and safe bikeways are one way forward. The high streets offer a natural focus to activity, give locational flexibility along the route for businesses and services, and avoid the problem of fixed catchment areas – discussed in Chapter 13.

The principle of linearity can be compatible with compact or multi-nucleated forms. Since it echoes the historical patterns of urban development out along main public transport routes, older towns and cities could plan in the long term to enhance linearity as a means of improving access both to local facilities and greenspace. Newer suburbs could be strung together to improve accessibility while preserving open space.

Five key urban form decision areas

The broad urban patterns above give images of overall form, but are a long way from everyday development decisions. Such decisions tend to be taken on a disaggregated basis – a residential proposal here, a retail application there, a road improvement somewhere else. In order to relate such incremental decisions to the overarching strategy, it is necessary to have a clear view of each of the critical facets, or decision areas, which go to make up urban form. Figure 12.7 identifies five critical aspects of spatial development: greenspace, movement, jobs/services, housing and density. It is possible to specify a healthy strategy for each decision area, irrespective of whether the evolution of a city region follows a more compact, multi-centred, linear or blended form. This section provides a brief summary to clarify the choices that are available, and point the way forward.

Planning the greenspace network

The two dimensions on Figure 12.8 represent the critical choices: Are greenspaces treated as discrete entities, disconnected, or are they seen as part of a linked green network? And are greenspaces single function, or multi-functional? Chapter 10 explained the multiple functions of the green infrastructure on which the health of the city depends. Its form, as outlined above, is largely determined by natural features and historic allocations. The greenspace system is unique to the geography and traditions of each city. Continuity is important, linking between varied features, for recreational routes, wildlife corridors and climatic/pollution management.

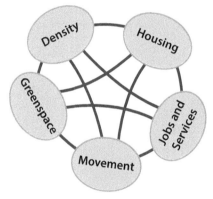

The five key decision areas of urban form

Fig 12.7 *Five facets of urban form*

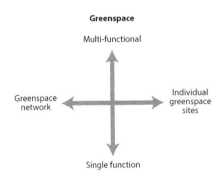

Fig 12.8 *Greenspace decision options*

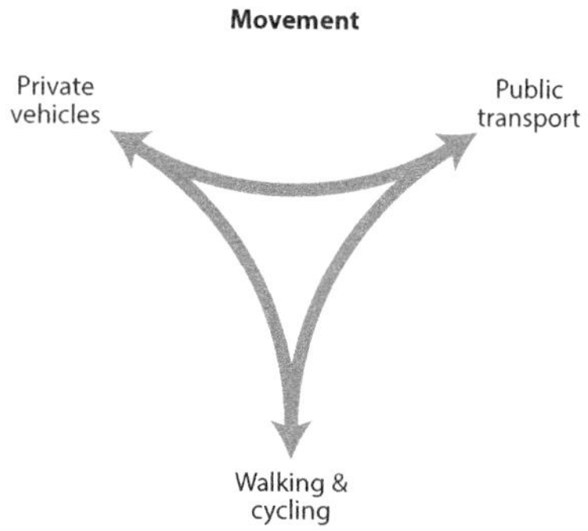

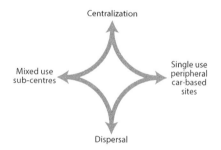

Movement

Private vehicles

Public transport

Walking & cycling

Fig 12.9 *Movement decision options*

Transport issues are examined throughout the book, in particular transport/ land use integration in Chapter 5, travel behaviour in Chapter 6, transport equity in Chapter 8, streets and networks in Chapter 13, transport and economy in Chapter 14.

Location of Jobs and Facilities

Centralization

Mixed use sub-centres

Single use peripheral car-based sites

Dispersal

Fig 12.10 *Jobs and facilities locational options*

Transport priorities

Transport or movement policy can be angled in three different ways: is the movement of private vehicles the dominant concern, or public transport, or walking and cycling (Figure 12.9)? In the city of well-being, walking and cycling are priority. Public transport is part of the active travel priority and also key to city-wide and inter-city trips. Tram and bus routes which are frequent, cost-effective, reliable and comfortable, provide the structure of the city. The implications of such a strategy for land use distribution are profound – as illustrated by the strategy for Freiburg (see Chapter 5). Historic radials are often the principal routes, because they lead directly from centre to periphery via the higher density areas, where custom is high. Bus and tram priority is vital along the route, in order to avoid the problem of traffic congestion and give public transport the edge over the private car. The aspiration must be to have a service that allows people just to turn up on spec, knowing a vehicle will be along shortly. A frequent service of this kind is every 10 minutes or more often.[31] Real-time information further helps to encourage use. Ease of interchange between services, and at the rail station, is important.

Commercial, retail, educational, health and leisure facilities

Conventionally, employment allocations are treated separately from shopping and social facilities (Figure 12.10). But in terms of location policy a retail unit, a school and a hospital have much in common with an office: they all provide jobs, and all have visitors – whether shoppers, children, patients or clients. The question is whether such facilities should be in city centres, major sub-centres, local centres, edge-of-town estates or dispersed.

Since the structure of the city should enable people to make the vast majority of their trips by public transport, foot or bike, facilities serving a city-wide or regional hinterland – including universities, major hospitals, football stadia and concert halls, as well as major office and retail functions – should be located where there is excellent access by public transport from the whole city, and good inter-city rail services, facilitating inter-city business travel as well as longer distance commuting, shopping and leisure trips. Following Dutch practice, these are *A-locations.* There may be several in a large city, or there may be one in each town in a polycentric region.

Other facilities can be divided into those serving a wide part of the city or a whole small town, those with a very local catchment, and industrial centres that employ few people but rely on good freight access. We will deal with the local neighbourhood facilities in Chapter 13. The wider catchment facilities – such as district shopping centres, superstores, leisure centres and professional services – should be clustered in mixed use high streets or district centres, embedded in the urban area and well served from all directions by bus, bike and road networks. If the public transport services are good, then facilities can be given locational flexibility along high street bus/tram routes, so that the market can respond more easily to changing opportunities. These are *B-locations.* The catchment population of such a centre might be 30,000 or more.

Large industrial and distribution activities are normally highly automated, and employ few people per hectare. Their prime need is for efficient movement of goods. While in many cases that indicates closeness to major roads, avoiding residential areas, the ambition is to give long-term sustainable transport choice, locating them by railways or waterways. These are *C-locations* (Figure 12.11).

There is of course an element of artificiality about such neat hierarchies, in part, because planning powers are often not sufficient. Also because businesses evolve, and may grow to serve wider catchments, or decline and become more local, while staying in the same location. For example, a local butcher, or coffee shop, may start as a

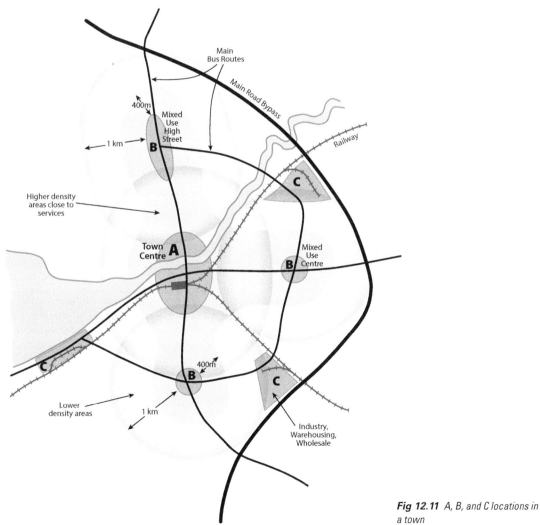

Fig 12.11 *A, B, and C locations in a town*

neighbourhood facility, but then establish a wider reputation, drawing customers from much further afield. Any strategy needs to recognize the ebb and flow of economic and social activity, hence the benefit of the high street principle, which can mix local and town facilities.

Housing location

New housing proposals often cause controversy. The issues of housing supply and affordability are addressed in Chapter 14. In terms of location, the choices are: first, about the balance between urban renewal (brownfield) development and greenfield development; second, the degree to which development is concentrated on a few major sites, or dispersed onto many small sites. The essential principles of a healthy spatial strategy are:

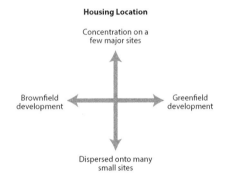

Fig 12.12 Housing location options

- *Accessibility*, so that housing is located where residents can easily get to jobs and facilities by walking, cycling and public transport (Figure 12.12). This is critical.
- *Brownfield sites*, preferred when available in suitable locations, so that infrastructure is reused and open land retained.
- *Infrastructure provision*, so that new areas benefit from existing facilities, or developers enhance the social and physical infrastructure for depleted parts of the town. The latter implies fewer larger sites, able to support such investment.
- *Choice*, so that different kinds of household, irrespective of income, have options to choose between. This implies many smaller sites, so that housing provision is not dominated by a few developers, and there is locational choice for households.
- *Mix*, so that every area of city, and every town, has affordable, middle-income and expensive properties, helping to sustain the local economy as well as provide choice (see Chapter 7).
- *Density gradient*, so that the higher density housing, including housing for the elderly and disabled, is close to facilities and bus services.

There are tensions here, not just politically but in terms of the 'healthy' answer. Brownfield sites, for example, are sometimes in inaccessible locations and should not be redeveloped for housing. Also, large sites and small both have advantages: it rather depends on the implementation mechanisms available how best to shape policy. The final part of the book addresses such issues.

Urban densities

Density policy is something of a minefield. It is not simply a matter of housing. Density applies equally to other land uses: should business be high density (as in city centres) or low density (as in business parks)? What about schools, superstores or distribution centres? And how much land is needed for urban greenspace? Figure 12.13 summarizes these dilemmas. There is little point in higher residential densities if other development is not higher density too. It is the

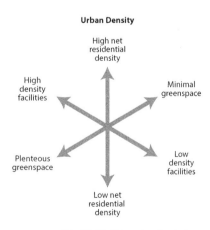

Fig 12.13 Urban density choices

combination of activities in an area which affects the general level of service viability and accessibility.

Part of the problem lies in confusion of what is meant by density. It is sensible to distinguish three kinds of density, which nest within each other as illustrated in Figure 12.14.

- Net residential density is just of the housing area and its access streets.
- Gross neighbourhood density is of the housing area plus neighbourhood uses such as parks, schools, shops, local industries.
- Gross urban density is based on the whole urban area.

In British policy debate, the *net residential density* is conventionally adopted as an indicator. But the net residential area often constitutes only around a third of the urban area. It is necessary to be precise about what is being measured. Is it dwellings, bed-spaces or people? If people, does it include workers and students as well as residents? In the UK the conventional planning measure is *dwellings per hectare* (dpha). Sometimes *bed-spaces per hectare* is used. Dwelling occupancy varies widely. So it is sensible to complement dpha with *population per hectare* (ppha), which relates more directly to demand for services.

Density is an important urban form variable, influencing healthy behaviour and transport-related emissions. Figure 12.15 positions

Three types of density

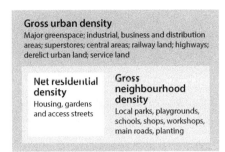

Fig 12.14 *Types of density*

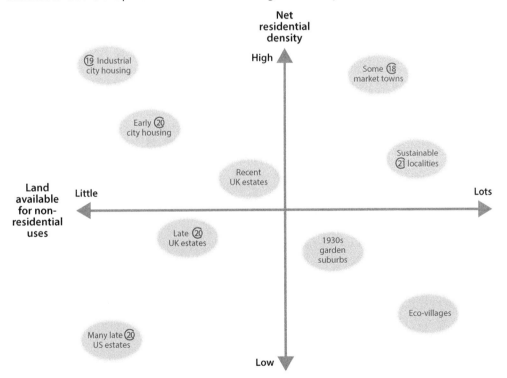

Fig 12.15 *The density of some typical urban environments*

Source: *Developed from Barton et al. 1995 (note 28), p.80.*

various settlement types on a density diagram. Note: this is an impressionistic diagram. But location, shape, design and management all play their part. The next chapter explores these themes at the scale of the neighbourhood.

Conclusion

Each city, each region, has its own unique geographical character, social and economic dynamics and political pressures. No *one* answer to the question of future urban form is universally applicable. Any plan has to marry principle and pragmatism. But the danger is that pragmatism rules principle, so cities evolve as a result of making the *easiest* decisions rather than the *best* decisions. The exemplary cities described in Chapter 5 demonstrate the possibility of principled planning in a range of cultural contexts.

Urban form policy is at the heart of planners' responsibility. The urban geographers of the Chicago School encouraged planners to visualize urban form as dynamic and evolving. Every new development, renewal or change of use contributes to trends that over time alter the structure of the city region and the opportunities open to people living, working and playing within it. The criteria for healthy and sustainable urban form presented at the beginning of Part III, emerging from the research and evidence presented in earlier chapters, give an unequivocal sense of direction for spatial policy. It is not a matter of promoting the 'compact city' at all costs, but recognizing that the whole complex web of land, network and building decisions requires an integrated and consistent approach. This does not mean undue restriction on market freedom; on the contrary, in certain ways it means opening up market options. It *does* mean that business needs to share responsibility for creating a good quality of environment that supports human and ecological well-being.

Linearity emerges as a key feature of natural and humane systems. Rivers and streams and associated flood plains help to give spatial structure to cities. The multiple functions of green infrastructure reinforce linearity in the form of greenspace networks. Public transport by its nature serves linear catchments, which can act as the focus for business and services. Access to bus and tram services by foot gives scale to linear concentrations, enabling people to live within easy walking distance of open space, facilities and public transport. Linear principles at neighbourhood and township scales, debated in the next chapter, can be incorporated into wider strategies for compact cities or multi-centred sub-regions. The essence is to ensure that gradually as city regions evolve the options for people to make healthy choices are enhanced, and settlements become more resilient in the face of potential climate change.

Further reading

Abbott, C. and McGrath, M. (2015) 'Planning a healthy city: progress and challenges in Portland, Oregon', in H. Barton, S. Thompson, S. Burgess, and M. Grant (eds) *The Routledge handbook of planning for health and well-being*. London: Routledge, pp. 566–577.

Breheny, M. (ed.) (1992) *Sustainable development and urban form*. London: Pion. Some classic articles, mostly as relevant now as then.

Falk, N. (2015) 'Creating healthier, smarter places: learning from European cities', in H. Barton, S. Thompson, S. Burgess, and M. Grant (eds) *The Routledge handbook of planning for health and well-being*. London: Routledge, pp. 359–370.

Hedicar, P. (2015) 'Settlement patterns, urban form and travel', in H. Barton, S. Thompson, S. Burgess, and M. Grant (eds) *The Routledge handbook of planning for health and well-being*. London: Routledge.

Jenks, M. and Dempsey, N. (eds) (2005) *Future forms and design for sustainable cities*. Oxford: Architectural Press. One of a series of research-based compendiums. For 'sustainable' read 'healthy'.

Jenks, M. and Jones, C. (eds) (2010) *Dimensions of the sustainable city*. Dordrecht: Springer. A very useful book, with linked papers on most of the elements of urban form.

Pacione, M. (2005) *Urban geography: a global perspective*, second edn. London: Routledge. A comprehensive, detailed and authoritative review.

Notes

1 Palladio was an influential sixteenth-century Italian architect.
2 Urban Task Force (1999) *Towards an urban renaissance* (London: Spon/Department of Environment, Transport and the Regions).
3 Burgess, Hoyt and colleagues called themselves (and are known as) urban ecologists, but would not be recognized as such by current ecologists – a better term for them would be urban geographers.
4 Burgess, E. (1925) 'The growth of the city', in R. Park and E. Burgess, *The City* (Chicago: University of Chicago Press), pp. 47–62.
5 Hoyt, H. (1939) *The structure and growth of residential neighborhoods in American cities* (Washington, DC: Federal Housing Administration).
6 Harris, C. and Ullman, E. (1945) 'The nature of cities', *The Annals of the American Academy of Political and Social Science*, 242: 7–17.
7 Adams, W. and Brock, J. (1986) *The bigness complex: industry, labor and government in the American economy* (New York: Pantheon Books), and others, reported in Haughton, G. and Hunter, C. (1994) *Sustainable cities* (London: Jessica Kingsley Publishers).
8 European Environment Agency (EEA) (2006) *Urban sprawl in Europe: the ignored challenge* (Copenhagen: EEA).
9 See the two volumes of *The containment of urban England* by Hall, P., Thomas, R., Gracey, H. and Drewitt, R. (1973) (London: George Allen & Unwin) for a magisterial analysis.
10 Ibid. See in particular Volume 2: *The planning system: objectives, operations, impacts*.
11 Owens, S.E. (1986) *Energy, planning and urban form* (London: Pion).
12 Breheny, M. (1992) 'The contradictions of the compact city: a review', in M. Breheny (ed.) *Sustainable development and urban form* (London: Pion); Jenks, M., Burton, E. and Williams, K. (eds) (1996) *The compact city: a sustainable urban form?* (London: E & FN Spon); Williams, K., Burton, E. and Jenks, M. (eds) (2001) *Achieving sustainable urban form* (London: Spon Press); Jenks, M. and Dempsey, N. (eds) (2005) *Future forms and design for sustainable cities* (Oxford: Architectural Press).
13 Owens (1986), op. cit.
14 Some of the text in this section is taken from Barton, H. (2000) 'Urban form and locality', in H. Barton (ed.) *Sustainable communities: the potential for eco-neighbourhoods* (London: Earthscan), pp. 106–107.
15 *Ecologist* Magazine (1972) *Blueprint for Survival* (whole issue, Jan.); Harper, P., Boyle, G. and the editors of Undercurrents (1976) *Radical technology* (London: Undercurrents Limited).
16 Fairlie, S. (1996) *Low impact development* (Oxfordshire: Jon Carpenter).
17 See Barton (2000), op. cit.
18 Halcrow Ltd. *et al.* (2009) *Planning for sustainable travel and research report and practitioner guide*. Prepared for the UK Commission for Integrated Transport. www.plan4sustainabletravel.org
19 For example, Elkin, T., McLaren, D. and Hillman, M. (1991) *Reviving the city: towards sustainable*

urban development (London: Friends of the Earth/Policy Studies Institute).

20 Urban Task Force (1999), op. cit.

21 Based on Newman, P. and Kenworthy, J. (1990) Cities and automobile dependence (Aldershot: Gower Technical).

22 See studies reviewed in Hedicar, P. (2015) 'Settlement patterns, urban form and travel', in H. Barton, S. Thompson, S. Burgess, and M. Grant (eds) The Routledge handbook of planning for health and well-being (London: Routledge); and Barton (2000), op. cit., pp. 109–112.

23 Barton, H., Horswell, M. and Miller, P. (2012) 'Neighbourhood accessibility and active travel', Planning Practice and Research, 27(2): 177–201.

24 Jenks, M. (2001) 'The acceptability of urban intensification', in Williams, et al., op. cit.

25 Melia, S., Parkhurst, G. and Barton, H. (2010) 'The paradox of intensification', Transport Policy, 18(1): 46–52.

26 European Environment Agency (2006), op. cit.

27 Lautso, K., Speikermann, K., Wegener, M. et al. (2004) PROPOLIS (Planning and Research of Policies for Land use and Transport for Increasing urban Sustainability) final report, second edn. Funded by the European Commission Fifth Framework Programme (Brussels: EC).

28 Barton, H., Davis, G. and Guise, R. (1995) Sustainable settlements: a guide for planners, designers and developers (Luton: Local Government Management Board, and Bristol: University of the West of England), p. 95.

29 Breheny, M., Ghent, T. and Lock, D. (1993) Alternative development patterns: new settlements (London: Department of the Environment).

30 Tjallingii, S. (1995) Ecopolis: strategies for ecologically sound urban development (Leiden: Backhuys Publishers).

31 Barton, H., Grant, M. and Guise, R. (2010) Shaping neighbourhoods: for local health and global sustainability (London: Routledge).

CHAPTER THIRTEEN

HEALTHY NEIGHBOURHOOD DESIGN

Fig 13.1 *Quality matters*
Source: Courtesy Rob Cowan –
www.plandemonium.org.uk

Introduction: the significance of locality

An important strand of urban form thinking has been at the neighbourhood level. As we saw in earlier chapters, neighbourhoods have been part of the lexicon of spatial planning since Howard, Unwin and Stein. They were a critical aspect of new town thinking in Britain, the Netherlands, and many other countries.

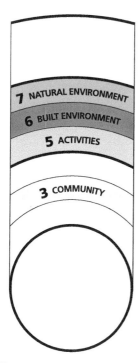

Fig 13.2 *Focus on local urban form*

'The feel of a place is highly influential when families choose their home. The feel is related to aesthetic quality, the social milieu, to historic and cultural associations, to the sense of safety and convenience.'

After a period when they were denigrated by sociologists, the revival in Anglo-American practice since the 1990s has been largely due to the belief that localism is good for sustainability. Designers such as Andres Duany and Peter Calthorpe in America, and David Lock and URBED in the UK, have given it new impetus.[1]

Neighourhoods are the places where people live. They imply a sense of belonging and of community, with shared educational, retail, health and leisure activities that provide a focus for social life. While for some people the neighbourhood is just their place of residence – their activities and social networks are elsewhere – for others, especially families, young people, older people, the poor and the less mobile, the neighbourhood can provide a lifeline: facilities and friends that are easily accessible, a sense of community and identity. As we have seen in earlier chapters, such neighbourhoods are recognized as important for mental well-being, physical activity, social inclusion and environmental sustainability.

Even when people's lives take them away from their neighbourhood, and they treat it more as a dormitory, they mind about its character. The *feel* of a place is highly influential when families choose their home. The feel is related to aesthetic quality, the social milieu, to historic and cultural associations, to the sense of safety and convenience. *Scale* is an important variable. For some people, all they are concerned about is the feel of their immediate vicinity – the street where they live. For others, it is the wider area as well – the quality of urban district or town (Figure 13.3).

Trends and policies in the second half of the twentieth century have tended to work against neighbourhoods. Households have become more inward-looking, drawn to television, social media, the internet and virtual reality. Mobility has been transformed for many by rising car ownership: people insulate themselves from their environment and neighbours by parachuting in and out in the cocooned luxury of their vehicle. Increased work specialization and job insecurity, as well as housing availability, lead to longer commuting. Larger, more distant food stores, hospitals and leisure facilities replace local shops. Neighbourhood services decay for want of a ready market. That decay can be further exaggerated in areas where population (and therefore demand) fall as a result of smaller households or vacancy.

But these patterns are not inevitable. The examples of exemplary cities illustrate the potential for livable neighbourhoods, catering for all sections of the community, with excellent local facilities and access to greenspace. The first section of this chapter looks at the spatial structure of localities – both accidental forms and intentional neighbourhoods. Later sections examine questions of density, lifetime neighbourhoods and urban design.

The shape of neighbourhoods

Neighbourhoods come in many shapes and sizes. In some suburbs they do not really exist at all because of low densities and disjointed, incremental development lacking clear focus. Careful interpretation of form can help with problem diagnosis and problem solving in existing urban areas as well as when designing new places. Each new

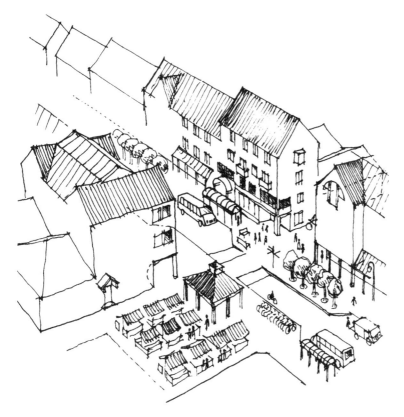

Fig 13.3 Nodal point along a high street. The centre of a neighbourhood with bus stops, shops with flats over, market square, shelter, bike park and pedestrian priority crossing.

Source: Drawing by Richard Guise, in Barton et al. 2010 (further reading).

development contributes to incremental change that over time tends to support or undermine well-being. Analysis suggests there are five archetypal local urban forms.[2] The first two of these are non-neighbourhoods. The others are neighbourhoods by accident or design. There are some parallels with the strategic urban forms presented in Chapter 12. The analysis here draws on research undertaken by myself and my colleagues in 2004–2008.[3]

'Analysis suggests there are five archetypal local urban forms. The first two of these are non-neighbourhoods. The others are neighbourhoods by accident or design.'

'PODS': car-oriented campus and cul-de-sac development

Pods are typical of many outer city areas developed in the last half century. Particular sites are developed independently for one specific use, with no attempt at neighbourhood planning. The wider pattern of development is dictated by a road hierarchy designed to facilitate traffic flows. Sites of varying size hang off the main/distributor road system like bean-pods off a stalk (Figure 13.4). Each pod is separately accessed by a cul-de-sac or loop road so that there is no direct connection between them. Residential pods may be long cul-de-sacs, gated enclaves for the rich or large limited-access estates, often lacking any facilities. Other land uses form campus-style developments, with buildings typically surrounded by car parks and landscaped areas. They may be business parks, retail parks, schools, universities, hospitals or industrial estates. Walking and cycling distances are invariably

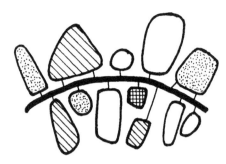

Fig 13.4 *Use-segregated 'pods' archetype*

'While pods are popular with investors, they create an environment that is anathema to pedestrian movement, compromises accessibility, exacerbates inequalities, impedes community networking and generates high levels of greenhouse gases.'

much longer than would be possible with a permeable network. In extreme examples such is the assumption of universal car use that it is dangerous to walk from one pod to another.

This pattern of development is still happening, especially in 'edge city' areas and the urban penumbra – sometimes in renewal schemes too. It is common across the developed world, and in affluent parts of less affluent countries. Its huge advantage is versatility. Each development can be treated as a separate entity, designed and built without having to worry about tying in with the neighbouring areas or collaborating with other landowners. The structure tends to be defined by land ownership and road access. Market forces play a strong role, determining density, use and design. Pods are what tends to occur when traditional traffic engineers dominate the advice given to municipal decision-makers, and planning authorities are reactive not proactive. Social agendas, such as the provision of public open space or community facilities, are only addressed when regulation dictates.

While pods are popular with investors, they create an environment that is anathema to pedestrian movement, compromises accessibility, exacerbates inequalities, impedes community networking and generates high levels of greenhouse gases.[4] New pods should therefore be outlawed – particularly campus-style 'parks' that block connections between places. The single-use character of such pods undermines the potential for town and district centres. Older pods, when they come up for intensification or renewal, should be obliged to retrofit use-diversity and good connectivity (Figure 13.5).

Sprawl: low density development lacking pedestrian foci

'Sprawl' is a justifiably pejorative term. Suburban and exurban sprawl is typified by low densities, poor pedestrian accessibility

Fig 13.5 *Retrofit of pod-land. Diagrammatic representation of pods in Backworth, Newcastle-upon-Tyne, where pedestrians are forced into indirect car-based routes; new pedestrian connections could be made, taming traffic on main roads.*

Source: Barton 2011 (note 2b), figure 35.

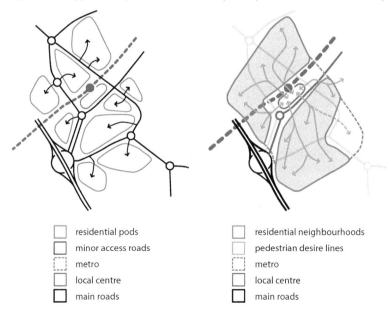

☐ residential pods	☐ residential neighbourhoods
☐ minor access roads	☐ pedestrian desire lines
☐ metro	☐ metro
☐ local centre	☐ local centre
☐ main roads	☐ main roads

and high car dependence. It is distinguished from pods by its scale. There may be many pods within it. It has attractions in terms of privacy, greenery, large gardens for household activities, vehicle storage and adaptability of buildings. But these private advantages come at an environmental cost (congestion, pollution, carbon emissions, high land take) as well as long-term health risks from lack of active travel and social isolation. Sprawl tends to grow in a disaggregated way, as landowners and developers capitalize on market opportunity. Employment and other facilities tend to be widely dispersed and single use – commercial strips and campus developments – designed purely for car access, with very poor pedestrian connections – or none.

For the future, sprawl needs to be outlawed. Existing areas of sprawl should be gradually evolved to diversify housing opportunities, increase the viability of local facilities and travel choices. Gradual renewal has to be done with care so that intensification occurs in the optimum locations and restructuring creates intentional neighbourhoods. Often there are undeveloped or redundant sites that create opportunity. In some cultures travel choice can be fostered through the cycling strategy discussed later. Figure 13.6 shows an approach to restructuring, increasing the population and service levels.[5]

Fig 13.6 *Restructuring the outer city. Large mid/late-century residential and business pods, with poor connectivity and service provision, needing renewal; plan for gradual intensification and transformation, triggered by new stations.*

Source: Barton et al. *2010 (note 5).*

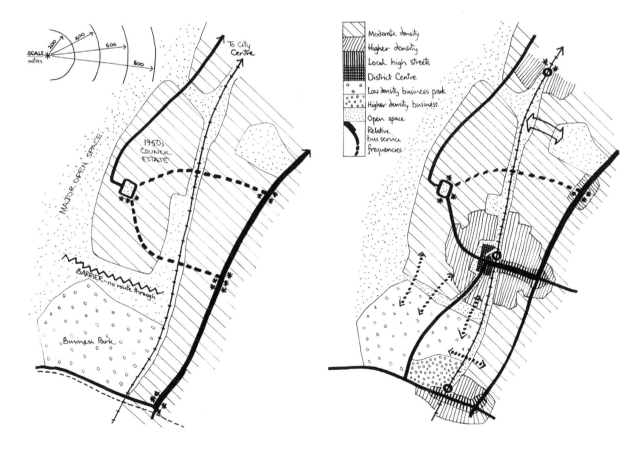

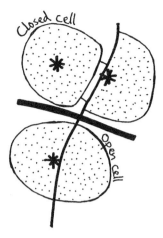

Fig 13.7 *The neighbourhood cell archetype*

Cells: intentional pedestrian-scale neighbourhoods

In contrast to pods and sprawl, the idea of 'neighbourhood' is to foster and facilitate a sense of local community. The 'neighbourhood unit' signifies a distinct, bounded residential area with a local centre – the nucleus of the cell. Based on British and European examples, population ranges from 4–12,000 people, and scale is defined by easily walkable distance. Many outer estates and new settlements have adopted this model. Like a traditional village, a neighbourhood cell should be centred on local shops, primary school and other community facilities (Figure 13.7). At the upper end of the population spectrum the neighbourhood may support a supermarket, library, secondary school and leisure centre. The term 'urban village' was coined in the 1990s to try to capture the sense of a homely, interactive neighbourhood.

Cells come in a variety of forms. The normal image is of an inward-looking *closed cell*[6] with open space, main roads and industrial areas defining a distinct edge. Bus or tram stops give a focus for pedestrian movement and therefore for clustered local facilities. The closed cell has the advantage of clear identity and low traffic volumes, but can suffer depending on its social composition. The viability of local facilities relies on the people living locally, their income levels and lifestyle choices. If the population falls as household size decreases, or is relatively poor, or inclined to travel by car to larger facilities elsewhere, then local shops and services may close. Those reliant on local services become disenfranchised.

An alternative model is the *open cell*, where a main distributor road passes through or adjacent to the centre of the neighbourhood. Facilities benefit from passing trade as well as local trade, and bus services can be more direct. An open cell is often not fully separated from surrounding localities: so although there is a definite centre, the neighbourhood edge is fuzzy and permeable, allowing greater interchange with neighbouring areas (Figure 13.8). Calthorpe's idea of *Transit-oriented development* (TOD) is an example of open cell design.[7]

Neighbourhood cells do not normally exist in older parts of towns, unless designed as part of a large regeneration scheme. In outer areas typified by sporadic pods and sprawl, 'fuzzy' cells can sometimes be designed so that they integrate development and provide the basis for better local facilities and improved public transport services (Figure 13.9). New commuter settlements can also be designed from scratch as cells. However, the size and connectivity of cells are critical to their success in attracting commercial investment; high car ownership allows people to choose bigger centres offering more choice.[8] Looking at good European examples, larger neighbourhoods are the norm.

Cluster: group of interlocking cells around a district centre

The cluster is a further development of the 'fuzzy' open cell model. But unlike the separate cell neighbourhoods, these neighbourhoods

'An alternative model is the open cell, where a main distributor road passes through or adjacent to the centre of the neighbourhood. Facilities benefit from passing trade as well as local trade, and bus services can be more direct.'

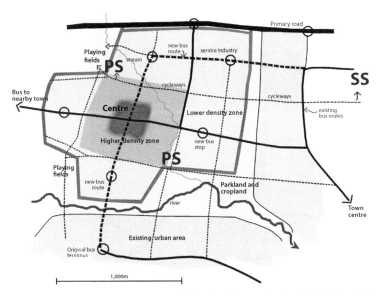

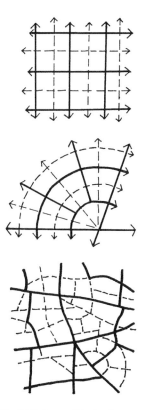

Fig 13.9 *Design for a new open cell neighbourhood. Located so that it is closely tied into the existing urban area by road, bus, bike and foot, showing a mixed use centre, graded densities, primary schools, accessible greenspace and 'scruffy' zone for service industry.*

Source: Barton et al. 2010 (further reading), figure 5.27.

are clustered and overlapping within a district or township that provides higher level services and a good range of jobs, serving perhaps 30–50,000 people (Figure 13.10). This model has been strongly advocated by the Urban Task Force as a means of achieving compact cities.[9] If it is to work as intended, based on walkable distances, then it relies on quite high densities. Judging by current behaviour in English cities, the maximum distance from centre to periphery to allow most people to walk should be no more than 1,000 metres. This implies a *gross* neighbourhood density of c. 40 dpha, and much higher net residential density, with many apartments. Greenspace is largely squeezed out to the edges in the interests of compactness. People living near the centre find themselves rather far from major open space, inhibiting participation of poorer households in active recreation.

The pattern exists, in rather random configuration, in some higher density inner city areas (see Figure 13.11). The cluster form can in theory give excellent levels of local accessibility to urban facilities, but the much greater choice offered by the district centre means that some local centres will not be able to compete, resulting in longer trips and the risk that more people then choose to go by car. It is difficult to apply in existing suburban and peri-urban areas, because of its size, complexity, and the timescale needed for realization. Overall, while the cluster model has theoretical attractions, it is problematic in practice.

Linear townships: localities clustered along a public transport spine

The linear form is evident in many older suburban areas where development occurred along main radials served by bus or tram

Fig 13.8 *Permeable street patterns. Neighbourhood cells require good permeability, but the network can take many forms. These show alternate streets for pedestrians, cyclists, and children's play, with vehicles access only.*

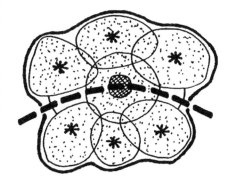

Fig 13.10 *The neighbourhood cluster archetype*

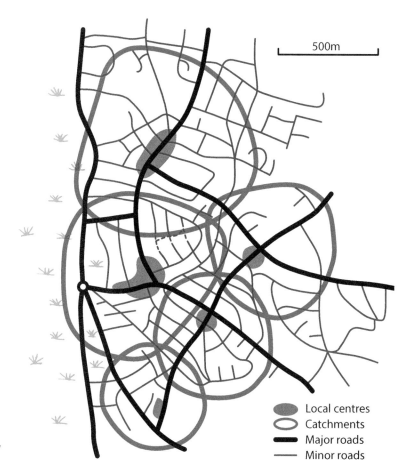

Fig 13.11 A cluster of overlapping neighbourhoods in north Bristol

Legend:
- Local centres
- Catchments
- Major roads
- Minor roads

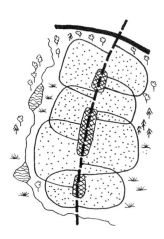

Fig 13.12 The linear township archetype

(Figure 13.12). Local high street services are strung out along the spine road. Typically the localities that are identified by residents as 'neighbourhoods' are not astride the main route but on either side of it, merging into each other. The high street acts as a 'uniting seam'[10] where people from different neighbourhoods mingle and meet. Taken together, the inter-linked neighbourhoods form townships of very varying size. Some older high streets declined in the latter part of the twentieth century, becoming almost moribund as populations fell, inner areas became predominantly occupied by poor and marginal populations, and traffic congestion undermined environmental quality. But recently in many cities they have revived as gentrification, renewal and more pedestrian-friendly policies have taken over.

The historic linear configuration has been adapted and re-defined in some new and expanded town designs – and becomes a key determinant of overall city form, as discussed in Chapter 12. It can take tangential or radial forms. Critically the linear township should as far as possible be paralleled on both sides by greenspace. It has been advocated as a sustainable model because it aims to maximize public transport efficiency, pedestrian accessibility to high street facilities *and* greenspace. If the noise, intimidation and dangers of

Legend
- **M** Metrostops
- **P** Primary Schools
- **S** Secondary Schools
- ╫╫╫ Metro Line
- ⋯ New Bus Route

Land Use
- Industrial
- Open Green Space
- Residential High Density
- Residential Medium Density
- Residential Low Density
- Mixed Use High Density

Fig 13.13 *Newcastle Great Park, reimagined as a linear township. Despite the good intentions of the city planners, the new urban extension of Newcastle Great Park has been developing as a series of large single use estates with limited connections ('pods'). This alternative linear scheme shows what could have been achieved if developers had been willing. In the assessment it scored highly on walkable accessibility, public transport and facility viability, and efficient use of land.*

Source: Based on Barton 2011 (note 2b), figure 27.

traffic on the spine road can be effectively reduced, then the form offers a healthy environment.

The starting point for gaining the benefits of linear townships in the future is an overall city plan that progressively reduces traffic levels while improving accessibility by other modes, at the same time reinforcing and extending existing high streets and strengthening the green backcloth (Figure 13.13). Unlike the cluster, the linear form is relatively easy to design in outer city areas. However, implementation through the market is inevitably contentious, relying on strong co-ordinated processes.

'The starting point for gaining the benefits of linear townships in the future is an overall city plan that progressively reduces traffic levels while improving accessibility by other modes.'

Cycling-based towns

In some settlements in the Netherlands, cycling accounts for the majority of trips. This frees up the pattern of a town. Instead of distances being geared to easy walking, they are related to easy cycling distance. The radius of a cycling neighbourhood can be three times that of a walking neighbourhood, so the density can be more relaxed, the population thresholds higher and able to support more services – equivalent perhaps to a whole cluster of walking neighbourhoods. There are potential problems for non-cyclists and those with limited mobility: they need the option to live close to services.

The cycling option may provide a possible way forward for low density, car-dependent suburbs. However, if cycling is currently not the norm, changing behaviour will take a generation. If streets were to be re-assigned to cycling, creating a network of routes, junctions designed for cycle safety, and a strong community campaign pursued, targeting all school children initially, then perhaps a positive transition to healthy lifestyles could begin.

Spatial analysis and density

Using form analysis to assist prescription

These archetypal neighbourhood forms can help describe and explain the function of suburbs and towns. Figure 13.14 illustrates their application to Hays, West London. The big picture is a series of linear townships (blue dashed ovals) which provide a fair range of services, two of them centred on an important radial route, the

'The radius of a cycling neighbourhood can be three times that of a walking neighbourhood, so the density can be more relaxed, the population thresholds higher and able to support more services.'

Fig 13.14 *Neighbourhood form analysis of Hays, West London*

Source: Barton 2011 (note 2b), figure 17.

third tangential and linked to a main line station. Parkland parallels the townships to a certain extent. Motorways, dual carriageways and railways slice across the urban area, impeding connectivity (red dashed lines). Pods of various sizes (surrounded by red lines) reduce permeability. Away from the spine routes there are areas of sprawl with few easily walkable facilities. The high streets are critical to the area, but have suffered from excessive traffic and competing car-based retail parks and superstores elsewhere.

The priority for the area is probably to reinforce the viability and attractiveness of the high streets by focusing new commercial development along them, while working to reduce traffic flows, improve the pedestrian environment and bus operational efficiency. Given the age of the area, there is opportunity for gradual residential densification close to the high streets as renewal occurs, bolstering the demand for services, and allowing diversification of the population. A concerted cycling strategy could bring outlying estates into easier active travel connection with facilities, and gradually reduce the level of car reliance. Any opportunities to link greenspaces should be seized.

Graded densities, social diversity and viable facilities

Density is an integrating concept in neighbourhood planning. Figure 13.15 relates issues of health and sustainability to the three tiers of density introduced in the last chapter: net residential, gross neighbourhood and gross urban. Ideal densities depend on context. In the UK, medium *net residential* densities of 40–50 dpha (around 100 ppha), imply mainly terraced development, and have been widely advocated.[11] If well designed, this density can provide energy-efficient built form, solar power, some limited outdoor space for homes; it can support viable public transport and facilitate

Fig 13.15 Health and sustainability factors in relation to density

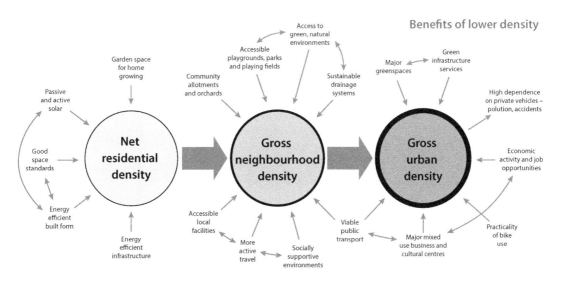

pedestrian accessibility to facilities. As an average, it works well, but this does not mean standardized. Different types of household, and different cultures, need varied provision.

The idea of *lifetime neighbourhoods* is that each locality should create options for people at all stages of life. Consider the respective preferences of single young adults, young families with children, older families with teenagers, empty-nester couples, frail elderly people. Consider those who love gardening and those who don't. Consider affluent households and poor households, those used to apartment living (as in Poland, for example) and those habituated to on-ground living. There is not one size fits all. *Variety* is therefore of the essence: variety of built form, of dwelling size and garden size, of price, of density, of accessibility to town or city facilities. Lifetime neighbourhoods mean catering for the needs of children and young families on the one hand and old and disabled people on the other. A place that is well designed for kids and elders is likely to be good for everyone else as well.

From the health angle, the differential between net residential and *gross neighbourhood* density is critical. If there is ample provision of parks, playgrounds, playing fields, allotments, schools, shops, workshops and other facilities, then the opportunity for active travel, the likelihood of social cohesion, are much greater than if such opportunities are absent. So moderate to high average housing densities are compensated by generous provision for 'ancillary' activities.

The grading of densities for all uses – *high* density close to high streets, *lower* further away and towards the main greenspace network – gives logic to locational decisions. The point is to maximize accessibility and choice. The higher densities at the core of townships, mainly in the form of apartments, create opportunities for single people, young couples, elderly and infirm people who value direct access to facilities and public transport above gardens. Facilities that do not involve high levels of use, or serve only very local clientele, can be scattered through the neighbourhoods. But most facilities should cluster along the high streets, facilitating flexible catchments, multi-purpose trips and reinforcing mutual viability.

The problems come when trying to achieve social diversity in areas dominated by social housing, or expensive private housing. Setting aside the views of residents (which may of course be critical politically), the market is loath to move into the former, while social housing providers find it expensive to buy in the latter. Nevertheless, every part of a town or city needs a broad balance of different housing opportunities to allow different income groups locational opportunities and overcome the dire effects of ghettos of poverty.

The quality of place

The enjoyment and identity of residents are tied up with the physical (as well as the social) character of their neighbourhood. This character is about sights, sounds, smells and feel. It is about the history and associations of the place – expressing local culture and continuity. The quality of the buildings, streets and spaces provides

'Lifetime neighbourhoods mean catering for the needs of children and young families on the one hand and old and disabled people on the other. A place that is well designed for kids and elders is likely to be good for everyone else as well.'

More on neighbourhoods for all

See Chapter 7 for discourse on housing and social mix. See Chapter 8 for a typology of social needs, and understanding the nature of community. See Barton *et al.* (2010) for more on local population diversity, housing for all and social capital.

the fixed context. There is also the living experience of the place: the wind in the trees, the people on the street, cyclists and vehicles moving – thus a *kinetic* reality.

The visual character always has prominence in people's minds – whether concerned with building conservation, the streetscape or trees. But it is important to see the visual appearance as part of a more holistic experience. For example, an urban square can inspire with its sense of space shaped by noble buildings, with active social uses creating a centre of community, with the movement and inter-action of people bringing human sounds and vitality.

The aesthetic perspective on planning was developed to a remark-able degree in the early 1960s. Building upon new insights into how people perceive their environment, Kevin Lynch wrote *The Image of the City* (1960),[12] exploring what the spatial form of a locality or a city means to the people who live there, and what planners can do to ensure a city is memorable. He was concerned not only with aesthetic pleasure but also with 'legibility': the ease with which the parts of a city can be recognized and organized into a coher-ent pattern – how people find their way around. Gordon Cullen wrote *Townscape* (1961),[13] developing a language of urban design. He analysed the sequential experience of people walking through urban spaces, the feelings they have, and how different kinds of space function. Interestingly, Cullen's inspiration was diametrically opposed to that of Le Corbusier and the Modernist architectural movement. Where Modernists valued sculptural clarity and uni-formity, he valued the organic informality and the rich diversity of mediaeval towns.

Both these texts are classic, and remain valuable today. They illus-trate the degree to which the view of town planning as design led to highly sophisticated theoretical and practical expositions, gener-ally in tune with the tradition of Howard, Unwin and Geddes. Like Jacobs, their shared starting point was not simply aesthetic taste but how people experience space (see Chapter 4).

In the contemporary era Richard Guise has written extensively about the related idea of local character and distinctiveness (Figure 13.16). Good design, he says, is about an integrated approach embracing

> responsiveness to the existing context, compatible mix of uses, appro-priate buildings to accommodate activities at the right rent, appropriate location and level of accessibility, all brought together in a place which is attractive and feels safe – that can create the conditions where a sense of neighbourliness and belonging is more likely to develop.[14]

A neighbourhood is an expression of local cultural continuity, embedded in the memories of longer-term residents. In the UK, listed buildings, tree preservation orders and conservation areas are available tools to preserve and enhance local distinctiveness. Used wisely, they can facilitate gradual evolution of historic areas as needs change. But they are limited in scope. Enhancement of neighbourhood character should be applied generally, not just in conservation areas. Some mundane environments need

Aesthetic appreciation

Consider a red rose and a Cotswold stone wall. The rose is not just pretty. It is perfumed. It is associated with love, and (for some) with England. It moves in the breeze. The wall is attractively textured and a home to lichen and moss. It speaks of local geology, history and traditional skills.

'Enhancement of neighbour-hood character should be applied generally, not just in conservation areas. Some mundane environ-ments need enlivening by attrac-tive new buildings, spaces and trees.'

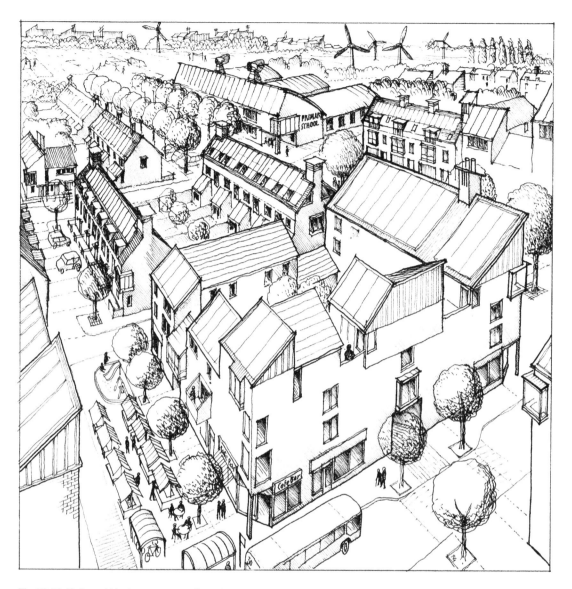

Fig 13.16 Variety within the
neighbourhood. A neighbourhood
offering choice of housing, with
graded densities from high street to
parkland; café, market and shops
are close to bus stops on the high
street; the primary school is close
to the open space; renewable
energy sources are part-owned
by the community; street trees will
grow to give shade.

Source: Drawing by Richard Guise, in
Barton et al. 2010 (further reading),
figure 5.13.

enlivening by attractive new buildings, spaces and trees; some
disjointed areas of sporadic development require integration, with
infilling and renewal aimed at creating more sustainable, healthy
environments.

Good practice in urban design developed fast in the 1980s and
1990s – in sharp contrast to the dominant market approach of the
time. In terms of publications an early winner was *Responsive
Environments*.[15] This manual for designers explained the new urban
aesthetic taking over from Modernism. The chapter headings give an
impression of the priorities:

• permeability – how easily can people, especially on foot, get
  to places?

- variety – what range of activities are locally available to people?
- legibility – how well can people orientate and understand opportunities?
- robustness – how easily can an area adapt to changing needs?
- visual appropriateness – is its appearance appropriate to its use?
- richness – does the environment give a rich sensory experience?
- personalization – are there opportunities for individual expression?

Subsequently many designers have added their own thoughts on the process and details of urban design, including in Britain, for example, Llewelyn-Davies, in America, Duany and Plater-Zyberg, in Denmark, Jan Gehl.[16] Many inner city regeneration schemes have been designed in accordance with sound principles, and consistent with the ideals of healthy cities. However, the generality of contemporary development in Britain, Australia, America and most of Europe is still at odds with them, driven by commercial pressures and conventional political attitudes.

The guides to design listed in the further reading section consider all aspects of function and character. A critical issue is how to relate plots and layout to the structure of neighbourhoods. Figure 13.17 suggests a systematic approach. Key to this is the notion of *perimeter blocks,* with streets or alleys all round, which allow for a permeable environment where people can move easily in any direction. Such blocks are of course visible in many traditional towns, and in the grid layouts of pioneer cities. But as illustrated earlier, the blocks do not have to be based on orthogonal principles; it depends on context.

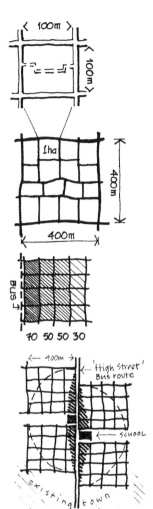

Fig 13.17 *Block, grid, graded density and neighbourhood, 1 hectare block, average 50 dpha @2.3 persons per dwelling, builds up to an open cell neighbourhood of 3,200 dwellings at varying densities, and 7,360 population. Everyone within c. 4–500 metres of high street and schools.*

Source: Barton et al. 2010 (further reading), figure 5.12.

Residential streets are for people

Powerful imagination has always been at the heart of changing streets and making them places for play and community. To gaze at a traffic-dominated rat-run of a residential street, and re-imagine it as a space where skipping, vibrant chalking, the soothing sounds of chat and the chinking of tea mugs take over, requires a real imaginative effort. And often the process of changing streets' atmosphere and space depends on the power of small actions which can gradually make streets more friendly and playful.[17]

There are two aspects of the new design orthodoxy that remain controversial. The first is: what makes a place feel safe, and therefore welcoming? The urban designers, influenced by the need for a permeable environment that encourages walking and cycling, favour a connected network of streets, with uses mixed. But the *Crime Prevention Through Environmental Design* (CPTED) guidelines, widely used in many countries, advocate single use zones and cul-de-sacs without linked pathways – i.e. pods. Some researchers claim the evidence backs CPTED.[18] However, the nature of street layouts is not an independent issue. It plays into the wider form of settlements and the behaviour, either encouraged or deterred. The CPTED guidelines emerge out of a car-oriented tradition, resulting in few people on the street. But safety on the streets is a function of use: if there are people around, going to local schools and shops, meeting casually, and there are 'eyes on the street', then (as Jacobs was at pains to argue) places can feel convivial and safe. Much of the research showing that mixed use is bad was undertaken in old inner city areas of mixed industrial and residential use, typified by poor environments, deprivation and economic decline. However, there is no need to polarize the debate: an overall permeable pattern of perimeter blocks can include *short* cul-de-sacs (maximum <50 m) that do not extend walking distances very much while providing a safe play environment and sense of enclosure, contributing to residential diversity.

The second area of continued controversy is about pedestrian priority on main roads and in town centres. This is essentially an argument between traffic engineers and urban designers, and again it is the tension between safety and accessibility. The engineers have traditionally tried to ensure safety through segregating traffic and pedestrians, resulting in barriers, traffic lights and signage. The urban designers tend to favour a more open system with some shared surfaces, where pedestrians, cyclists and drivers negotiate their way through, catching each other's eyes. Residents, shoppers, shop-keepers and politicians are often at loggerheads, unable to agree. From the healthy planner's point of view, the progressive extension of pedestrian and cycling priority – including new short-cuts, full pedestrianization, cycle streets, bus/tram/pedestrian streets, shared surfaces and protected and voluntary crossings – is highly desirable, fostering active travel and social interaction (Figure 13.18). Many cities, especially in Western Europe, demonstrate the practicality of returning the public realm to people, not traffic. The precise methods for achieving this in any particular place depend on local circumstances, but the direction of change should not be in doubt.

Conclusion: urban design

The design of perimeter blocks, the layout and use of streets, the quality of the public realm, the integration of nature into the scene, are all critical to healthy localities, whether in outer suburb, inner city or city centre. It has not been possible in this brief review to do justice to the large and swelling theory and practice of urban design. However, there are many books and guides which go much further. Some of those are listed below for further reading. There are also examples of masterplans for regeneration projects and urban extensions, from which much can be learnt, positively or negatively. Some masterplans are at the scale of neighbourhoods.

The five forms of locality distinguished in this chapter – two of which are anti-neighbourhood – give a sound basis for analysing the internal structure of existing cities, and initial ideas for planning or retrofitting healthy environmental conditions. It is clear there is no one form that is universally applicable. It depends on context. The

Fig 13.18 *Residential street design: taming the car. New Hall, Harlow, and Reiselfeld, Freiburg*

open cell neighbourhood and the linear township are more likely than the closed cell or neighbourhood cluster to be relevant. Whatever the form, one essential requirement is *connectedness*, allowing choice for users and flexibility for services and businesses. Another requirement is *accessibility* for residents to local facilities and greenspace, so that physical activity, social interaction and enjoyment of nature are attractive options. A third is *choice* of housing and, linked to that, diversity of social group, avoiding both the poor ghetto syndrome and the affluent gated communities.

The principles are fine, and becoming better established. Action is another matter. Despite the growing body of evidence about how people are affected by place, design decisions continue too often to build unhealthy conditions into the structure of settlements. Chapters in Part V tackle this issue. They explore the mechanisms of change in relation to fundamental attitudes to land, property, and the collaborative processes necessary to achieve progress.

Further reading

Barton, H. (ed.) (2000) *Sustainable communities: the potential for eco-neighbourhoods.* London: Earthscan.

Barton, H., Grant, M. and Guise, R. (2010) *Shaping Neighbourhoods – for local health and global sustainability.* London: Routledge. The most comprehensive and practical guide to neighbourhood planning available, tackling social, health, economic, environmental and design issues.

Duany, A. and Plater-Zyberg, E. (1991) *Towns and town-making principles.* Rissoli, New York: Howard University Graduate School of Design.

Gehl, J. (2010) *Cities for people.* Washington, DC: Island Press. An inspirational text from this world-famous designer.

Neal, P. (ed.) (2003) *Urban villages and the making of communities.* London: Spon Press. A useful review of practice, with some good examples from a range of countries. Contributors include Andres Duany and David Lock.

Rudlin, D. and Falk, N. (2009) *The sustainable urban neighbourhood: building the 21st century home.* Oxford: Architectural Press.

Guides to urban design skills

DTLR and CABE (2001) *By design: better places to live.* London: DTLR and CABE.

Llewelyn-Davies (2000) *The urban design compendium.* London: English Partnerships and the Housing Corporation.

Placecheck – place appraisal: a method of assessing the qualities of a place, showing what improvements are needed, and focusing people on working together to achieve them. Devised by Rob Cowan and Urban Design Skills. See the Placecheck website: www.placecheck.info

Notes

1   See, for example, Neal, P. (ed.) (2003) *Urban villages and the making of communities* (London: Spon Press) and Rudlin, D. and Falk, N. (2009) *The sustainable urban neighbourhood: building the 21st century home* (Oxford: Architectural Press).

2   Building on Barton, H. (ed.) (2000) *Sustainable communities: the potential for eco-neighbourhoods* (London: Earthscan), Chapter 8, and Barton, H. (2011) *Reshaping suburbs.* A report produced as part of the EPSRC SOLUTIONS project, Bristol, University of the West of England. Google 'Reshaping Suburbs' or available at: www.uwe.ac.uk/et/research/who/publications

3   See Barton (2011), op. cit.

4   Ibid.

5   Barton, H., Grant, M. and Guise, R. (2010) *Shaping Neighbourhoods – for local health and global sustainability* (London: Routledge), Figures 5.35 and 5.36.

6   Barton (2000), op. cit.

7   Calthorpe, P. (1993) *The next American metropolis: ecology, community and the American dream* (New York: Princeton Architectural Press).

8   Barton (2011), op. cit.

9   Urban Task Force (1999) *Towards an urban renaissance* (London: Spon/Department of Environment, Transport and the Regions).

10 This graphic metaphor was first used by Kevin Lynch in *A theory of good city form* (Cambridge, MA: MIT Press, 1981).

11 See, for example, Owens, S. (1986) *Energy, planning and urban form* (London: Pion); and Barton (ed.) (2000), op. cit.

12 Lynch, K. (1960) *The image of the city*, vol. 11 (Cambridge, MA: MIT Press).

13 Cullen, G. (1961) *Townscape* (London: Architectural Press).

14 Barton *et al.* (2010), op. cit., p. 101.

15 Bentley, I. (1985) *Responsive environments: a manual for designers* (London: Routledge).

16 Gehl, J. (2010) *Cities for people* (Washington, DC: Island Press).

17 Text from Playing Out (residents campaign group), 148 North Street, Bristol, UK, BS3 1HA.

18 Cousins, P. (2015) 'Crime and community safety: challenging the design consensus', in H. Barton, S. Thompson, S. Burgess, and M. Grant (eds) *The Routledge handbook of planning for health and well-being* (London: Routledge).

CHAPTER FOURTEEN

URBAN DYNAMICS

Society is faced with a profound dilemma. To resist growth is to risk economic and social collapse. To pursue it relentlessly is to endanger the eco-systems on which we depend for long-term survival.

Tim Jackson[1]

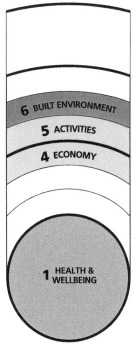

Fig 14.1 *Focus on strategic planning*

Introduction: strategic planning issues

This chapter explores the key strategic questions around economic development, employment, population, housing and transport. The central issue in a dynamic situation is to match human needs, economic development and infrastructure provision. The tensions between the different elements are often manifest: local politicians keen to encourage economic activity, but less keen to ensure housing supply matches demand; economic expansion causing polluted and congested environments; social provision such as schools and parks not keeping up with population growth. Such tensions are symptomatic of a lack of healthy balance between the elements of the city. Imbalance can occur in declining urban areas as much as in growth zones.

Figure 14.2 illustrates the dynamic relationship between four of the key elements, and the primary direction of influence. A basic realization is that population is not an independent variable. It is largely dependent on the level of economic activity. In other words, if there are jobs available, then people will be drawn to the city region, there will be net migration in; if there are few jobs, they will look elsewhere, and there will be net migration out. This pattern is sometimes overlaid by specific factors, such as people choosing to retire to the area.

The level and nature of the population are then the main trigger for the provision of services by private and public organizations. For example, shops and schools exist to serve the population. Population growth and change are also the triggers for new housing and renewal. The retail, leisure, educational, health, building and other trades that directly serve the population contribute to the level of economic activity, sometimes constituting most of the employment opportunities.

The urban system may go through long periods of growth – a spiral of progressive reinforcement – or of decline, as key industries close. No city is an island. It interacts with other cities and is part of a global market. Its attractiveness for business and people depends on its relative position in terms of geographical advantage – its reputation, jobs, services, skills and environmental quality.[2] The economic and spatial planners of the city have the task of trying to maintain equilibrium through any process of change, avoiding the problems of unequal expansion and 'over-heating', on the one hand, and the problems of rising unemployment and poverty, with their severe health implications, on the other. The aim is to achieve a good match between the different elements of the place. Critical 'sea-saw' balances include:

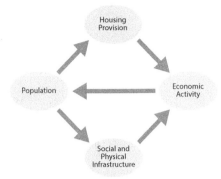

Urban Dynamics

Fig 14.2 Urban dynamics

- The see-saw between jobs available, in different industrial sectors, and people seeking work, with varied skills – in the context of globalization and competition between cities which mean the status quo is rarely an option.
- The balance between commuting in and commuting out, given the desire to encourage local employment and reduce the need to travel.
- The availability of housing to match economic development and changing social patterns – such as an ageing population.
- The provision of schools, training, health services, social and recreational facilities to match the needs of the changing population.
- The level of retail provision and commercial leisure services, so that the settlement is reasonably self-sufficient, retaining trade locally.
- The adequacy and safety of the road and rail networks, pedestrian and cycling networks, to allow easy movement, underpin local activity, and avoid high levels of air pollution.
- Investment in sustainable technologies for energy, water, materials and waste reuse/recycling to reduce the carbon and broader ecological footprint.

This chapter concentrates on economic activity and the relationship to population, housing and transport infrastructure at the level of the city region: how to conceive and understand the dynamics of change.

Understanding the economic base of a city

As we have seen in earlier chapters, having a job is critically important for health. Employment, income, and satisfaction at work are determinants of mental and physical well-being. A strong economic base also enables a city to invest. Local politicians typically prioritize the safeguarding of existing and the creation of new jobs, keeping the curse of unemployment at bay. Land use planners, transport planners, economic development officers and regeneration agencies share a responsibility with entrepreneurs and elected representatives for the health of the economy.

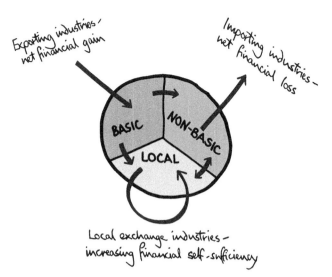

Exporting industries'
net financial gain

Importing industries
net financial loss

Local exchange industries -
increasing financial self-sufficiency

Fig 14.3 *Basic, importing and local economic sectors*

'Economic base theory works on the assumption that basic (i.e. exporting) industries are vital to the well-being of the settlement. They are selling to the world, and thus draw surplus (the value added) into the local economy.'

How, then, should we conceptualize the local economy and devise strategies for economic success? The *economic base* model provides a starting point. It aggregates industries into two broad categories: basic and non-basic. *Basic (or exporting) industries* are those which provide goods and services for external markets (Figure 14.3). Their success waxes and wanes with national and international economic trends. They export their products, and money flows back in, providing employment and boosting the local economy. Most manufacturing firms fall into this category. So do most primary industries (minerals and agriculture) and service industries with markets elsewhere – including some architectural and planning practices. The tourist industry, which relies on visitors from elsewhere spending their money in town, can be included too.

Non-basic industries rely on the local market, serving the needs of the city population. They thrive and grow when the population increases and/or becomes more affluent. Conversely they shrink when the city hits hard times. Most construction firms fall into this category, along with retail outlets and professional services. Public services such as education and health are directly population related. Figure 14.3 is innovative in distinguishing two kinds of non-basic industries – those which import materials and services from outside the city region (*importing industries*), and those which are purely internal, relying on *local trading*, keeping wealth within the community and reducing the environmental impact of transport.

Economic base theory works on the assumption that basic (i.e. exporting) industries are vital to the well-being of the settlement. They are selling to the world, and thus draw surplus (the value added) into the local economy. So economic development officers (and governments concerned about declining regions) go to considerable lengths, including subsidy in some cases, to attract large industrial or institutional investors which can act as exporting keystones of the local economy. Many such basic industries (car firms are a case in point) rely on components from tributary suppliers – and many of those may be local. The people newly employed in both the main company and the suppliers then demand local services and thus boost the non-basic sector as well. As more people are employed in local private and public services they too increase demand for those same services, and there is a virtuous circle of city prosperity.

This is the *multiplier* effect. The theory has led to econometric models which are widely used and influential in economic and transport planning. The *Lowry model*, for example, is used in complex land use/transport models. The modelling process takes as its starting point assumptions (i.e. best guesses) about the likely growth and distribution of basic employment and related population. It then predicts the resulting non-basic employment and population, leading on to the testing of alternative land use strategies and transport networks.[3] However, many have questioned the validity of such processes. According to some, the task of distinguishing basic from non-basic industry is almost impossible – there is no clear dividing line.[4] More fundamentally, others challenge the economic assumptions, arguing that boosting local trading and local control, and reducing dependence on externally owned firms which suck profits out of the area, is a more robust strategy. The New Economics Foundation has raised the profile of this agenda, for example through its surveys of high streets across Britain, showing that diversity of shops has been lost as national chains take over, and such 'clone towns' are more vulnerable to shop closure.[5]

Many initiatives are encouraging more localized economies: farmers markets, community agriculture schemes, credit unions, local banks, charity shops, Local Employment and Trading Schemes (LETS), internet-based local exchange systems (e.g. Freecycle) and 'Transition Towns' projects. City authorities, through their influence on land, can frustrate or support such initiatives. Local trading overall (including some conventional shops, trades, professional and public services) can be very important, contributing to economic diversity. Diversity makes for a resilient economic base, with better potential to innovate and adapt as circumstances change. If a city is dominated by a few major firms, the risks associated with failure are greater, and there may be less opportunity for aspiring entrepreneurs to find new market niches. Conversely, if there are large numbers of small and medium-sized businesses, entrepreneurial activity is in the DNA of the population. Such economies act as incubators for growth. While some new firms will fail, some will succeed. The growing firms, expanding their workforce, will be in a position to take over from others that are coming to the end of their life. The economy is in creative flux.

Economic growth and decline

The ideal scenario for the economy of a city is steady but not spectacular growth. It allows high employment levels, population structure retaining a balance between different ages and groups, and planned provision of infrastructure. There are problems with very rapid expansion. It tends to result in undue pressures on resources: shortages in social and physical infrastructure; increasing congestion and declining accessibility; polluted air; increased risks of water and land contamination; escalating land and building prices as demand exceeds supply; hardship and health hazards for the poor. Many of the cities of the developing world, faced with rural in-migration, exhibit these characteristics, mirroring the worst excesses of early nineteenth-century industrial cities in Europe.

Conversely, when the economic *raison d'être* of a city is lost, demand for land and buildings declines in parallel – unless a new economy grows within the shambles of the old. Detroit is a classic, and extreme, case. The decline of the car industry led to out migration and the collapse of demand, with consequent empty buildings and vacant land. The population of the central city fell from 1.8 million in 1950 to 0.7 million in 2010. The same, on a less apocalyptic scale, happened to Liverpool, where in places the absence

'When the economic raison d'être of a city is lost, demand for land and buildings declines in parallel. Economic theory suggests that cheap property entices in new entrepreneurs who can then flourish because of low overheads. But market failure is contaminating.'

of demand led to negative land values, reflecting the cost of de-contaminating old industrial sites or clearing vacant housing and dead shops. Faced with this situation, Liverpool adopted a grass-it-over strategy. Sites were levelled and seeded, to give an impression of urban tidiness. Economic theory suggests that cheap property entices in new entrepreneurs who can then flourish because of low overheads. But market failure is contaminating. Recovery tends to be painfully slow: basic industries find the potential workforce has moved away; non-basic industries have no market. Sustained state effort is needed to try to turn things around – or acceptance of a reduced, but new, status. Detroit, suffering bankruptcy in 2013 and many abandoned neighbourhoods, shows signs of renaissance. People are hopeful again. Liverpool's population has bottomed out and started to grow again.

Population and housing

The availability and quality of housing are other key determinants of health, alongside employment. As noted above, population and therefore demand for housing tends to follow economic development. Population change is made up of four components: birth rate, death rate, in-migration and out migration. The birth rate can vary significantly within a generation, and varies between different cultures and classes. The death rate overall is more stable, though it too varies between different population (income) groups. Net migration is strongly influenced by the job opportunities available, but there are other factors as well: in more affluent societies people (in work and in retirement) are attracted or repelled by the quality of the physical and social environment, especially the housing quality, the public realm and cultural life. So while birth and death rates are largely *independent variables*, subject to their own dynamics, *total* population is a mainly *dependent variable*, influenced by the characteristics, trends and decisions in the economy, housing, environment and facilities.

In Britain, many politicians and communities are adept at ignoring the problems of housing. The UK Treasury 'Barker' Report into land use planning cogently argues that the relationship between supply and demand for housing influences not only price, but also the locational choices available to households (especially poorer households), and the flexibility of labour markets.[6] It follows that, when households are constrained by the housing market to live in places that are far away from their main work and social connections, this will affect their travel mode options and choices. Often it means households living in outlying commuter exurbs with few local facilities. The health implications are manifold: housing stress for many poorer households, longer commuting distances as people search for accommodation they can afford, increased traffic with concomitant air pollution, carbon emissions, accidents, noise and visual intrusion, social exclusion of the transport poor. More households feel obliged to purchase one car *per adult* if they can afford it (or even when they can't), car dependence increases and active travel declines.

'When households are constrained by the housing market to live in places that are far away from their main work and cultural connections, more households feel obliged to purchase one car per adult if they can afford it (or even when they can't), car dependence increases and active travel declines.'

Household formation, housing need and demand

At the strategic planning scale the number of households and the changing nature of those households are critical factors. The general trend across the world in the last century has been for average household size to fall. Where a century ago the average size in Britain was over three, it is now 2.4.[7] In some European cities the average size has fallen below two. If fertility rises or housing is in short supply, forcing people to share accommodation, trends can reverse. Changes in household size are often more important than population change in determining the number of dwellings needed.

Housing need estimates are based on an objective assessment of changing population and household formation. They assume a 'social welfare' approach to policy-making, in other words, that the local and state governments have a responsibility to try to ensure that needs are met. The UK has adopted this welfare stance since soon after the First World War, and in principle it is good for health. Apart from forecasts, unsatisfied needs can also be assessed more directly through, for example, waiting lists for social housing, the degree of household sharing and information garnered from estate agents. The trends in household formation are often assumed to be purely the result of social change, independent of supply. In England, recent evidence suggests otherwise. There is a striking difference between the 2011 household projection, based on trends, and the results of the 2011 census. There are fewer one-person households, and more couples with other adults living with them.[8] Demand is latent, suppressed by lack of supply.

The average household size conceals much variety, as illustrated by the list in the sidebar. Different categories have different space and location needs. However, it is false to assume that, for example, a one person household necessarily wants a one bedroom dwelling. A parent whose children have flown the nest may want space for anticipated grandchildren to come and stay. Their ability to satisfy their wants depends on their ability to pay.

Housing demand is a market-based concept, based on the ability to pay. House-builders react to price signals, and will build more homes when they can see the opportunity to make a profit, comparing the price of land and construction with potential sale value. The mismatch of estimated housing need and supply in parts of the UK and many cities across the world has reached crisis proportions, with high prices and the shortage of affordable housing causing stress for many families.

The reasons for this endemic mismatch are complex. It may be simply geographical – such as a lack of buildable land in a narrow constrained valley. It can be due to bottlenecks in the availability of building materials or skilled workers. It can also be due to rationing of supply – whether by planning authorities protecting greenfields, or house-builders hoarding land in order to increase its value, deliberately building fewer houses than they could sell. Either way these are restrictive practices that, as we have noted, compound problems of health and equity. The question arises: how to free up

Types of household

- One-person households
  - young, middle-aged, empty-nesters, elderly
- Couples living alone
  - young, middle-aged, empty-nesters, elderly
- Couples with children living with them
  - one, two, three+ children
- Lone parents with children
  - one, two, three+ children
- Couples with adult(s) living in
  - often a 'child' or a parent
- Other multi-person households
  - e.g. students or people sharing

Housing Provision

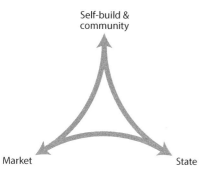

Fig 14.4 *The principal housing provision sectors*

'In the first decade of the twenty-first century the cost of housing doubled in the UK, while in Germany it stayed level.'

the supply system? In part inertia relates to the balance of different sectors of housing provision (see Figure 14.4). In Britain, the market sector dominates. Most housing is provided by house-builders, who then sell to owner-occupiers and 'buy-to-let' landlords. Prices and rents are high, especially in the South, reflecting shortage. This was not always the case. In the mid-twentieth century, dwellings built by local authorities accounted for a third to a half of new-build, and total house-building was commensurately higher. Other countries maintain much higher building rates in relation to population. In Germany the tradition of self-build and community housing is strong. Households buy serviced plots on which they have a dwelling built to their own specification. Rents and prices are also subject to controls by local authorities, in both public and private sectors. In the first decade of the twenty-first century the cost of housing doubled in the UK, while in Germany it stayed level.[9]

Sufficient land in accessible locations and diversity of supply mechanisms are the essential ingredients, with all three sectors positively supported. Innovative mechanisms – such as Community Land Trusts and Co-housing projects – could be supported. Private tenants need reasonable security of tenure encouraging longer stay, putting down roots in the local area. Social housing tenants need pathways to home ownership which do not denude the social housing stock. All this is difficult to achieve if prices are unaffordable in relation to average wages. The end of the next chapter discusses ways in which municipalities could open up the options.

Matching economic activity and population

The relationship between people available for work and economic activity is central to strategic planning. The *activity rate* measures the proportion of the working age population that are actively in work (including training) or seeking work. In high-income countries the general trend in the activity rate since the Second World War has been upwards, as progressively more women enter the labour market. The rate for England and Wales now hovers around 70 per cent and seems to have reached a plateau. The definition of 'working age' (16–64) is something of a historic anachronism. It fails to give the whole picture in an age when many young adults continue schooling beyond 16 and enter higher education, and when people are entitled to work beyond 64. The Herefordshire example given here highlights some key variables which apply elsewhere.

Herefordshire economic activity rate

The population of the county is 175,000. The economic activity rate for the 'working age' population (16–64) in 2012 was 76%, with the rate for men being significantly higher than for women: 82% and 71% respectively. The 76% is made up of 56% employees – equally men and women; 15% self-employed – mainly men; and 5% registered unemployed. Total employment in the county has risen with the population since 2001, with a small increase in full-time employment, a rise of 12% in self-employment, and a substantial 20% rise in part-time employment. The economically *inactive* account for 24% of the working age population, and the vast majority of these do not want a job. Of that 24% a quarter suffer from long term sickness; a quarter are carers or look after the home (mainly women); a fifth are students; another fifth have taken early retirement; the remaining 10% have other reasons.[10]

The activity rate allows us to calculate the *job ratio*. This compares the working population with the jobs available within an area. It is calculated by dividing the number of local jobs by the number of people working/work-seeking. A score over one indicates more jobs than people. The hope for a large urban area or city region is a rough balance of work and workers, giving a good opportunity for local work, and potentially minimizing the need for out- or in-commuting. If the friction of distance (the cost of travel) is low, as in 2016, job-search areas become more extended. If the friction of distance is high (perhaps due to a carbon tax), then a job ratio over 1 and a wide diversity of opportunities increases the city's resilience.

At the scale of the village or urban neighbourhood jobs are often in short supply. Yet diverse work opportunities within walkable distance are important for some groups in the population – carers wanting part-time work, teenagers, students, low-paid workers. There is some indication that a neighbourhood job ratio threshold of over 0.7 allows a significant number of people to find local work.[11] Though this would depend on the nature of the jobs and skills available.

A good balance between population and employment has become a talisman of sustainability. It has been written into countless plans as an aspiration devoutly to be wished, but often very difficult to achieve. As suggested earlier, forecasts of both population and economic activity are not firm predictions, just best guesses. The tools above (activity rate, job ratio, etc.) can help us to assess the resilience of the city, and take action accordingly. However, the trajectory of both elements depends not just on each other, but the supporting infrastructure. The utilities, transport networks, public spaces, services and facilities that go to make the city. We will concentrate here on transport infrastructure.

'A good balance between population and employment has become a talisman of sustainability. It has been written into countless plans as an aspiration devoutly to be wished, but often very difficult to achieve.'

Transport infrastructure and economic development

Transport infrastructure is vital for economic activity, but debate persists over what kind of infrastructure. Across the world urbanized areas are experiencing very significant transport problems, and they are getting worse. Road investment is widely seen as vital to economic success. Cars are promoted by images of status, power, and sexual desirability – side-lining healthy forms of movement. Many cities in the developing world are at the level of car and lorry use experienced in Europe in the 1950s and 1960s, but growing at a much faster rate and failing to learn the painful lessons.

Governments also compete to promote air travel through heavy subsidization, and cities invest in airports which further pollute the environment.[12]

The assumption that economic success is dependent on growing car use is not borne out by the evidence. Health damage caused by vehicles is the cause of many millions of days off work, therefore reduced productivity.[13] The significance of road transport for health and well-being has been rehearsed in earlier chapters: road accidents, air pollution, noise, car dependence and reduced physical activity, severance of communities, social exclusion of the transport poor ... the list is long. Cities that try alternatives based on pedestrian-friendly environments, active travel and public transport offer many attractions. Copenhagen and Freiburg, cities featured in Chapter 5, strengthened their competitive position, increased footfall in the centre and experiences rising commercial rents.[14] The Chamber of Commerce in Groningen, the Netherlands, opposed the new strategy introduced in 1977 for many years, because of the perceived threat to business, but now backs it to the hilt: not one business wants to return to the car-based system.[15] If done well, a healthy strategy pays off.

The transport infrastructure is there for a purpose, to get from one place to another. From an economic as well as a humane perspective, considerations of *efficiency* are paramount. Road space is limited. As demonstrated conclusively by the Buchanan Report, *Traffic in Towns*, over half a century ago, providing for full motorization is both very destructive and very expensive, and in large cities impossible.[16] Car use is notoriously a selfish affair, most cars occupied by one person alone. Buses hold up to 80 passengers, a tram perhaps 300. Cyclists can crowd together, four, five or six in the space of one car. Pedestrians require little space. Efficient use of road space, and efficient movement in cities, depend on making the public transport, cycling and pedestrian systems work effectively, serving the interests of both shorter- and longer-distance urban travellers, thereby reducing vehicle use to the point where congestion, air pollution and accidents are no longer great problems.

Reversing car-oriented habits requires concerted action on land use patterns, transport investment, tariffs and subsidies, organizational travel plans and public engagement. There are plenty of cities (especially in Europe) which demonstrate the potential for success, for example:

- Manchester (UK) – the Metrolink tram has reduced car trips to the centre from the area it serves by 50 per cent, replacing over 1 million car journeys each year.
- Aachen (Germany) – traffic into the city centre in the 1990s was reduced by 85 per cent, the car's share of overall city trips fell from 44 to 36 per cent, and NOx emissions reduced by 50 per cent.
- Groningen (the Netherlands) – by 1990, after a concerted effort to make the city bike-friendly, 48 per cent of trips within the city were by bike, 17 per cent foot, 5 per cent bus and 30 per cent car.

- Germany and Switzerland: car owners who have joined a car-sharing scheme have reduced their car mileage by 50 per cent.[17]

The essence of all schemes is to increase travel choices available, and make people aware of those options. Instead of the default option being the car, with all its inequities and health impacts, people have freedom to choose. Schemes do, however, require very careful design, and the city needs the ability to learn from experience, and adapt in the light of experience. Some rapidly developing cities seem to have a death wish. Beijing was a city of bicycles 50 years ago. Then as it grew, and grew more affluent, there was a massive transfer of road space from bike to car. The entirely predictable results: congestion, appalling levels of air pollution and smog – health hazards so bad the city has to periodically close itself down.

'Reversing car-oriented habits requires concerted action on land use patterns, transport investment, tariffs and subsidies, organizational travel plans and public engagement.'

Land use transport models

The conventional way transport analysis has been tackled at city region scale is through the use of mathematical models. Initially developed in the mid-twentieth century in the USA, Land Use Transport Models (LUTM) normally relate to a city region, which is divided into several hundred zones. Each zone is given a baseline level of population, housing and economic activity, derived from the census and other data sources. Mathematical formula are devised relating these variables to each other, trying to match reality as closely as possible. The Lowry model (see earlier) and gravity models are frequently used. The model estimates the likely number of trips, by transport mode, between zones, and the allocation of those trips to the existing infrastructure. Then new levels of population, economic activity and transport infrastructure are assumed as a strategic plan for a future date, and the trip calculations are repeated, to test the quality of the plan. In some models the location of new businesses and housing is determined by economic assumptions, and it is possible to estimate land values, household and business costs. It is also possible to tie in assumptions about traffic pollution, carbon emissions and other variables.[18]

Such models have the advantage of taking an integrated, interactive view of a city region. The disadvantages, though, are many. They are time-consuming and expensive, sucking energy from other processes. They are based on past behavioural patterns, assuming they continue into the future. The zones are often quite large, so that local actions and shorter trips are lost from sight, and walking and cycling options cannot be properly explored. The model assumptions are not transparent, and the results all too easily reflect the attitudes of the modellers.[19] A wide-ranging 1970 review of strategic planning in America concluded that models did not improve plan-making, indeed, they were counterproductive because they took resources away from other tasks.[20] Since then, computing power has massively increased, but the questions remain.[21]

If transport policy is to be changed and the varied decision-makers brought on board, then we need more transparent and flexible, less conservative, and much cheaper approaches – collaborative, holistic, experimental, learning from experience.

Afterword

This chapter has introduced some, but not all, of the key elements that go to make up a strategic plan. Economic development, population, housing and transport provide a core of matters that the plan should attempt to keep in balance with each other, so that the city works well economically and socially. Other aspects – social and green infrastructure and urban form – have been examined in earlier chapters. A flexible, coherent strategy is required, setting the context for incremental decisions at both policy and spatial levels, if human well-being is to be improved. All too often, however, consistent and effective strategies are not forthcoming. The final part of the book looks at some of the political and technical reasons, and suggests ways forward.

Further reading

Glasson, J. and Marshall, T. (2007) *Regional planning*. London: Routledge.

Hall, P. (2014) *Good cities, better lives*. London: Routledge. Chapters on economic, housing and transport planning in Germany, France, the Netherlands and Scandinavia.

Lowe, S. (2011) *The housing debate*. Bristol: The Policy Press.

Melia, S. (2015) *Urban transport without hot air*. Cambridge: UIT Cambridge, a populist format but full of well-researched analysis.

Notes

1 Jackson, T. (2009) *Prosperity without growth: economics for a finite planet* (London: Earthscan), p. 187.

2 Forrester, J.W. (1969) *Urban dynamics*, vol. 114 (Cambridge, MA: MIT Press).

3 See, for example, Echenique, M., Hargreaves, A. and Mitchell, G. (2009) 'Spatial planning, sustainability and long-run trends', *Town and Country Planning*, 78, Sept. 380–385, reporting on the SOLUTIONS Project.

4 McCann, P. (2013) *Modern urban and regional economics*, second edn (Oxford: Oxford University Press).

5 New Economics Foundation (2005) *Clone town Britain* (London: NEF).

6 Barker, K. (2006) *Review of land use planning* (London: HM Treasury, HMSO).

7 Office for National Statistics, available at: www.ons.gov.uk/census/2011census

8 Holmans, A. (2013) *New estimates of housing demand and need in England, 2011 to

2031 (London: Town and Country Planning Association).

9 www.forbes.com/sites/eamonfingleton/2014/02/02 (accessed 26 Jan. 2016).

10 Herefordshire County Council Research Team (2012) *Economic Activity in Herefordshire*. Available at: www.researchteam@herefordshire.gov.uk

11 Stead, D. (1994) 'Reducing travel distances through land use planning', unpublished MA dissertation, Faculty of the Built Environment, University of the West of England, Bristol.

12 Whitelegg, J. and Haq, G. (eds) (2003) *The Earthscan reader on world transport policy and practice* (London: Earthscan).

13 Ibid.

14 TEST (1987) *Quality streets* (London: TEST).

15 Melia, S. (2015) *Urban transport without hot air* (Cambridge: UIT Cambridge).

16 Buchanan, C. (1964) *Traffic in towns: The specially shortened edition of the Buchanan Report* (Harmondsworth: Penguin).

17 All examples from Whitelegg and Haq (2003), op. cit.

18 Echenique *et al.* (2009), op. cit.

19 To see the limitations of a major modelling exercise, see Barton, H., Grant, M. and Horswell, M. (2011) 'Suburban solutions – the other side of the story', *Town and Country Planning*, July/August: 339–345.

20 Boyce, D., Day, N. and McDonald, C. (1970) *Metropolitan plan making: an analysis of experience with the preparation and evaluation of alternative land use and transportation plans* (Philadelphia, PA: Regional Science Research Institute).

21 Lautso, K., Speikermann, K., Wegener, M., Sheppard, I., Steadman, P., Martino, A., Domingo, R. and Gayda, S. (2004) *PROPOLIS (Planning and Research of Policies for Land use and Transport for Increasing urban Sustainability) Final Report*, second edn. Funded by the European Commission Fifth Framework Programme (Brussels: EC).

V   Perspiration

Land, power and process

The previous parts of the book identify, beyond reasonable doubt, the characteristics of a 'city of well-being'. What we need to achieve is clear. How we realize it, is much more problematic. All the positive images are just so much wishful thinking if the mechanisms for delivery are not available. We need clear pathways forward. Chapter 11 provided a 'reality check', observing the way the development process works in a pluralist, market-oriented society. Chapters 12–14 explored some of the tensions between common practice and healthy planning principles. As has often been said about composing music, getting it right is 5 per cent inspiration and 95 per cent perspiration. Part V offers a window on how to approach this mammoth task.

Underlying assumptions and political philosophies are at stake. So Chapter 15 goes back to basics: how far is planning necessary, and who is really doing it? Planning is not an independent, self-sufficient activity. It is a reflection of societal values and cultural attitudes, as interpreted by political decisions.[1] Its official role varies between countries and even between provinces or states within one country. Fundamental to the role of planning is the attitude to property rights. Some societies consider private land ownership sacrosanct. In others, community land rights are deeply embedded. Planning systems, by their very nature, place constraints on private rights. Three systems – in the USA, Britain, and the Netherlands – represent a fair political range from liberal to social democratic. They contrast in their ability to be able to deliver healthy environments.

This leads on to the question of *how* to work with market and political processes to achieve social ends. Planning theory has over the years articulated radically different approaches ranging from heroic rationality to humdrum pragmatism. Chapter 16 takes a historical look at the development of ideas, trying to clarify the role of planners in a pluralist society. The conclusion is that planners in varied fields must be explicit about values and clear about the spatial and design 'bottom lines', while necessarily working collaboratively, building alliances and seizing opportunities.

Chapter 17 then presents a process that is principled, systematic and evidence-based, while at the same time being collaborative, inclusive and community oriented. Some planning systems require this kind of process, at least in theory. But it is appropriate irrespective of legislation. The creation of a healthy urban environment depends on it being effective. The chapter outlines the process and illustrates it with a relatively simple local example. Finally, the Epilogue draws overall conclusions.

Note

1   Nadin, V. and Stead, D. (2008) 'European spatial planning systems: social models and learning', *The Planning Review*, 44(172): 35–47.

CHAPTER FIFTEEN

THE GOVERNANCE OF LAND

Fig 15.1 *Parking rights*

Source: Courtesy Rob Cowan – www.plandemonium.org.uk

L and is the fundamental asset on which humans and other land animals depend. The way it is distributed, planned and managed largely determines the nature of human settlements and affects the well-being of the population. Earlier chapters showed that town planning in some form has occurred since the beginning of cities. But professional planners (of whatever kind) are only cogs in the machine, and the official planning system just part of the machinery. The governance of land varies greatly between countries. It stems from deeply embedded cultural attitudes that shape the actions of landowners, users and the policies of the state. Neo-liberals perennially question whether *governance* (in the sense of official planning diktat) is actually needed. It is vital to confront this widespread instinct, stemming from conventional economic thinking, with convincing arguments. So we start with this most basic of questions.

Is planning really necessary?

First, the case against planning. There are three contrasting strands of argument. The first is from a neo-liberal perspective. Many commentators take free market conventions as gospel. If there is a problem in society, then the solution is to roll back the state and increase competition, so as to drive up quality and drive down costs. Some states in the USA adopt a *laissez-faire* approach to development akin to that in nineteenth-century Europe. Landowners can develop land more or less as they choose – a basic human right. The state intervenes only in specific instances; for example, protecting public open space. In some former states of the USSR – where comprehensive planning was imposed by autocratic diktat – politicians have reacted against planning, and 'the market' has let rip, creating wealth for some. In Thatcherite Britain, a 1980s planning guidance note talked about 'lifting the burden' of planning off the market. The assumption of liberal economists and politicians is that bureaucratic constraints on capital are damaging, and central controls are liable to distort effective market response to problems and opportunities.

The irony is some on the left of politics have also been suspicious of planning. The social libertarians share with economic liberals an antipathy towards state interference. Colin Ward, the British communitarian anarchist, articulated

The theory of spontaneous order

'Given a common need, a collection of people will, by trial and error, by improvisation and experiment, evolve order out of the situation.'

> the theory of spontaneous order ... given a common need, a collection of people will, by trial and error, by improvisation and experiment, evolve order out of the situation – this order being more durable and more closely related to their needs than any kind of externally imposed authority could provide.[1]

Ward cited the plotlands along the English Channel coast as examples of anarchist development. The informal settlements of many great cities in poorer countries exhibit similar traits of self-management on a vastly greater scale.

The third strand of argument comes from Marxist-leaning academics who developed 'critical theory' of the status quo. They saw planning as innately technocratic, based on central control, unsympathetic and unresponsive to the needs of ordinary people. The role of the state in capitalist countries was perceived as a repressive arm of powerful capitalist interests, an instrument to maintain unequal power structures. In his 1973 book, *Social Justice and the City,* David Harvey[2] pointed to the coincidence of interest between develop- ment companies and local planning authorities; for example, the latter act to assemble major sites (buying up plots in different own- ership through compulsory purchase) on behalf of *one* developer, to facilitate comprehensive redevelopment. The local authority would presume this was in the community interest, because new investment was enabled, but in so doing effectively disrupted local community networks, displaced local businesses and curtailed small-scale builders and their employees who could not compete. The local state favoured capital accumulation by big business at the expense of local people. Profits would fly out of the area to distant shareholders, rather than reinforcing the local economy.

Thus in the last quarter of the twentieth century planning was attacked from both right and left. This twin attack was like a pincer movement on the role of town planners, undermining confidence. On both sides, however, there was grudging recognition that some degree of land planning was necessary. Even Hayek, the apostle of capitalism who preached the primacy of the market in the early twen- tieth century, recognized that market failures existed (such as long- term dereliction) which required a policy response. Planning was also needed to deal with neighbourhood effects (pollution, noise, traffic) and to supply essential communal goods such as roads, sewers and parks. There needs, he said, to be some protection for people or activities which cannot compete in the land market.[3] Some contemporary economists, despite being imbued with free market thinking, criticize the conventional wisdom that markets are rational and self-equilibrating.[4] Planning is seen as a necessary facilitator of effective market operation, providing essential infrastructure and compensating for market inefficiencies.

Harvey, too, considered that town planning was necessary – an institutionalized mechanism for the public good. He saw it as a poten- tial (though often ineffective) bulwark against the market, and pro- vider of the infrastructure and non-profit services on which markets and communities depend. As Allmendinger[5] points out, this position seems remarkably similar to those of Hayek and the free marketeers!

The argument *for* planning is thus already made by those who are (with some justification) wary of it. Beyond that there is the burden of earlier chapters: the market, left to its own devices, tends to produce settlement patterns and styles of development that are inefficient, inequitable and unhealthy. There are social goods that rely on good spatial planning. Economic efficiency itself relies on effective land use/transport planning that avoids the diseconomies of land shortage, poor accessibility, congestion, pollution and an unhealthy, less productive workforce. So all great cities in the devel- oped world attempt to exert effective planning control. In East Asia, for example, Tokyo, Hong-Kong, Singapore and Shanghai have highly developed strategies. Some countries depend for their very survival on centralized planning control. The classic example is the Netherlands. The Dutch have stolen one third of their land from the sea. The system of rivers, dykes, drains, and urban development requires constant vigilance, and people therefore accept a degree of integrated town and country planning that would be anathema in some other societies.

There is another plank to the argument. This concerns the practical difficulty of *avoiding* the planning of towns and cities. The question is: *who* is doing the planning? The broad definition of planning given in the first chapter is justified by the pluralist nature of decision-making in democratic, capitalist countries. The planning authority is not all-powerful – it has to negotiate with other public and private sector bodies which share in the planning of cities. Major transport and utility decisions, which help to define the shape and development of the city, are often determined by other agencies; health and education authorities invest in social infrastructure; major employers, retailers, commercial and housing investors plan development on a scale which means they help determine the shape of settlements. The lesser players in the game – households, community groups and small businesses – have to find wriggle room within the framework set by the bigger powers.

In a pluralist society, where decisions are incremental and disaggregated, not controlled by an authoritarian power, all the major players need to accept social responsibility for the outcome of their decisions. Just as they recognize employment laws, they should take account of health and environmental implications of their spatial decisions. This may be statutorily enforced to some extent, but necessarily means working co-operatively.

In summary, then, in modern towns and cities spatial planning happens, whether we like it or not. Planning is a ubiquitous activity. The question is not *whether* to plan, but *who* is planning, *what* they are planning, *how* they are planning, and in whose interests?

'In modern towns and cities spatial planning happens, whether we like it or not. The question is not whether to plan, but who is planning, what they are planning, how they are planning, and in whose interests?'

Private and community property rights

Land use planning is tied up with the issue of land ownership. Property rights in western democracies – the right to own property, to do what you want with it within certain limits – are taken for granted. Property is a commodity, like grain or natural gas, and therefore subject to the laws of supply and demand. It is also an expression of individual or group identity. In capitalist countries, we are so used to private property rights, to the sale and purchase of land and buildings, that it is easy to imagine this is the only way to have ownership of land. Conventional economic theories reinforce this assumption, because they treat any divergence from a competitive market in property as something of an exception, an intervention.

But property is not always treated as a commodity. In some countries and some situations land and/or buildings have a cultural value such that ownership is perceived as communal. In Europe, we can see the residue of different, non-commodified, systems of value. Urban parks, playing fields, streets and squares are owned by the municipality on behalf of the community, often vested in perpetuity for community use. Major development companies may be obliged to give over a proportion of land for community use, even when they cannot see a marketing benefit. Land is effectively taken out of the market system. Private land may also be subject to enduring public rights. 'Common land' in Britain is a case in point. While the legal ownership is vested in a trust or private company, the community has freedom of use in perpetuity. Commoners may have the right to graze livestock. This is a form of communal ownership. The *users* have inalienable rights.

A profound cultural divide can be seen in countries where tribal traditions have been submerged by European settlers. The difference is very evident, for example, in New Zealand. The British settlers – the 'Pakiha' – struggling to establish farming on an untamed terrain, had an assumption of private property rights: a family can do what it wants with its own land. But they came up against a culture that was alien to them. The Maori don't own the land in a narrow legal sense, they are *of* the land. The land is their mother, the home of their ancestors, their place on Earth. When the Pakiha settlers occupied land and established legal ownership they dispossessed Maori tribes who had traditional (but non-legal) rights of ownership. When these two systems of belief clashed, it took understanding and tolerance on both sides to thrash out an agreement. The Treaty of Waitanga (1840) became an international model, though some tensions have inevitably persisted.

This belief in communal rights over private property is evident in a more general way too. The English landscape is remarkable for the sharp visual divide between town and country. Sporadic, dispersed residential and commercial developments are generally outlawed. This is the result of powerful countryside protection policies, sustained over generations, supported by governments of left and right, reflecting a passionate (and romantic), widespread belief in the value of open country – green fields and hill-country alike protected. A sense of shared values in 'England's green and pleasant land' takes precedence over private rights, affecting land values profoundly. This equates to a non-legal, non-financial sense of community ownership.

Equivalently, routes from one place to another across private land may be public. In some European countries (Switzerland and Italy, for example) there is a traditional right for people to wander through pastures, orchards and vineyards, duly respecting crops and livestock, stemming from a time when rural communities were more co-operative in their land management. By contrast, in more recently settled lands (New Zealand, Australia, North America), there is no such right: the land is sacred to the owner: if you stray inadvertently across the holding, you are quite liable to get shot! England and Wales lie somewhere in between: there are specific (historic) rights of way threading through the fields.

'The English landscape is remarkable for the sharp visual divide between town and country, reflecting a passionate (and romantic), widespread belief in the value of open country.'

Privatization and land assembly

A related angle on ownership is the pressure for privatization of public space and routeways. The motivation can be the safety and security of residents and users: house-builders and residents may argue against connection between cul-de-sacs; gated communities may explicitly refuse casual entrants; urban shopping and leisure malls lock their doors once business is done. Most seriously major organizations acquire huge land holdings which create barriers to movement. Local authorities often assist in this through land assembly. The resulting impermeable environment frustrates desire lines, segregates one place from another, forces people to go the long way round, discouraging active travel. When small plots are lost, there is a reduction in opportunity for small businesses and community initiatives. In the *Rational Optimist*, Matt Ridley argues that the concentration of land owning power is counterproductive socially and economically. He shows evidence that well-distributed land ownership in developing countries releases the energy and initiative of the many.[6] Recent research in Dublin, Ireland, suggests that small plot shopping centres have the capacity to perform more responsively and employ more people, than big plot centres.[7]

In conclusion: the dominant form of land ownership in developed and developing countries treats land as a commodity, available to be traded in the market, subject to the economic forces of supply and demand and with a tendency to concentration of ownership. Other concepts of informal, social or community ownership operate in parallel to a greater or lesser extent, depending on country and culture, are necessary for effective functioning of settlements. Because non-market ownerships are by nature more egalitarian, they are also likely to be beneficial to equity and well-being.

Comparative planning systems

'Land use planning systems are just one of the mechanisms of governance that determine the way development happens.'

Land use planning systems are in a sense a sub-set of property rights. Planning systems give local authorities the right, on behalf of the community, to intervene in the land market and the development process. They are just one of the mechanisms of governance that determine the way development happens. The range of other mechanisms includes:

- the conventions of private and community land ownership already discussed;
- the relative powers and obligations of central, provincial, county and municipal government;
- the tax base and funding mechanisms available at each level;
- the degree of integration of different spatial topics;
- the potential for land value 'capture' by the community.

Each state has a different mix. The box gives thumbnail sketches of the system in three rich countries to illustrate the variety: (1) a pioneer model in the United States, where the progressive expansion of settlers into huge virgin territories has led to a very decentralized system of planning; (2) a comprehensive model in the Netherlands, where the need to safeguard reclaimed land from flood necessitated an integrated, legally binding approach; and (3) somewhere in-between, the British system – centralized in order to manage high population densities, with flexible, discretionary decision-making suited to economic liberalism.

Thumbnail sketches of three planning systems

The USA: a pioneer liberal model

The United States has many variants on the theme, but common to all is a belief in the almost sacred rights of property owners. There is no absolute obligation to create official plans, but most states and local authorities do. The most common role of strategic plans is to decide on transport infrastructure investment. The real power over land use lies at the local level. Each authority (often quite small townships in outer city areas) decides for itself the level and location of development. The sharp end of the plan is normally a *zoning map*, with specific plot size (or 'sub-division') rules and household-type rules in each zone, partly to retain the social exclusivity of some zones, protecting property values. An alternative to strict zoning plans are form-based codes, which allow some mixture of households and uses, depending on the location in a transect from rural to urban.[8]

The Netherlands: a comprehensive integrated model

The Netherlands' planning system comes from a European (Napoleonic) government tradition. Plans have the force of law – they are *legally binding* and not discretionary. Policies are very systematically developed as a result of negotiation between government, province and municipality. The plan expressly links transport investment, water management and land development and identifies the best places for growth following discussion with market interests. The local authority can buy development land with the aid of low interest loans from the state investment bank. It produces masterplans for brown and greenfield sites as the basis for joint ventures with developers, making effective arrangements for affordable housing and for sustainable energy strategies.[9]

Britain: a state liberal model

The UK's planning system (in 2016) is ostensibly plan-led, and those plans, prepared by local authorities, and at various stages of completion, cover the whole country. However, plan content is largely shaped by government diktat, including the amount of housing and commerce to plan for. Developer influence on land allocations is strong, such that housing land allocation is sometimes only weakly related to transport investment, despite obligations for plans to be logically based. Wider regional spatial planning does not currently exist, but economic planning is undertaken by separate non-elected bodies, and has wide spatial and investment implications. The development management process is *discretionary,* a matter of judging each case on its merits in the light of the plan and other relevant factors. Masterplans for major developments are normally developer-led. The local authority can buy up land to facilitate implementation, but the legal process is convoluted, and full market price is paid. At the very local level, village and neighbourhood plans can be undertaken by voluntary groups within the context of local authority plans, and are subject to referenda.[10]

Other countries have different models. The Australian system, for example, combines legal elements derived from the British system with zoning and sub-division based on American practice. Across the world, almost all countries have a system of some kind, sometimes more honoured in the breach than the observance. Belgium has a tradition of rural housing *laissez-faire,* which contrasts both with the comprehensive planning tradition of its neighbour, the Netherlands, and with the British countryside protection tradition. Ireland and Portugal have tended in the past to let the market dictate greenfield development – with unfortunate results of housing areas without physical and social infrastructure. In medium- and lower-income countries where cities are growing very fast from migration off the land, even quite proficient planning authorities have little hope of keeping up with development. Turkey and Brazil are examples of this. In some cities, informal settlements are the only way that people can survive.

A variety of approaches to planning, land ownership, local authority structures and powers is inevitable. But systems also evolve and develop with time, responding to political, environmental, economic and social pressures. It is clear from earlier chapters that some systems, as currently operated, deliver poor health outcomes, while others are much more successful. The poor outcomes are, one hopes, more by accident than by design. Health, well-being and even climate change are not seen as important drivers of spatial policy. Decisions are taken on other grounds altogether. If health, well-being and climate *were* fully recognized as motivation for planning, then systems and conventions would have to be adapted.

Local government powers

'No new urban extensions, no new settlements and few inner city redevelopments in Britain begin to compete in quality and healthy behaviours with the best European examples.'

Let us assume that the motivation, at political and technical levels, is strong. What governance mechanisms would facilitate cities of well-being? Peter Hall has made a study of this question in his book *Good Cities, Better Lives.*[11] He noted that no new urban extensions, no new settlements and few inner city redevelopments in Britain begin to compete in quality and healthy behaviours with the best European examples in Germany, France, the Netherlands, Sweden and Denmark. The key difference is the extent of local authority power: healthy, sustainable neighbourhoods are only achieved, he argues, when local authorities have the power both to buy well-located land without legal or financial penalties, and to set a clear spatial context for private and community investment. In the past in Britain, this was achieved by appointed, non-democratic 'development corporations' for new towns and urban regeneration areas. But European experience shows that it is possible through elected local authorities. The essential condition is that different political parties agree a consistent and shared vision, so that when power changes hands, the strategy remains intact. Land use and transport decisions are too long lasting and too important to be political footballs.

The funding regime for physical and social infrastructure is critical. One British study undertaken by private sector firms concluded that the existence of state banks, able to support local authorities with low-interest loans, was a crucial factor in making places attractive, and in keeping house prices affordable.[12] In Germany, the distinctive feature is *local* banks. Instead of breeding giant banks, the rules encourage provincial banks that are dedicated to the support of local businesses and municipalities. Another approach, exemplified by Freiburg (Chapter 5), is the local authority *right to buy development land* at a price that allows infrastructure (parks, streets, tramways, schools, community centres, etc.) to be constructed 'up-front', as or before people occupy their homes. Land approved in city plans for development or redevelopment can be bought at existing use value, plus generous compensation; then held by the authority through the development process so that the power of land ownership is added to that of planning to control the allocation of plots and the shape of development. Such a system is not anti-market. It is simply ensuring that some of the huge up-lift in value (see Chapter 11) resulting from community planning decisions, is kept by the community for essential infrastructure. Both households and businesses benefit.

More radical is the approach taken in the first garden city of Letchworth, until the 1980s (Chapter 4). All the land was held in trust for the community. The rents accruing to the municipality from commercial and residential properties support local services and improvements to the town, cutting costs for all.

Finance and land ownership, though, are not enough. What is different in Freiburg, Copenhagen, Stockholm, Utrecht and many other cities, is long-term strategic thinking. A city's political, commercial and professional leaders have the responsibility of setting a logical long-term course designed to fulfil their shared aspirations. To achieve this, there needs to be stability in the wider legal and institutional setting. Where governments change the rules after each election, local authorities are undermined. Consistent strategies across housing, community facilities, economic development, transport, energy, air quality, greenspace and urban form become impossible to sustain. Local authorities need sufficient autonomy to decide strategy locally, in the context of stable overarching goals set by government.

Transferability of such principles is problematic. Where central government emasculates local authorities, or commercial priorities take precedence over social and community priorities, the prerequisites for real progress are not there. The conclusion is that only when state, market and community interests get together behind common goals, accepting that co-operation is necessary, can governance be effective. The desire for healthy urban environments could be the trigger. The last two chapters develop the idea of collaborative cities.

'Where central government emasculates local authorities, or commercial priorities take precedence over social and community priorities, the prerequisites for real progress are not there.'

Conclusion

The earlier chapters made an overwhelming case for effective planning, in the interests of human health and well-being. This chapter has highlighted some of the governance issues that need to be wrestled with if this is to be achieved. We need to confront knee-jerk free market rhetoric with good arguments, and at the same time allay the fears of those who perceive planning as anti-democratic, anti-market and anti-freedom. By recognizing those fears and the values behind them we may also be able to refine ideas of how best to plan.

Societal positions in land law and institutional structures reflect attitudes in relation to three issues. The first is whether planning is necessary. The conclusion is that planning occurs anyway, and is accepted by all sides as necessary to deliver social goods. The big question is: who is doing it, and are they delivering social goods or just private gain? The second issue is attitudes to the ownership of land, where some cultures feel that private ownership is sacrosanct. The conclusion is that even in 'free market' societies, extensive community rights exist, and are necessary. The question is, how far should that necessity go? The third issue is the degree of centralization or decentralization. The conclusion is that local authorities need the power to act with a good degree of financial muscle and investment independence, to take the initiative, learn from mistakes, co-ordinate effectively in the public interest. Such authorities, or co-operating groups of authorities, must be large enough to make sensible strategic planning decisions.

One way of approaching the question of where authority should lie is the idea of *subsidiarity.* This is the principle that decisions should be taken at the lowest appropriate level. Some development decisions can be taken by property owners, when there is agreement from immediate neighbours. Some at local neighbourhood level; for example, the design and management of playgrounds, or proposals for house extensions where neighbours disagree. Some can be made at the city level: the layout of a new estate, the extension of green infrastructure or the pedestrianization of the city centre. Overall housing, employment, energy, transport and urban form strategies need to be made at the city region scale. Certain decisions may be necessary at provincial or national scale. Government sets the planning mechanisms and the overarching goals which lesser authorities have to try to achieve, but need not dictate major investment decisions or spatial strategies.

Within any given legal/institutional context, built environment professionals advising public, private and voluntary organizations have an obligation to work creatively to solve problems. But the role and responsibility of planners is a contentious issue. Chapter 16 reviews the theories of how the professionals should approach their task.

Further reading

Allmendinger, P. (2009) *Planning theory*. London: Palgrave Macmillan.

Barton, H., Thompson, S., Burgess, S. and Grant, M. (eds) (2015) *The Routledge handbook of planning for health and well-being.* London: Routledge.

Cullingworth, B. and Caves, R. (2014) *Planning in the USA: policies, issues and processes,* fourth edn. London: Routledge. An excellent, readable and comprehensive perspective.

Cullingworth, B., Nadin, V., Hart, T., Davoudi, S., Pendlebury, J., Vigar, G., Webb, D. and Townsend, T. (2015) *Town and country planning in the UK*. London: Routledge.

Greed, C. with Johnson, D. (2014) *Planning in the UK: an introduction*. Basingstoke: Palgrave Macmillan.

Kent, J. and Thompson, S. (2015) 'Healthy planning in Australia', in H. Barton, S. Thompson, S. Burgess, and M. Grant (eds) *The Routledge handbook of planning for health and well-being*. London: Routledge.

Lawrence, R. (2015) 'Mind the gap: bridging the divide between knowledge, policy and practice', in H. Barton, S. Thompson, S. Burgess, and M. Grant (eds) *The Routledge handbook of planning for health and well-being*. London: Routledge.

Oxley, M., Brown, T., Nadin, V., Qu, L., Tummers, L. and Fernandez-Maldonado, A. (2009) *Review of European planning systems*. Leicester: De Montfort University.

Rydin, Y. (2011) *The purpose of planning: creating sustainable towns and cities*. Bristol: Policy Press.

Thapar, M. and Rao, M. (2015) 'Managing city development for health in India: the case of Hyderabad city', in H. Barton, S. Thompson, S. Burgess, and M. Grant (eds) *The Routledge handbook of planning for health and well-being*. London: Routledge.

Thompson, S. (ed.) (2007) *Planning Australia: an overview of urban and regional planning*. Port Melbourne: Cambridge University Press.

Notes

1   Ward, C. (1973) *Anarchy in action* (London: Allen and Unwin), p. 28.
2   Harvey, D. (1973) *Social justice and the city* (London: Edward Arnold).
3   Hayek, F. von (1944) *The road to serfdom* (London: Routledge), as discussed in Allmendinger, P. (2009) *Planning theory* (London: Palgrave Macmillan), Chapter 5.
4   Turner, A., quoted by Kay, J. (2013) 'Circular thinking: models that offer universal descriptions of the world have led economists to repeat their mistakes', *Royal Society of Arts Journal*, 4. Kay quotes other eminent economists critical of orthodoxy, stressing the degree to which economists create simplified artificial worlds, 'more akin to Tolkien's Middle Earth, or a computer game like Grand Theft Auto'.
5   Allmendinger (2009), op. cit.
6   Ridley, M. (2010) *The rational optimist: how prosperity evolves* (New York: Harper & Row).
7   Norton, C. (2016) 'The significance of small plot, fine grain development and its potential as a tool in the sustainable regeneration of urban centres', PhD thesis, Bristol: University of the West of England.
8   See Cullingworth, B. and Caves, R. (2014) *Planning in the USA: policies, issues and processes,* fourth edn (London: Routledge).
9   See Nadin, V. and Stead, D. (2008) 'European spatial planning systems: social models and learning', *The Planning Review*, 44(172): 35–47.
10 See Cullingworth, B., Nadin, V., Hart, T., Davoudi, S., Pendlebury, J., Vigar, G., Webb, D. and Townsend, T. (2015) *Town and country planning in the UK* (London: Routledge).
11 Hall, P. (2014) *Good cities, better lives: how Europe discovered the lost art of urbanism* (London: Routledge).
12 PRP, URBED and Design for Homes (2008) *Beyond eco-towns: applying lessons from Europe* (London: PRP Architects Ltd).

CHAPTER SIXTEEN

THE PLANNING PROCESS AND THE ROLE OF PLANNERS

Overview

Chapter 15 stressed the importance of the *way* things happen, as well as *what* happens. Chapter 11 provided a 'reality check' on the process of urban change, demonstrating the sheer number of different interests involved. So how should planners plan? How should they work within a democratic, pluralist, capitalist society? Planners (in the broad sense used in this book) advise investors, politicians and communities what to do. How should they approach this task?

This is a vexed question that planning theorists have been arguing over for half a century. The chapter compares different ideas about what planning is (or should be) about. It follows a roughly sequential analysis. The main theories of planning may be typified, crudely, as the physical design approach, prevalent in the immediate post-war years; the rational comprehensive approach, in the 1960s and 1970s; the pragmatic, incremental style in the 1980s and 1990s; and the collaborative approach this century. These are set in the context of an understanding of the political, regulatory, technical and ethical dimensions of planning.

'Planning theory has become a rather academic subject – in the sense that it is discussed mainly by academics. We can learn much from each of the theories, no one of them has a monopoly of truth.'

Planning theory has become a rather academic subject – in the sense that it is discussed mainly by academics. Some might say is has also become academic in the other sense – that it is rather abstracted from reality. This has not always been the case, and what I try to do here is express the concepts in accessible ways that can be easily related to professional experience. The focus is on some of the key thinkers and practitioners who have pushed things forward. We can learn much from each of the theories and the critiques of them. In my view, no one of them has a monopoly of truth, but each contributes to our understanding of the nature of planning.

Dimensions of planning: technical, political and executive

At the outset, we consider the range of activities that planners are involved in. This helps to locate the different theories. Figure 16.1 defines three interlocking aspects: the technical, executive and political roles of planning. Given that planners are professional advisors, each of these aspects must be approached through the clear lens of professional ethics.

The technical dimension is about what are the best means of achieving given ends – understanding the nature and causes of problems that exist and the efficacy of possible courses of action. It is concerned with the substance of the plan or design. So, for example, if the perceived issue is congestion on the roads, how serious is it?, where is it serious?, how does it relate to other issues such as parking, public transport and active travel?, what are the possible avenues to tackle it and what might be the impacts on people and business?

The political dimension is about who makes decisions, and how to make them, and is therefore about power and influence. Elected representatives and key investors, as we have noted, hold many of the strings of power. But the wider politics of the situation may be complex, with residents groups at loggerheads with the local authority, neighbouring authorities competing rather than co-operating, landowners manipulating while trying to appear reasonable, key agencies not playing ball, officials and elected representatives with pet foibles, and so on! The problems of achieving co-ordination in a pluralistic society can be formidable.

The executive dimension is about how to get things done. It includes the administrative procedures and means of implementing agreed proposals or plans. A municipal planner preparing a plan has to fulfil certain statutory requirements. A consultant making a planning application for a client has to satisfy the legal niceties and the official design rules. An urban regeneration agency has to establish the mechanisms by which regeneration can happen. These procedures will strongly influence the outcome, but are not themselves primarily about content. They are the enabling framework – or maybe the frustrating framework – for development decisions.

These three processes – the technical, the political and the executive – are in practice of course entwined. They are concerned, however, with distinct questions: what are likely to be the 'best' answers to social, economic and environmental problems? Who should be involved in making decisions and how best to involve them? How can those decisions be effectively implemented? Professional ethics implies being well-informed, honest and skilled in answering these questions.

Fig 16.1 *Three dimensions of planning*

'What are likely to be the "best" answers to social, economic and environmental problems? Who should be involved in making decisions and how can those decisions be effectively implemented?'

From design to the rational planning process

The dominant view of town planners in the 1950s and early 1960s was of planning as town and civic design, a technical exercise applying experience and creativity to development problems. Post-war planners in Europe were charged with mammoth reconstruction, the creation of new settlements and planning for the motor car – highly influenced by the assumptions of Modernism. As noted earlier, this design emphasis was heavily criticized by some for its physical determinism, social blindness, and design uniformity (see Chapter 4).

During the 1960s there was a seismic shift in planning thought. There were two elements to this: a change to the way in which the urban environment was conceived, and a move towards an explicitly rational way of making planning decisions. The new perspective on the nature of the environment came to be called the *systems approach*. Whereas the early post-war planners, following the architectural and engineering traditions, saw plans as pictures, or blueprints – providing an intended end-state pattern of land uses, networks and layouts – the systems approach viewed plans as staging points in city evolution, based on an understanding of economic processes and human behaviour. The groundwork for this approach had been laid earlier in the century in fields of urban geography, land economics and urban ecology. The new insights were expressed in the seminal book *Urban Land Use Planning* by Stuart Chapin (1957 and 1965):[1]

> Land use is concerned with human activity in a very broad sense. It is concerned with the living pattern of households, productive patterns of industries, selling patterns of retail and personal service establishments, and the many other classes of activity that exist and interact as elements in the urban social system.[2]

The view of human settlements as 'systems' rather than designs was further articulated by Brian McLoughlin in 1969, whose book *Urban and Regional Planning: A Systems Approach*[3] became the new bible of British planners. He highlighted the significance of operational research and growing computing power in allowing (requiring) town planning to come of age – i.e. become more scientific. He distinguished four aspects of an urban system:

- spaces – buildings, open spaces, i.e. physical provision on the ground;
- channels – roads, railways, sewers, etc.;
- activities – living, working, shopping, learning, playing;
- communications – movement of people, and telecommunications.

He saw the interaction of these over time as the stuff of planning. Activities and communications represent *demand;* spaces and channels represent *supply*. The task of the planner is to try to match supply and demand in the context of the competitive market, taking the comprehensive overview, while households and firms seek to satisfy their own needs. In the Settlement Health Map, activities and communications are represented by sphere 5; spaces and channels by sphere 6.

Along with this more integrated view of human settlements went new awareness of the way in which decisions should be made. In a previous generation Patrick Geddes had made great play of the need to understand a town properly, to undertake surveys of places, routes and people, then analyse the results, before making a plan. He had not always been heeded, even by himself! But the principle of *survey-analysis-plan* was embedded in planning culture.

McLoughin took this principle a stage further. He stressed the need for *rationality* – rather than the normal reliance on trained intuition (at best) or knee-jerk instinct (at worst). Rationality, he said, involved first knowing (and agreeing with politicians/clients) what you are trying to achieve; then generating alternative possible courses of action and testing their relative proficiency. Having decided on the best way forward and put it into action, subsequent monitoring and review would assess the degree to which the decisions achieved the specified objectives, and the objectives themselves remained valid. The cyclic process is summarized in Figure 16.2.

What was (more-or-less) new in this process was the expectation that planning should be rational in respect of *ends* as well as *means*, and that the process was cyclic. McLoughin emphasized that we are dealing with a probabilistic system in which change cannot be foreseen with certainty. So the planning goals and mechanisms should be capable of frequent fine tuning and occasional comprehensive re-assessment. The blueprint plans of the design era, with their relative spatial inflexibility, could not cope with complex reality, and planning should move towards more reliance on policy statements.

Heroic versus humdrum planning

The central ideas of the systems approach and the rational process are, in principle, straightforward. But, as advocated by key thinkers such as McLoughin and particularly Chadwick,[4] they were elaborated in technically complex ways. They relied on extensive data gathering and sophisticated analytical tools to try to tease out the optimum and robust solutions. Andreas Faludi, writing about planning theories in 1972, called the approach *rational comprehensive*.[5] Practice followed theory with remarkable alacrity. Already transport planners in the USA had led the way, developing mathematical computer models to plan road networks. Broader models that integrated land use with transport then became an essential tool of systems planning (see Chapter 14). As computing power increased, they grew in sophistication, attempting 'total urban modelling'.

The problem with such techniques was that they relied on whole sets of prior assumptions for their inputs and internal equations, which then were difficult to get to grips with. They became black box 'expert' processes, difficult for amateurs to challenge. They were expensive and time-consuming, hungry for information, sucking the energy and creativity of the operators away from more immediate issues. In terms of Figure 16.1, the *technical* aspects dominated planning thought. Sometimes impressive plans were drawn up at great expense, only to discover they were too late – they had been overtaken by events. So ironically, the very techniques which were designed to facilitate both rational decision-making and an integrated understanding of the urban environment, undermined the credibility of the planning process. Rational comprehensive planning was too heroic by half.

'McLoughin stressed the need for rationality – rather than the normal reliance on trained intuition (at best) or knee-jerk instinct (at worst).'

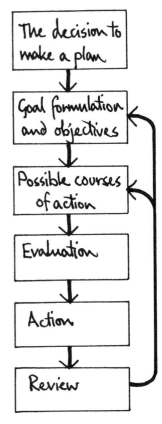

Fig 16.2 *The rational process of planning*

Source: Based on McLoughin 1969 (note 3), p.102.

'Ironically, the very techniques which were designed to facilitate both rational decision-making and an integrated understanding of the urban environment, undermined the credibility of the planning process.'

It is easy, though, to exaggerate the dangers of the scientific approach. Many studies developed systematic and logical analytical techniques that were not reliant on very complex mathematical models. Nevertheless there was (and is) often a gulf between the careful technical studies and messy reality. Even as the rational comprehensive approach was gaining ground, a counter-argument was being made which challenged its basic premises. This argument was concerned with the *effectiveness* of planning. In brief, planning might be more effective if heroics were put to one side, and a much more pragmatic, humdrum stance was taken.

Charles Lindblom wrote a fascinating article in 1959 entitled 'The science of "muddling through"'.[6] In it, he argued that where complex problems (such as planning a town) were concerned, the very attempt at rationality was counterproductive because of practical limits on time, information, human capabilities and the urgency of decisions. He observed that the actual process of decision-making was altogether different from the rational model. Administrators in public or private agencies were not free agents, able to comprehend all the relevant factors and options. In practice, they were constrained by financial, legal and political factors and had prescribed functions to fulfil. They had to survive in an uncertain world, and sometimes take far-reaching decisions with totally inadequate knowledge.

In this situation, Lindblom argued, it was better to make a virtue of necessity. Instead of the heroics of a rational comprehensive approach, destined to fail, he advocated a more humdrum, incremental, pragmatic approach searching for answers, on a step-by-step basis: accept the messy reality, don't strive for agreed values (people and politicians will always disagree) but work to achieve satisfactory decisions that most people can live with.

Later incrementalists took the theory further. John Friedman highlighted the problem of implementation. He chastised the rational planners as being concerned with making good decisions without understanding the difficulties of implementation: 'the problem is no longer how to make decisions more rational, but how to improve the quality of *action*'. Friedman argued that a policy and its implementation needed to be considered together, so that the policy was realistic, and the action was policy-driven. He saw that this required a new set of skills from planners: working constructively with diverse interests, negotiating for effective action despite conflicts, compromising without sacrificing essential qualities.[7]

Other commentators picked up the theme of implementation, and observed that far from being in control of development, planning authorities – lacking investment power – were actually at the mercy of the market, waiting for developers to come forward with proposals.[8] Plans often seemed to be a matter of giving sensible form to what the market would have done anyway. Sue Barrett and Colin Fudge (1981)[9] articulated what they called the *policy/action gap,* whereby grand plans were devised using all the best technical methods but then were never implemented because the planners had not sufficiently engaged with the market and political processes. They emphasized the centrality of the negotiation process between the many "actors" in the play of land use decision-making.

Planners in this situation, they suggested, need to be flexible in their approach, solving problems, tackling impediments, alert to opportunities, building support from other actors, seizing the initiative when possible.

There are real attractions with this image of planning. Planners become 'entrepreneurial', pragmatic and politically astute operators within the system. In relation to Figure 16.1, entrepreneurial planners focus on the *executive* field, while being very aware of the *political*. But there are endemic difficulties. The temptation is to go with the flow, bowing to pressures from powerful people – councillors, developers – risking the sacrifice of the general public interest. Unless the professionals have a very clear and well-evidenced ethical stance, and considerable negotiating and strategizing skills, humdrum planning can be a recipe for lowest common denominator outcomes – leading to an inequitable and often unattractive human environment.

'Planners need to be flexible in their approach, solving problems, tackling impediments, alert to opportunities, building support from other actors, seizing the initiative when possible.'

Mixed scanning and pragmatic rationality

McLoughlin himself was aware of both the strengths and weaknesses of his systematic model. When managing the Leicester and Leicestershire Sub-regional study in the 1970s, the impracticality of the ideal rational process became apparent – politics is more about gut reactions than rationalism – and he adjusted the process accordingly. His pragmatic rationalism ensured the success of the exercise, and the study was held up as exemplary.[10]

Other theorists were not deaf to the tensions described above, and tried to articulate a middle way. One of these was the *mixed scanning* process proposed by Amitai Etzioni (1967).[11] In this theory there is a broad (but shallow) scanning of the whole environment, so that the main issues and interactions are accurately identified, followed by narrow (but deep) examination of priority areas/questions, as determined by necessity or pressure from key actors. Friend and Jessop (1969)[12] developed refined techniques for the middle way. They studied the reality of local authority decision-making over four years in Coventry, England, adopting an operational research viewpoint. In the light of that they devised the *Strategic Choice* approach to planning, which was designed to apply logical thinking to the messy, complex situations that planners faced. Good decision-making by officials and elected representatives, they observed, is hampered by uncertainty: the uncertainty of market and community demands, the unpredictability of societal and environmental change, the uncertainty of resource availability, the uncertainty of what other agencies will do (Figure 16.3).

It is vital, they argued, for planners to understand their room for manoeuvre – to recognize the limits of power or influence in any given situation. There is tension between the need for *commitment* (making a clear decision) and the need for *flexibility* (keeping options open in an uncertain world). Plans need to be devised so that they are capable of adapting to changing circumstances. The Strategic Choice theorists went on to devise tools to cope with the multi-agency nature of government, so that different agencies with their

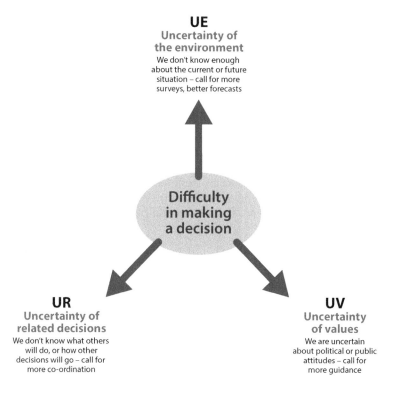

UE
**Uncertainty of
the environment**
We don't know enough
about the current or future
situation – call for more
surveys, better forecasts

**Difficulty
in making
a decision**

UR
**Uncertainty of
related decisions**
We don't know what others
will do, or how other
decisions will go – call for
more co-ordination

UV
**Uncertainty
of values**
We are uncertain
about political or public
attitudes – call for
more guidance

Fig 16.3 Three aspects of
uncertainty

*Source: Based on Friend and
Jessop 1969 (note 12), p.95.*

own remits can see clearly how their responsibilities interact with others. Some of these tools will be introduced in Chapter 17.

The more general point to make here is that the purely *technical* version of rational planning cannot survive in a pluralistic and unpredictable world. There is a need for a good dose of pragmatism, and the active involvement of influential players, if things are to happen.

The medium is the message: collaborative planning

A key principle of implementation theory is that all the groups with a stake in a decision need to be involved in that decision. That belief underpins the theories of collaborative planning developed in the 1990s. The basic contention is that planners are not in a position to determine the future of towns and cities, but they are in a position to *facilitate debate* about that future between competing interests in society. So their job is to make that debate as effective and as fair as possible. As Patsy Healey says in her book, *Collaborative Planning*, the planner is 'some kind of knowledge mediator and broker', a critical friend and enabler of co-operative decision-making.[13]

This definition of the planner's role sidesteps the questions of 'why plan?' or 'what are the spatial priorities?' Goals will be defined by stakeholders. The professional planner simply seeks to ensure that all the stakeholders are heard, are well informed, and together reach conclusions that work towards the agreed goals.

Part of the inspiration for the collaborative approach is from the concept of 'ideal speech' developed by Habermas (1984).[14] He argues that in a democratic society we should be striving for consensus based on full participation and equality between participants (free from power-play). Authority would not be vested in dominant organizations, but in the quality of argument. Ideal speech can realize what he calls communicative rationality. The essence of the collaborative approach is that all views are given space, each is respected as valid. Take the example of an urban development site: the house-builder wants profit, the local activists want greenspace, the local council wants affordable housing. The planner's job is to facilitate fair discussion. Healey talks about building 'relational bonds' between participants. As mutual understanding grows, the possibility increases of shared learning, breaking new ground, identifying possible courses of action that could solve the tensions. New ideas can then be taken forward and tested by the planning and design professionals in the group. A good decision is one that recognizes the interests of all with a stake in it.

'In a democratic society we should be striving for consensus based on full participation and equality between participants (free from power-play).'

In this situation the planner has a clear, normative role:

- to reach out to all stakeholders and try to draw them into discussion, ensuring that under-represented groups are assisted;
- to increase institutional and community capacities to participate effectively;
- to articulate policy/development choices and their implications clearly so that everyone can engage with the debate;
- to take forward and develop ideas/proposals that emerge from debate and try to make them work;
- to help forge alliances and reach sensible decisions with clear pathways of implementation.

The collaborative approach thus majors on the *political* facet of planning. It breaks down the distinction between ends and means. It suggests that what matters in a democratic society is how decisions are taken, rather than exactly what the decision is. If everyone has a good opportunity to put their case, then all relevant perspectives can be recognized in the plan.

Ends and means

The aspirations of collaborative planning are admirable, but just as in the case of rational planning, critics point to its utopian and unrealistic assumptions. The concept of *ideal speech*, which underpins collaborative planning, is not achievable. In reality there are huge inequalities. Susan Fainstein, in her book *The Just City* (2010),[15] challenges the assumption that open participation will of itself lead to better decisions. This is because the participants are far from equal in their propensity to get involved and their ability to put their case. Powerful vested interests, such as private and public sector landowners, house-builders, economic development agencies, etc., will ensure their message gets across, and seek to negotiate from strength. Articulate residents groups will promote their own, often defensive, interests. Difficult issues, lacking champions, are likely to be ducked. So the result of the collaborative approach will often simply support the dominant partners, not the whole community.

Fainstein goes further. She argues, 'Recent theory in both political philosophy and planning overly idealizes open communication and neglects the substance of debate.'[16] The real problems which people experience in the human environment – problems of unjust distribution of key resources such as housing; unjust exposure to environmental pollution; unjust climate impositions on succeeding generations – can be sidelined all too easily. If planners focus primarily on the *manner* of decision-taking not the *matter*, then the implication is that they are abrogating their responsibility. She advocates an explicitly normative stance, based on the principle of social justice. Planners should see their job as trying to foster a more equal and inclusive environment, not simply a more equal and inclusive process. Unless the planners themselves have ethical standards and knowledge of what makes a good environment for all, and articulate their position with conviction, sub-standard environments will be the norm.

'If planners focus primarily on the manner of decision-taking not the matter, then the implication is that they are abrogating their responsibility.'

Testing theory against practice

Much of the discussion above – and the texts it is based on – has remained at the level of theory. The question arises, how do the theories relate to practice? Working back through the main theories, it is clear that the collaborative approach has much to offer. Most planning systems in the developed world place obligations on public sector planners to involve interested parties in a two-way participatory process. Community engagement is in principle embedded in the system, and there is an obligation to try to reach non-participant sections of the population. Increasingly there is also a requirement for investors to show they have consulted widely before putting in their proposals. So collaborative planning principles are very relevant.

However, Fainstein's critique rings true. Collaborative workshops can be frustrating affairs. The planners may work hard to get all stakeholders. Speaking from personal experience, there can be general agreement on the need for a healthy urban environment. But some key interests (such as landowners or transport providers) may not consider it is worth their while to engage. Yet they hold many of the cards. Without them, discussion is hypothetical. At the same time, while the views of existing residents are well represented (normally anti-development), the interests of future residents are not. The emerging masterplans fail to deliver agreed social and environmental goals. Such collaborative processes only 'work' when the powerful bodies want them to.[17]

In many situations the pragmatic approach of the implementation theorists represents the reality. Land and development agencies are the drivers of change. Decisions are taken incrementally by the many different public, private and voluntary sector agencies, each with their own remit, seizing opportunities, reacting to each other and to wider economic and political dynamics. At worst, this means that the local authority planners fall back on legal and administrative processes, reacting to events as they occur, just trying to mitigate the worst impacts of a sporadic process. At best, it means an entrepreneurial approach, building public/private partnerships, seeking pathways through the morass of regulation and finance to achieve a client's or municipality's objectives.

Having said that, the rational approach remains the standard against which practice is judged. Rationality, or at least the appearance of rationality, is obligatory when defending plans and development decisions. Plan preparation in the EU, for example, has to include Strategic Environmental Assessment (SEA), which involves examination of goals, evidence and options, and the rationale for the chosen strategy. Major infrastructure and development projects are subject to the equivalent process of Environmental Impact Assessment (EIA). In practice, SEA and EIA may fail to live up to their billing, but rationality still provides the scale against which they are measured. In Britain, the current requirement for all plans to be 'sound', means based on evidence and logic, not political prejudice or vested interest.

Systems theory – often falsely elided in discussion with the rational process – is concerned primarily with substance not process. Professional debate on policy has been profoundly affected by systems thinking, which encourages the proper recognition of complex interactions between spatial elements, activities and people. It has acted as a corrective to an atomized view of urban development. The mathematical models derived from systems thinking – analysing land use transport interactions and retail investment strategies, for example – are in regular use. Population and housing forecasts, ecological and climate studies, rely on systems thinking. Such models profoundly affect the process of planning, orientating professional work. Despite improvements, models often suffer from 'black box syndrome', where underlying assumptions are hidden from view, but the idea of systems – ecological, social, economic and spatial – underpins modern planning.

The design theories of the mid-twentieth century were prescriptive rather than analytical, and are often sidelined by planning theorists. However, key texts by Gibberd, Lynch, Cullen, Buchanan, Jacobs and others provide a platform of knowledge and controversy which has influenced practice ever since. Since the 1990s, design theories have been enlivened by the sustainability agenda. The concepts of compact cities, safe cities, 'smart growth', new urbanism, eco-villages and sustainable communities have influenced practice hugely – to the extent that policy discourse is shaped by them.

It is evident that none of the planning theories, whether concerned with process or substance, is an adequate base by itself for planning practice. Each reflects a different facet of planning, and has influenced current practice to a significant degree. Contemporary planners, designers and facilitators can pick up what they need from the theory menu. No one theory should claim the monopoly of wisdom.

'The rational approach remains the standard against which practice is judged. Rationality, or at least the appearance of rationality, is obligatory when defending plans and development decisions.'

Ethical planning

Figure 16.4 elaborates on Figure 16.1, recognizing that all the main theories of planning have their place. Each also has a distinctive ethical stance that has merit. The political dimension, informed by collaborative planning theories, requires planners to be enablers of a democratic process of consensus-building between all the interested parties, able to value the contribution of each, engaging with communities while working with key players. The question is 'how to facilitate open discussion and fair decisions?' The executive dimension, informed by incremental theories, requires pragmatic operators of the system, managing legal and administrative processes effectively. The ideal is that of the implementer, the entrepreneurial planner, seizing opportunities, using the systems to good effect. The question is 'how to get things done?'

The technical dimension is split into three. First, there is scientific knowledge and understanding of urban systems, people and policy. Parts III and IV of the book explore this huge area. Systems theory encourages an integrated, dynamic perspective. The questions are: how do settlements function? How are people's health and well-being affected? What can we learn from experience elsewhere? Second, there is the creative process of problem recognition,

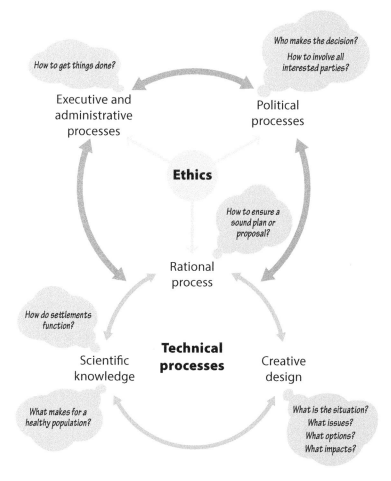

Fig 16.4 *Theories of the planning process in their place*

strategy-making and design, matters of skill and trained intuition. The questions are: what are the problems and their causes? How can they be solved? What spatial and design options are there? Can we devise better solutions? Then, third, there is the rational process, building on the principles of rational planning theory, trying to ensure, and demonstrate, that the aims of the plan are justified, and the plan likely to achieve the aims. The questions are: is the plan logical? Can we show it is sound?

The task of planning is to marry these various dimensions. The process of logically working through issues, options and evaluation has to recognize the practical means of delivery in the cultural and legal context, and match those processes with political, business and community engagement that can lead to good decisions. It would clearly be unethical to give credence to plans/decisions that are technically unsound, or have a democratic deficit, or have little chance of being implemented. The technical skills, the 'political' skills and the action skills are essential elements in the planners' armoury.

'It would clearly be unethical to give credence to plans/decisions that are technically unsound, or have a democratic deficit, or have little chance of being implemented.'

All is in vain if the good *ideas* are not there. They may come from any of the stakeholders, but seeing them clearly, developing and promoting them often depends on planners accepting a *leadership* role, not just enabling. Persuasive powers, negotiating skills and clarity about where to give ground and where to hold firm, are essential.

So too is clarity about values. Town planners (as opposed to planners in the broader sense) are charged with taking an overview of the future shape of settlements. No one else has that job. If good ideas are to win backing from diverse stakeholders, then some shared values are needed. As argued in earlier chapters, the ambition of *health for all* (or 'healthy urban environments' or 'health and well-being') could draw people together, help forge alliances, providing a common ethical platform as the launch pad for coherent plans, programmes and projects.

Unless planners accept a good measure of responsibility for pursuing the fundamentals of healthy, equitable, and climate-resilient cities, spelling out the significance of spatial decisions in unambiguous terms, even in the face of powerful forces, we will look back with shame on this age: 'fiddling while Rome burns'. Elaborate decision processes and pragmatic inventiveness are only worthwhile if devoted to noble ends, not mere expediency.

Further reading

Fainstein, S. (2010) *The just city*. Ithaca, NY: Cornell University Press.

Faludi, A. (ed.) (1973) *A reader in planning theory*. Oxford: Pergamon Press.

Healey, P. (2006) *Collaborative planning: shaping places in fragmented societies*, second edn. Basingstoke: Palgrave Macmillan.

Taylor, N. (1998) *Urban planning theory since 1945*. London: Sage.

Notes

1 Chapin, F. S. (1957 and 1965) *Urban land use planning* (Champaign-Urbana, IL: University of Illinois Press).

2 Ibid. (1965), p. 98.

3 McLoughlin, J.B. (1969) *Urban and regional planning: a systems approach* (London: Faber and Faber).

4 Chadwick, G. (1971) *A systems view of planning* (Oxford: Pergamon Press).

5 Faludi, A. (1972) *Planning theory* (Oxford: Pergamon Press).

6 Lindblom, C.E. (1959) 'The science of "muddling through"', *Public Administration Review*, pp. 79–88, reprinted in Faludi, A. (ed.) (1973) *A reader in planning theory* (Oxford: Pergamon Press).

7 Friedman, J. (1969) 'Notes on societal action', *Journal of the American Institute of Planners*, pp. 311–318, as quoted by Taylor, N. (1998) *Urban planning theory since 1945* (London: Sage), p. 117.

8 Pickvance, C. (1977) 'Physical planning and market forces in urban development', in Paris, C. (ed.) (1982) *Critical readings in planning theory* (Oxford: Pergamon Press).

9 Barrett, S. and Fudge, C. (1981) *Policy and action: essays on the implementation of public policy* (London: Methuen).

10 Allmendinger, P. (2009) *Planning theory* (London: Palgrave Macmillan), p. 77.

11 Etzioni, A. (1967) 'Mixed scanning: a third approach to decision-making', *Public Administration Review,* December, reprinted in Faludi (1973), op. cit., pp. 217–229.

12 Friend, J. and Jessop, W. (1969 and 1976) *Local government and strategic choice* (Oxford: Pergamon Press).

13 Healey, P. (2006) *Collaborative planning: shaping places in fragmented societies,* second edn (Basingstoke: Palgrave Macmillan), p. 309.

14 Habermas, J. (1984) *The theory of communicative action,* vol. 1: *Reason and rationalization of society* (London: Polity Press).

15 Fainstein, S. (2010) *The just city* (Ithaca, NY: Cornell University Press).

16 Ibid., p. 23.

17 This paragraph is based on extensive personal experience and conversations with activists, practising planners and academics.

CHAPTER SEVENTEEN

PUTTING PRINCIPLE INTO PRACTICE

If you don't decide which way to go, you'll end up going the way you were already heading.

Lao tsu

It is only the first bottle that is expensive.

French proverb

Introduction

Chapter 16 has given us a hard task: to marry the logical, systematic preparation of a plan with the active involvement of all the stakeholders, and achieve a plan that promotes the well-being of all. How can planners develop sound policies, work collaboratively, get things done?

The substance of a plan is in principle established by dispassionate analysis of problems, trends, options, impacts, feasibility, drawing on the views and information from stakeholders – an assessment of what the plan is trying to do, and how best to achieve it. The professional planner, though, is rarely in a position to finalize decisions. Most aspects of the plan are likely to be dependent on politicians, private investors and public departments (transport, housing, education, health, etc.) over which there is limited leverage. The politics of the situation may be complex, with local parishes or residents at loggerheads with the local authority, and neighbouring authorities competing rather than co-operating. Eventually the planner in the middle of all this is recommending courses of action to development interests or elected representatives who have their own preferences and prejudices. The whole plan is likely to be both Political (with a big P) and political in the much broader sense – about power and influence, who gains and who loses.

This chapter presents a coherent approach to policy-making. It starts by briefly outlining good practice in relation to inclusive and co-operative decision-making and the cyclic process of plan preparation. These principles are then illustrated with a case study of a relatively simple, small-area plan, leading to a review of the way in which health and sustainability goals can be effectively incorporated in the plan, especially through plan and project appraisal. The

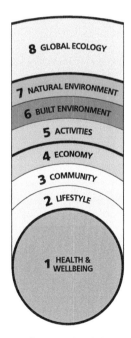

Fig 17.1 Focus on the whole agenda

chapter is only of course a short introduction to the issues, and any process has to be adapted to legal requirements. The principles are relevant whatever the official rules.

Community engagement: making decisions in a pluralist society

There are different levels of involvement in any planning process:

- *Partners* – who share the decision-making and accept responsibility for making things happen. They may be linked by formal contractual agreements. In a regeneration area, for example, key partners may be the regeneration agency, a housing provider and a major developer.
- *Participants* – who actively participate in the plan-making process (through a stakeholder forum, for example), but are not prime movers or final arbiters. Examples might be the chamber of commerce and the civic society. See Figure 17.2.
- *Consultees* – who are formally asked for their views about issues and solutions, but do not necessarily engage in collaborative forums. Normally this includes statutory consultees and all local residents, businesses and organizations.

While all need to have the opportunity to be involved at an appropriate level, *leadership* and clear decision-making are critical. The lead partner (such as a local authority, parish council, regeneration agency or developer consortium) has to instigate and co-ordinate in

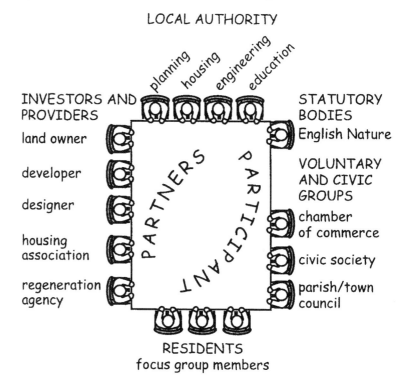

Fig 17.2 *A stakeholder forum: illustrative membership*

Source: Barton et al. *2010* (further reading), figure 2.5.

a timely, open and effective manner. The positive attitude, support and leadership qualities of the mayor or managing director (whether deeply involved or not) help determine the outcome. Planners and designers working for the lead partner(s) have the responsibility of providing information, concepts, policy options, and design inspiration to match the aspirations of the partners and the forum.

The WHO Healthy Cities (HC) network has very clear and helpful guidelines for municipalities that want to join, insisting on both *top down* and *bottom up* approaches.[1] The Mayor (or Chair) of the council has to sign the HC charter and be actively committed to the project. Political support at the outset, and throughout the process, is considered critically important. At the same time the authority needs to ensure that local communities have been consulted and are actively engaged, involved in a transparent process. Collaboration also has to occur between departments, breaking down traditional silos. This is critical when considering whether cities have built the capacity to achieve 'healthy urban planning'. Senior professionals in transport, housing, economic development, public health, recreation and greenspace have to be involved as well as in planning.

The involvement of stakeholders is part of a democratic approach, and assists the three dimensions of planning discussed in Chapter 16. Politically, it can help build constituencies of support for the plan; technically, it can provide vital information and evidence to improve the logic of the plan; from the executive perspective, it can be fundamental to implementation: the various departments and agencies feel part of the plan and are more liable to commit the funds to realize it. The benefits of collaboration are expressed by Figure 17.3.

'Political support at the outset, and throughout the process, is critically important. At the same time the authority needs to ensure that local communities are actively engaged in a transparent process.'

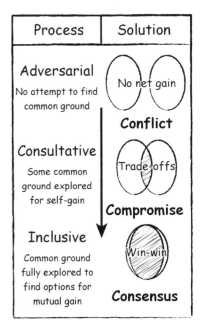

Process	Solution

Fig 17.3 *The benefits of working together*

Source: Barton et al. 2010 (further reading), figure 2.2.

Community engagement

Achieving community acceptance and 'buy in' to proposals for change is often problematic. So it is important to have a systematic strategy for community engagement that goes right through the planning and development process. Paternalistic attitudes are counterproductive. It can be tempting for investors and even local authorities to treat participatory obligations in tokenistic fashion (see Figure 17.4).[2] Instead residents and businesses need to be seen as equals, providing vital information (local knowledge, ideas, values) that can help shape the plan and increase its chance of improving health and well-being. The 'ladder of participation' illustrates the range of approaches possible, several of which may apply at the same time, depending on the stakeholders involved.

The question arises: who represents 'the community'? Given the diversity of interests there is no simple answer. Voluntary sector groups are important participants in the forum. However, they cannot necessarily be taken to represent everyone. Typically only 10 per cent of adults are 'joiners', and voluntary groups often have small, self-perpetuating committees. They can gain greater credibility by reaching out to a large membership. Elected representatives have a broader remit, but often quite idiosyncratic views. The partners in settlement planning – policy-makers and investors – may be tempted to accept the views of the active associations and councillors as

Rungs of the ladder

	Neighbourhood-level characteristics	Attitude of the local authority	Comments
7. Autonomous powers	An elected neighbourhood council with substantial powers, legally and financially independent of local authorities.	Confrontational	The ideal of social anarchism, requiring new legislation. Reality might fall short of the ideal, and be prone to NIMBYism.
6. Delegated powers	Community Development Trust or parish/town council with substantial responsibilities delegated by the local authority.	Collaborative	Achievable without legislation; gives some sense of local control; can be innovative and radical.
5. Partnership	Neighbourhood Forum or regeneration agency with power-sharing between local authority, business and citizens' groups.	Collaborative	Widely practiced; relies on shared ownership, effective leadership, co-operative skills and capacity building in the community.
4. Genuine consultation	Public meetings, stakeholder groups, web votes, focus groups, planning for real, etc. A real attempt to encourage local debate and respond to it.	Enabling	Widely practiced. Positive attitudes, openness and community engagement skills on the part of the authority are vital.
3. Two-way information	Good quality information from authority to citizens and from citizens to authority via community newspapers, social surveys, etc.	Technical	Not adequate in itself, but a vital part of an inclusive strategy, reaching the non-joiners.
2. Tokenism	Consultation too little, too late, going through the motions.	Manipulative	All too common, after all the major decisions have been taken – especially by development companies.
1. Spin	Decisions made and publicized, but no consultation considered necessary.	Autocratic	Quite normal in major urban investment areas such as energy, water, education, health, even local authority housing.

Fig 17.4 *A revised ladder of citizen participation*

Source: Detailed in note 2.

proxies for the wider population. This makes for a good and easy start. But many community interests may be inadequately represented. The professionals should therefore, where possible, reach out to the wider resident and business population, for example by undertaking social surveys.

Communication across political, professional and community divides is not straightforward (Figure 17.5). Words can get in the way of shared understanding. Every profession devises its own language, its distinctive jargon and logic, which may alienate or confuse other people. Finding the common touch, the common word, to express often complex ideas, needs careful cultivation.

Fig 17.5 Communication, or not!
Source: Courtesy of Rob Cowan –
www.plandemonium.org.uk

A cyclical planning process

The process of producing and realizing a plan falls into a well-established cycle, based on the idea of the rational process discussed in the last chapter. Stakeholders are involved at every stage. So too is the collection of evidence. Figure 17.6 is a summary of each stage.

Taking the initiative

Many plans are produced because there is legislative obligation to do so. Other plans may be responding to particular development opportunities or political concerns. The decision by a local authority, agency

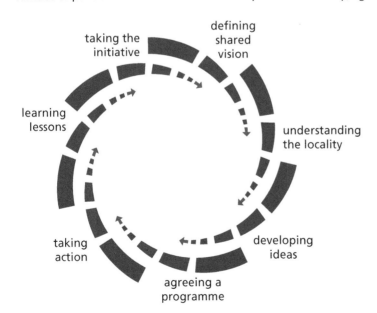

Fig 17.6 The seven-stage cyclical process of plan-making

Source: Barton et al. (2010), Figure 2.1.

or master-developer to make/review a plan requires consideration of the context and informal soundings with key interests. Early and open consultation can result in greater awareness of the issues and opportunities, leading to the plan being better angled to the situation. This initial scoping exercise should aim to answer the questions:

- What is the purpose and scope of the plan?
- What area should it cover?
- Is it potentially in line with broader goals and strategies?
- What stakeholders should be invited as partners or participants?
- Has the initiating agency the capacity to carry it through?

Defining a shared vision

'A vision presupposes a clear view of what the current situation is, what issues need addressing, and what the potential of the plan could be.'

Once partners and participants are on board, the 'vision' gives a sense of direction to the plan, and helps motivate partners, politicians and public to 'buy into' the plan. A vision presupposes a clear view of what the current situation is, what issues need addressing, and what the potential of the plan could be. Figure 17.7 gives an insight into defining scope. The vision should be informed by analysis of available sources of data (e.g. population census, traffic surveys, flood risk data) and public/stakeholder views. The lead organization has the responsibility to ensure that the vision is both realistic and inspiring, and puts health and well-being centre-stage. It might consist of broad aspirations (aims or goals) and more specific criteria of achievement (or objectives). The resulting *project brief* should set out:

- the scope of the exercise;
- the area, its characteristics and the policy context;
- the broad vision for the area;
- more specific objectives or criteria for the plan (to be refined later);
- the partners, and other stakeholders involved;
- the process of community engagement, policy-making and appraisal;
- the way the project will be managed (by whom? what oversight?).

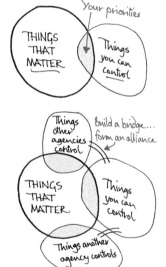

Fig 17.7 Defining the scope of a plan

Understanding the locality

This is something that continues throughout plan-making. But the biggest effort needs to come early, and is used to define the *baseline* situation against which progress can be measured, gaining a proper understanding of the nature of *problems and opportunities* that exist before fixing on policy choices. The temptation is to study just those aspects that directly impinge on the subject of the plan or project. But in line with the mixed scanning approach (Chapter 16), it is important to open eyes to all that is relevant. The Settlement Health Map gives a full possible agenda of study:

- people, their diversity of needs and concerns, health and well-being;

- behaviour, levels of physical activity and inhibiting factors, lifestyles;
- community activity, cohesion, levels of social support and capital;
- economic activity, market conditions, growth problems and potentials;
- activities and movement, current use of space, traffic volumes, services, footfall, issues arising;
- the built environment, the quality of buildings, renewal processes, route networks use and adequacy for different modes, quality/use of urban and greenspaces;
- the local natural environment, landscape, air quality, water systems, wildlife habitats;
- global impacts, climate emissions, settlement resilience.

It is not possible to know it all, nor is it appropriate. The judgement is about what is helpful, and where extra, in-depth information is necessary to formulate or assess the proposals. The vision and objectives, together with public and political concern, help to focus attention where it matters. The professionals involved then have the responsibility to investigate specific problems and opportunities further – the 'known unknowns' that will affect policy or design.

Developing ideas

Plan-making is not a linear process. Before the decision to make a new plan, there were no doubt established policies, inherited proposals and expectations, and specific ideas from influential bodies, which required to be followed up. 'Developing ideas' means exploring these and other possible courses of action. Increasing knowledge, derived from context analysis, physical and social surveys, and stakeholders, allows more precision in the development of options. Simple tools can assist analysis. Let us assume there is a specific problem (say, of poor bus services). Figure 17.8 suggests questions that should be asked. Figure 17.9 is a *decision graph* showing how the issue of bus policy is related to other transport decisions. Figure 17.10 then takes

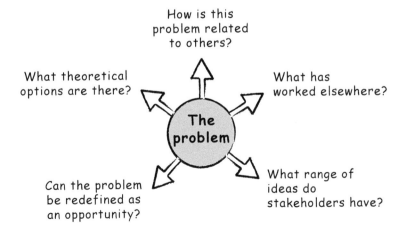

How is this problem related to others?

What theoretical options are there?

What has worked elsewhere?

The problem

Can the problem be redefined as an opportunity?

What range of ideas do stakeholders have?

Fig 17.8 *Searching for a solution*
Source: Barton et al. *2010 (further reading), figure 2.10.*

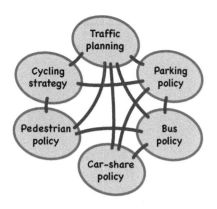

Fig 17.9 *The interdependence of decision areas*

two related decision areas and uses a *compatibility chart* to evaluate how options in each are likely to impact on each other – relying on evidence from studies elsewhere. It becomes apparent that some parking policies undermine good bus services while others reinforce them. While the whole issue is of course much more complex, this sequence illustrates an approach to analysis. It is useful when a number of different agencies are involved – each can relate to a particular decision area and see the relationship with others.[3]

There are systematic ways of working through spatial plan-making in order to ensure that environmental and health aims are central. The *twin-track* model of urban form (see Chapter 12) highlights the two tracks of the greenspace/water system and the public transport network. One enables the ecology of the settlement to work effectively. The other provides the focus for diurnal human activity. The morphology of the settlement is defined by the pedestrian accessibility to local high streets and the bus/tram spine on the one hand, and access to greenspace on the other. This process illustrated in Figure 17.11 is relevant for both regeneration areas and new urban extensions.

Simple tools and processes are useful in the political domain. Often there will be potential conflict between political, commercial and community interests. It is vital to grapple with these, and to express them in open debate between stakeholders so that all parties can recognize the issues. The planners and designers have the opportunity to be creative, learning from experience elsewhere, searching for solutions to intractable problems. Health and wellbeing are at stake. It is a matter of finding good answers and persuasive arguments.

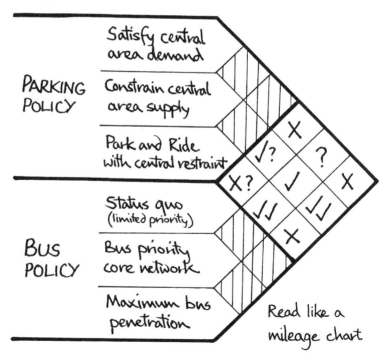

Fig 17.10 *A compatibility chart of policy options*

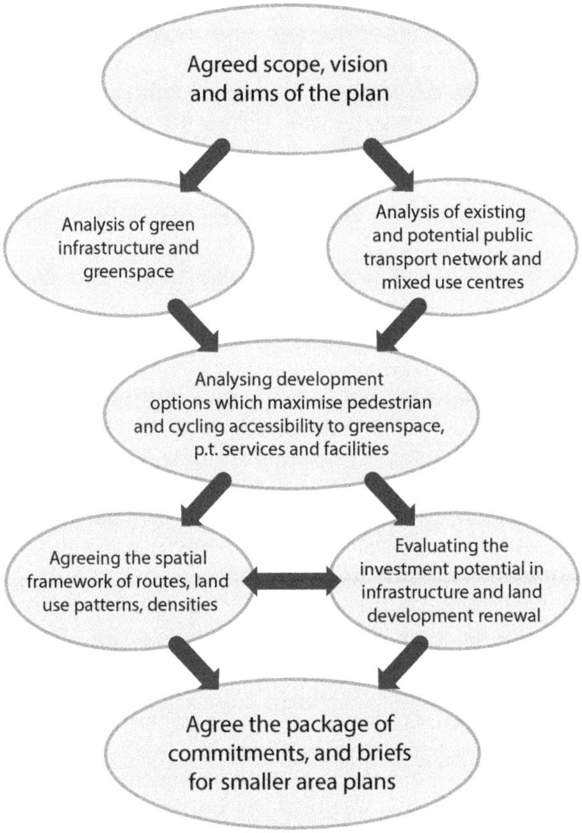

Fig 17.11 *The twin-track approach to spatial strategy*

Agreeing a plan or proposal

Official plans come in a variety of forms, according to context. The degree to which they consist of policies, spatially specific allocations or urban design schemes depends on their scale and purpose. Below are different types of policy intervention:

- Policies: normally intended to guide development management decisions; can apply to the whole of a plan area or a part.
- Commitments: tasks or projects which the planning agency or other body undertakes to fulfil or promote.
- Quotas: amounts of population, housing, employment or other variables allocated to particular sub-regions, settlements or zones.
- Zoning map: areas defined for specific land uses: residential, commercial, mixed use, greenspace, education, main routes, etc.
- Spatial framework: guidelines for development in an area of change identifying route networks, special zones, projects.
- Design code: set of principles for the design and layout of streets, buildings and spaces, often linked to a spatial framework.

- Masterplan: a schematic layout for a development area, often with a three-dimensional element, providing the context for detailed design.
- Development or design brief: specification for what should happen on a particular site – may be very simple or very detailed.
- Detailed layout: precise measured plan of streets, buildings and spaces on a site, required for a full planning application.

The plan or project planners need to choose the best combination of forms for a given situation. At a point when the options have been honed sufficiently they need formal evaluation. Large-scale projects, such as tram systems, power stations, major renewal schemes or urban extensions, normally require *Environmental Impact Assessments* (EIA). Other projects sometimes require simpler forms of environmental or sustainability assessment. In Europe, most plans, policies and programmes need to have a *Strategic Environmental Assessment* (SEA); in the UK, SEA has been incorporated in a wider *Sustainability Appraisal,* which includes social and economic as well as environmental criteria. *Health Impact Analysis* is occasionally used, but is not a statutory form. The trefoil sustainability model shown in Figure 17.12 offers a 'quick and dirty' test for specific proposals.

As discussed later, appraisal is not intended as end-point evaluation, but a means of improving the plan or project. Public and political engagement at this stage can also trigger changes. The comparison between options will require extra information and further refinement of the favoured plan or scheme. Eventually a clear recommendation can be put to the politicians or investors who make the decision.

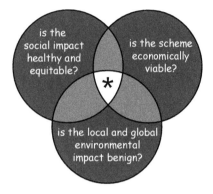

Fig 17.12 *The trefoil test of healthy development. All three criteria need to be fulfilled.*

Source: Barton et al. *2010 (further reading), figure 2.11.*

Taking action

A plan has been called a *commitment package*. It is a mechanism for gaining the commitment of all the partners, and the support of participants. The roles and tasks of different agencies should be specific, with each agency agreeing its own programme as part of the overall scheme. A conventional land use plan relies primarily on investors (public and private sector, large and small) coming forward with projects, applying for planning permission and subject to development management decisions.

Given the incremental nature of implementation, it is important to identify some 'early wins', where action can be taken and help to boost the credibility of the plan. Gaining early momentum can help protect the plan against derailment by events. The planning authority can try to trigger development proposals by preparing development briefs for particular sites. Public ownership of land can be put to good use, with exemplary projects that demonstrate confidence and give a sense of direction. Effectiveness depends on:

'Given the incremental nature of implementation, it is important to identify some "early wins", where action can be taken and help to boost the credibility of the plan.'

- long-term consistency of vision, strategy and tactics;
- a proactive and joined-up approach from the planning authority and other public agencies;

- the ability to seize opportunities, such as transport investments or land ownership changes, and to solve problems as they arise;
- a continuing open and collaborative approach, contributing to a sense of shared ownership of the plan, including among councilors and major investors.

Learning lessons

Planning policies are often pursued for decades without checking on their effectiveness and continued relevance. As the plan is implemented, it is vital to keep tabs on its progress: what has actually happened on the ground, and is it in line with the plan's intentions? Monitoring the plan and its context is more active than the word implies. There are several monitoring pathways, all of them useful: the observation and thoughts of actors (elected representatives, officials, investors, professional advisors); public, civil society and business representations; media debate; data collection and analysis. We will concentrate on the last of these.

The essential questions that monitoring should seek to answer are threefold:

- Is the policy or design being implemented? If not, why not?
- Is it resulting in the changes that were hoped for, or are there unintended consequences?
- Are the objectives of the policy or design still valid, or has the situation changed?

At the scale of a town or city trends in health, social inclusion, perceived well-being, environmental conditions, economic development, employment, population and housing, the availability of services and transport facilities are all critical. They can be monitored and recorded annually in a 'State of the city', 'Quality of life' or 'Health and Sustainability' report, which can then act as a stimulus to further action. Primary indicators are direct measures of health and well-being, for example 'years of healthy life'. Secondary indicators are measures of environmental conditions, such as air pollution levels, and of behaviour, for example the amount of active recreation. Tertiary indicators are measures of the urban environment, such as the extent of cycleways. Ideally there are a few 'headline indicators' that have intuitive public and political significance. Seattle, in Washington, is famous for introducing an intuitive measure of air pollution: 'can you see the mountain?' The Kuopio technique (Chapter 5) of identifying the three urban fabrics – pedestrian, transit and car – is a tertiary indicator, and a graphic way of integrating a number of key variables: the quality of the pedestrian environment and of public transport services, the level of accessibility afforded, the inclusiveness of the transport system, and by implication (not directly) potential levels of active travel and carbon emissions (see later discussion and Figure 17.19).

At some point (five years is typical) the plan or major aspects of it will need review and up-dating. But meanwhile the emerging issues can be anticipated by careful, collaborative alertness.

Case study: Stroud town centre Neighbourhood Plan[4]

'Stroud is a market town set in the Cotswold Hills, in Gloucestershire, England. Its economy was originally based on woollen mills and water power; now on engineering and services, with growing IT and cultural activities.'

The purpose of this case study is to tell a story which conveys something of the complexity of the planning process: the way technical, legal, community and political aspects interplay in practice. Having said that, this is no more than a sketch of a small-area plan. Stroud is a market town set in the Cotswold Hills, in Gloucestershire, England. Its economy was originally based on woollen mills and water power, supported by canal and rail access; now it is based on engineering and services, with growing IT and cultural activities. Its population is around 30,000, and it sits in the much wider Stroud District. The parish of Stroud – which has its own 'town council' – is less than half of the town.

Neighbourhood Development Plans (NDP) have been established by the UK government as a means of giving local communities greater say in the future of their area. They are undertaken by parish councils, town councils or community fora, nesting within the strategic policy context set by District authorities in the 'Local Plan'. If approved (by the District, an inspector and a community referendum) they have legal force, and can be used in development management.

Stroud town centre NDP was initiated by Stroud Town Council (STC), after a voluntary sector study and a public meeting, which highlighted some urgent questions about the future of the area (Figure 17.13). There were four main justifications for a plan:

- the re-opening of the canal, giving a new dimension to the town centre;
- vacant and underused sites in key locations;
- the desire to reverse the decline of retailing in the centre;
- poor pedestrian connectivity inhibiting active travel to the centre.

Two retired professional planners took the lead in advising STC. A 'steering group' was formed including the STC Clerk, elected representatives from the District and Town councils, Stroud Preservation Trust and Civic Society. It was agreed that the plan should include

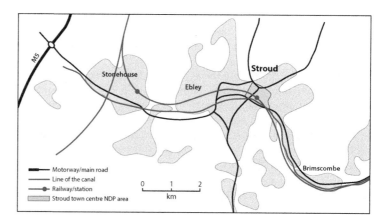

Fig 17.13 *Stroud area, and the town centre Neighbourhood Plan*

not just the centre but areas immediately around it that could influence its future. A proposal was put to the District Council and approved. Following the formal launch of the project in July 2014 many residents and a few business people volunteered to help. Those who agreed to co-ordinate working groups for the plan (movement, trading, housing, environment, etc.) were co-opted onto the steering group. Considerable enthusiasm and mutual commitment were established, and the momentum carried the plan preparation through subsequent trials.

Vision and understanding

These two stages – defining the vision and understanding the locality – were elided in the Stroud process. The main focus was two periods of public engagement in September and November 2014. The aim in September was to discover what people using the town centre felt about its strengths and weaknesses, and therefore the issues that should be addressed. The aim in November was to decide on the vision and priorities. In preparation for public exhibitions and seminars, the working groups on different topics produced survey reports, highlighting the facts and their implications. For example, the analysis of the population living in the plan area (from the 2011 census) showed only 500+ people lived there, mainly in rented flats, with young single men over-represented, and higher levels of unemployment and disability than average. This information impressed people in general and the steering group in particular with the need to increase the population and diversity of housing options, in order to support social inclusion and bulwark the viability of shops in the centre. Another survey showed the extent of problems facing pedestrians – such as awkward routes and potentially intimidating road crossings – helping to explain very high car dependence and low levels of active travel. Analytical maps were produced showing the land use pattern (Figure 17.14), greenspaces, conservation policies and the pedestrian network.

Most people using the town centre had a lot of positive things to say about its character, its social and cultural dynamism, but also had concerns. They highlighted issues such as the various difficulties of getting into the centre by foot, bike, car and bus; poor street quality; and the decline of retailing. So a cluster of objectives began to emerge which shaped the plan. The planners on the steering group ensured that issues were seen through the lens of healthy, sustainable development, and in line with government policy. The agreed vision was for the town centre to be 'welcoming, healthy and thriving'.

'Most people using the town centre had a lot of positive things to say about its character, but also had concerns. The agreed vision was for the town centre to be "welcoming, healthy and thriving".'

Developing ideas

The period from the November consultation on the vision, to the March 2015 exhibition on policy options, was intensive. The options often took the simple form of doing something or doing nothing. Many of the volunteers found it difficult to move from issues and aims to policies. There were also conflicts between different

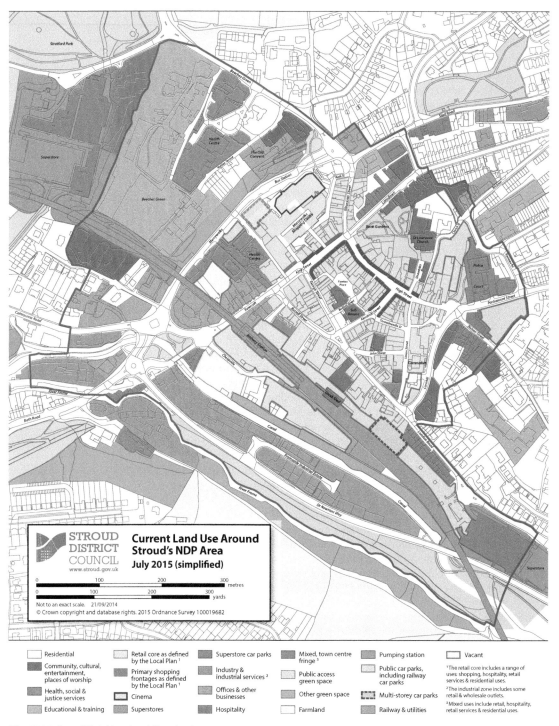

Fig 17.14 *Stroud Neighbourhood Plan: land use pattern*

Source: Stroud Town Council 2016 (note 9), p.17.

priorities and beliefs. For example, traders were very suspicious of extending pedestrianization, and wanted as much on-street parking as possible to allow 'pop and shop' visits; by contrast the environmentalists were in favour of greatly extending the pedestrian areas. The draft plan was somewhere in-between, trying to keep both parties on board: a set of modest proposals which improved safety at awkward junctions and enhanced the quality of some key spaces – each justified in its own right. This was a *softly, softly* approach. If people liked these improvements, once implemented, then that would establish a precedent for more ambitious schemes.

The outcome of public engagement and political consultations was positive. Indeed, some of the most ambitious proposals – for new pedestrian and bike routes and bridges to connect parts of the town currently separate – won strong support. The emerging strategy included policies for the following:

- encouraging investment in good quality retail, office, service and social facilities;
- providing opportunities for more and varied housing, increasing the number of people within easy walking distance of the centre;
- progressively up-grading the quality of streets and spaces to improve the pedestrian experience and enhance the setting of historic buildings;
- transforming the convenience, safety and attractiveness of access to the town centre for pedestrians and cyclists, thereby encouraging more physical activity and less car dependence;
- reducing the exposure of people to traffic danger and air pollution;
- promoting better directions and charging systems for car parking, more welcoming 'gateways' into the centre, especially in relation to train and bus stations;
- creating an attractive canal frontage, much better linked into the town, and a canal basin for narrow boats;
- greening the town centre and its environs, protecting greenspaces in perpetuity, preserving tree belts and encouraging biodiversity;
- promoting Stroud as a canal-based market town, capitalizing on rail and waterway improvements.

Agreeing the plan

The journey from the options to the submitted plan was long and arduous. Most of the volunteers fell away. Tasks were left to a core group of two planners, the STC Clerk and one councillor, the chair of the Preservation Trust, and the part-time administrative assistant. The staging posts were: approval by the Town Council, formal public consultation in October 2015, and submission to the District Council in December 2015. On the way it was essential to establish that the plan was based on sound evidence, satisfied criteria of sustainable development, and was 'deliverable'. Several special

'It was essential to establish that the plan was based on sound evidence, satisfied criteria of sustainable development, and was "deliverable".'

studies by consultants were commissioned to assist. Despite the earlier surveys by the working groups, extra evidence was needed to demonstrate, for example, the poor quality of the pedestrian experience. Consultation with official bodies and independent testing of policies in a Sustainability Appraisal were needed, partly to ensure that government guidance was being adhered to.

The form of the plan was a critical consideration. The town centre 'neighbourhood' is not like a village with greenfields around it. Most parts have well-established urban uses. However, incremental renewal occurs unpredictably and there are certain sites that are vacant or underused. So the plan took the form of a range of measures:

- *General policies* that apply to any situation in the plan area, guiding development without being prescriptive, covering topics such as retailing, employment, housing, greenspace, movement and design.
- *Zonal policies* which apply to parts of the centre or specific sites – with some flexibility of use because of market imponderables.
- *Spatial Framework* – which shows the specific sites, locations where particular policies apply (e.g. gateways), the pedestrian routes and crossings that must be planned for when change occurs, and the civic spaces which require improvement (see Figure 17.15).
- *Design code* – to which any new development or public realm improvements must adhere.
- *How it will happen* – spelling out the mechanisms, in particular through private investors and development management; also the partners and the funding sources which will, it is hoped, realize the pedestrian and public realm improvements.
- *Advocacy policies* – such as road improvements and parking controls – which are outside the remit of the plan, but where the STC has a clear view and will seek to influence events.

Showing how things could realistically happen is essential for the approval and credibility of the plan. This required several things: the creation of more specific proposals for development sites, which could then be assessed for viability; contact with all landowners and building users who would be potentially affected by proposals; meetings with specific sets of interests (e.g. housing, culture and environment) to refine the plan, and with major land owners, hoping to interest them in the proposals. All this had to happen before the town council could give the go-ahead for the legally required six-week public participation process. Then after comments and representations from the public, businesses, charities and official bodies (including different parts of Stroud District Council [SDC]), the plan was either further modified, or explanation given as to why that was not necessary. The plan was then approved by the Town Council and submitted to SDC. SDC accepted the plan as consistent with its recently approved Local Plan, and initiated the final part of the process.

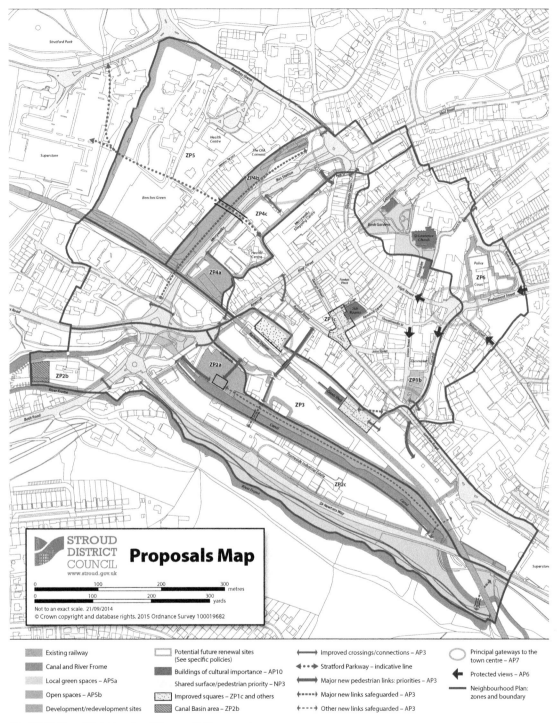

Fig 17.15 *Stroud Neighbourhood Plan: spatial framework*

Source: Stroud Town Council 2016 (note 9), p.103.

Taking action

At the time of writing (January 2016), the final stages of plan approval still have to be completed: examination by an independent inspector, and public referendum. It could still fall at one of these final hurdles, but the signs from NDPs elsewhere in the country are promising. None have yet been thrown out by the community. The referendum is expected in August 2016. That means that the plan will have taken something over two years from conception to final validation. Yet this is a small-area plan, with limited remit. Most other neighbourhood plans in the District are taking longer. The complexity of the community-oriented process, together with legal requirements, mean that quick plan-making is not an option.

Even before it becomes legally valid, however, the plan begins to have influence. It starts changing the assumptions and mind-set of landowners and councillors. Some new initiatives have been launched. For example, STC has embarked on negotiations for improvement and up-grading of the station forecourt, as one of the 'gateways' to Stroud. And the future of several vacant sites is under discussion. The NDP core group has been involved in detailed discussions with the prospective developers of a critically important site by the canal: Cheapside waterfront. The plan incorporates a simple *development brief*. The investors have in principle accepted the recommendations, and the main elements have been incorporated in the plan: access along the canal frontage, a public square with retail space adjacent, a direct route from the canal to the station and the car parks (Figure 17.16).

Learning lessons

Monitoring change in the plan area, and assessing the impact of policies, needs to be an on-going process. There are several simple indicators – such as the amount of new housing, the extent of public realm improvements and the footfall in the main shopping streets. The plan will come up for review in 2020, in parallel with the Local Plan for the whole District.

Figure 17.17 illustrates the overall process for the Stroud town centre plan. It shows how the 'technical' process of developing the plan is integrated with stakeholder and public engagement and with the legal obligations, i.e. the political and administrative processes. It is clear that the process is complex. Even for this small plan, a high degree of expertise is needed, plus volunteer commitment, political nous, and consistent clarity of purpose.

Converting healthy rhetoric into healthy decisions

There is many a slip between intention and realization. The case study above illustrates the difficulties of making even a relatively simple plan consistent, when many different interests are at stake, and decision-making is not centralized. So how can we ensure that

'The NDP core group has been involved in detailed discussions with the prospective developers of a critically important site by the canal.'

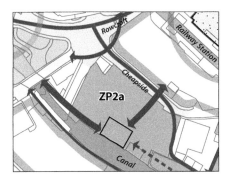

Fig 17.16 Cheapside waterfront spatial requirements

Source: Stroud Town Council 2016 (note 9), p.56 – an extract from the Proposals Map.

Appendix 8

Plan process diagram

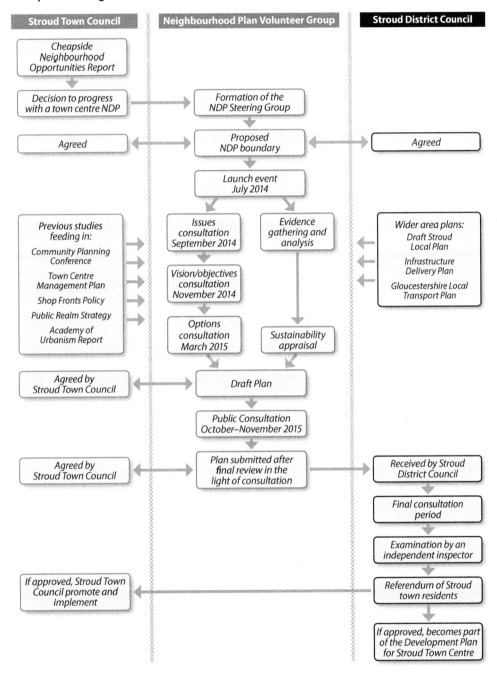

Fig 17.17 *The Stroud Neighbourhood Plan process*
Source: Prepared by the author for the NDP team.

the rhetoric of health, well-being and sustainable development is converted eventually into appropriate decisions on the ground? There is no magic bullet. There can be no guarantee. But at each stage of the process the professionals and decision-makers require unambiguous honesty.

Many health agencies, trying to influence development decisions, have turned to plan and project appraisal – particularly *health impact assessment* (HIA).

In Britain, the Department for Health, Health England and NICE (the National Institute for Health and Care Excellence) have all become concerned about the degree to which health and well-being are effectively incorporated in appraisal, and in spatial plans. A comprehensive study for NICE in 2010–2011 reviewed all the available evidence in Britain and worldwide. The study concluded that appraisal does not generally consider health impacts in any depth, if at all. Even HIAs tended to be partial in their approach, good on physical activity and environmental pollution but inadequate on mental well-being and health equity. Key barriers to full health-integration were lack of knowledge of those involved, the segmentation of knowledge and the absence of strong health goals in the plans.[5]

'Appraisal does not generally consider health impacts in any depth, if at all. Even HIAs tended to be partial in their approach, good on physical activity and environmental pollution but inadequate on mental well-being and health equity.'

Some authorities manage to make it work. In England, the Plymouth Plan is held up as an exemplar, winning the RTPI Award for excellence in plan-making in 2015. It is a single strategic plan for the city acting not only as the spatial development plan, but also as the Council's strategy for health, housing, children and young people, culture, transport and the economy. Land allocation is a key function of the plan relevant to all departments. The legal and professional processes of plan-making shaped the integrated process.[6] The RTPI judges were impressed by the evident cross-discipline and cross-political support for the integration of policies and the extensive engagement of the public in the process. They concluded that the Plymouth Plan is a ground-breaking example of 'joined-up' government.[7]

The Settlement Health Map can act as an effective trigger to joined-up thinking. Take for example the proposed construction of a new town bypass. The map can be used dynamically to identify effects, which could then be estimated before the decision to proceed is taken. Figure 17.18 shows by arrows the primary and secondary impacts then the effects from all spheres on personal health.

The primary (or direct) impacts are on the landscape, wildlife habitats and farmland, on the one hand, and on travel patterns, on the other. Travel by vehicle increases because of the new facility; new connections are possible, changing the pattern of accessibility. Increased vehicle mileage leads to more air pollution along the bypass route. Whether pollution and carbon emissions are increased or reduced overall depends on the degree to which the transfer of some trips from the centre of town does not simply release suppressed demand. That will depend on parallel action to deter traffic in the centre and positive support for alternative modes. Failing that, the bypass will reinforce the trend towards increased car use.

The new road profoundly alters vehicle accessibility. Land values along the bypass would be transformed, and both commercial and

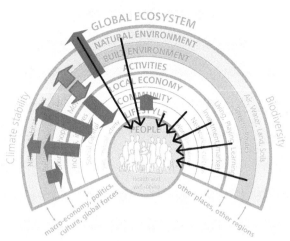

Fig 17.18 *Analysing the health impacts of a town bypass, using the Health Map to identify primary, secondary and health impacts*

Source: Barton et al. 2010 (further reading), p.68.

The settlement as
the local human habitat
in its global context

residential developers will be seeking sites. New business parks and retail outlets may attract extra economic activity, with benefits to employment opportunities in the town, but will also cost jobs in older areas. There would be a transfer of trips from central and local destinations, often walkable, to edge-of-town car-based destinations. Active travel would be reduced. Neighbourhood facilities might close, penalizing those who rely on them.

Once the likely effects have been assessed, the Health Map gives the agenda for estimating health, social, economic, environmental and sustainability impacts. If employed as part of an HIA it allows estimates of overall health costs and benefits. The road proposal is treated not just as a transport decision, but as something which changes the whole urban system, and alters the balance of people's lives.

Another trigger to action discussed earlier – this time in relation to a comprehensive urban plan – is the three urban fabrics approach (Figure 17.19). Walking, public transport and accessibility to jobs and facilities are so critical to health and sustainability outcomes that the three fabrics provide good overarching indicators. Monitoring the three fabrics is a relatively simple matter, which can be done using Geographical Information Systems (GIS) and up-to-date information on land uses, roads, bus services, and pedestrian connections. A fourth 'cycling fabric' could be added. No social surveys or complex modelling are required. The results feed directly into professional and political debate. Developers can gain credit and elected representatives can be honoured, for extending the walking and transit fabrics. Or shamed for reducing them. When the physical environment facilitates healthy behaviour, then more

Fig 17.19 *The three city fabrics test of healthy progress provides urban indicators that capture fundamentals of spatial structure, network quality and transit services*

Source: Author's illustration based on Leo Kosonen's ideas. See Chapter 5.

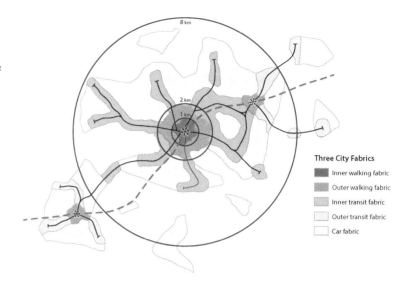

Three City Fabrics

■ Inner walking fabric
■ Outer walking fabric
▨ Inner transit fabric
☐ Outer transit fabric
☐ Car fabric

people will choose healthy lifestyles, and health inequalities will be reduced.

Conclusion

Earlier chapters in the book are mostly about building up a holistic understanding of the urban environment in relation to people's health and global health, then reflecting on the nature of planning. This chapter provides a brief insight into what happens in practice. Somehow, through the varied pressures – institutional, political, commercial – planners need to maintain a clear professional and ethical perspective. The planning process needs to do the following:

- Be explicit and holistic in relation to objectives, encompassing all the relevant aspects of health and well-being, social inclusion, environmental sustainability, and economic vitality, ensuring that these are incorporated in the plan at an early stage.
- Be inclusive of stakeholders, valuing the involvement of varied public, private and community interests in a shared learning programme that enables the progressive, mutual development of understanding and ideas.
- Focus attention on critical issues through effective scoping, recognizing the interaction of policies and behaviours, so that resources are used wisely and expertise of all kinds – local, cultural, specialist, generalist, political, market – is tapped appropriately.
- Be both rational and creative through the plan process, uncovering the truth of problems, providing a positive incentive for the team to devise innovative solutions, testing options systematically and honestly.

- Build towards legitimized and well-supported, logical decisions, with the pathways to implementation clear and practical, and with commitment from partners.[8]

Further reading

Addison, L. (2010) 'Building collaborative partnerships', in H. Barton, M. Grant, and R. Guise *Shaping neighbourhoods: for local health and global sustainability.* London: Routledge.

Barton, H., Grant, M. and Guise, R. (2010) *Shaping neighbourhoods: for local health and global sustainability.* London: Routledge. This provides much greater detail on the practical processes and techniques needed to make healthy spatial policies.

Cave, B. (2010) 'Assessing the potential health effects of policies, plans, programmes and projects', in H. Barton, M. Grant, and R. Guise *Shaping neighbourhoods: for local health and global sustainability.* London: Routledge.

Corburn, J. (2009) *Towards the healthy city: people, places and the politics of urban planning.* Cambridge, MA: MIT Press. A book from a Californian perspective, including stories and analysis of attempts at healthy planning.

Kurth, J., Iqbal, Z., Southon, P., Weston, C. and Robinson, C. (2015) 'Health-integrated planning and appraisal in the English Midlands', in H. Barton, S. Thompson, S. Burgess, and M. Grant (eds) *The Routledge handbook of planning for health and well-being.* London: Routledge.

Notes

1   In the UK, www.healthycities.org.uk/ membership/howtojoin
2   Figure 17.4 is from Barton *et al.* (2010), freely adapted from Burns, D., Hambleton, R. and Hoggett, P. (1994) *The politics of decentralization* (London: Macmillan), itself adapted from Arnstein, S. (1969) 'A ladder of citizen participation', *AIJP, XXX4*, pp. 216–224.
3   These tools are derived from AIDA (the Analysis of Interconnected Decision Areas) – part of the *strategic choice* approach. See Barton, H. and Bruder, N. (1995) *A guide to local environmental auditing* (London: Earthscan), Chapters 2 and 8. For a more in-depth description of AIDA, see Hickling, A. (1974) *Managing decisions: the strategic choice approach* (Rugby: Mantech Publications); reprint digitized (2010).
4   The following section is my own summary of the process and the plan (having been involved in it) simplified for a general readership. The *Stroud Town Centre Neighbourhood Development Plan 2015–2035* documentation is available on www.shapingtheheartstroud.org
5   Gray, S., Barton, H., Carmichael, L., Mytton, J., Lease, H. and Joynt, J. (2011) 'The effectiveness of health appraisal processes currently in addressing health and well-being during spatial plan appraisal: a systematic review', *BMC Public Health*, 11: 889. And Carmichael, L., Barton, H., Gray, S., Lease, H. and Pilkington, P. (2012) 'Integration of health into urban spatial planning through impact assessment: identifying governance and policy barriers and facilitators', *Environmental Impact Assessment Review*, 32: 187–194.
6   Plymouth is a city of 200,000 people in SW England. See www.plymouth.gov.uk/ plymouthplan
7   RTPI South West magazine *Branchout*, Autumn 2015. See www.rtpi.org.uk/southwest
8   Barton, H. and Grant, M. (2008) 'Testing time for sustainability: striving for inclusive rationality in project appraisal', *JRSPB*, 128(3): 130–139.
9   Stroud Town Council (2016) Shaping the heart of Stroud – Stroud town centre Neighbourhood Development Plan 2015-2035: Submission draft. Stroud, Stroud District Council and Stroud Town Council. Maps reproduced with permission of Ordnance Survey.

EPILOGUE

Whatever you can do, or dream you can, begin it! Boldness has genius, power and magic. Begin it now!

Goethe

Seven conclusions if we are serious about planning cities for well-being

If it is accepted that the purpose of planning is to promote health, well-being and quality of life, for all groups in the population, then urban planning has a clear moral purpose. Yet inappropriate policies and development fashions persist – whether because of vested interest, governance systems, expediency or misconception. In many places we are still building unhealthy, unsustainable conditions into the very fabric of human settlements. Health service costs (and social inequity) escalate, partly as a result. But there is no longer any excuse for misconception. Spatial planning, working with the market and communities, can be a means of achieving livable, healthy and resilient environments. It is not valid to claim that we do not know the answers. The scientific evidence needed to underpin healthy environmental planning is increasingly comprehensive. Planners and designers have examples of excellent practice, as well as examples of poor, even disastrous, practice to learn from. By way of summary, below are seven conclusions for healthy cities.

1 The scientific evidence

It is no longer open to doubt that the form and function of human settlements has profound implications for the health of people and of the planet. The evidence is overwhelming. The shape, design and management of cities and their hinterlands influence the options that are open to people in terms of housing affordability and quality, physical activity, social contact, access to jobs, facilities, healthy food and nature. Air pollution, greenhouse emissions, water security and flood risk all relate to spatial planning. Spatial inequities tend to exacerbate health disparities, leading to increasing costs to individuals and society in relation to health and social care. We ignore this evidence at our peril.

2 The evidence from exemplars

Looking at the history of urban planning from the earliest times to the present, there are many examples of places designed for well-being. We can learn lessons from the past, and gain inspiration from current good practice. Creating healthy urban environments was the prime motive of the pioneers of modern planning. Informed now by research findings, it should be so again.

3 Healthy spatial strategies

The principles of sound city planning apply across countries, cultures and economic status. While application depends on context, the concept of the city and its environs as providing the human habitat is fundamental. The settlement health map embraces all the elements – social, economic, spatial and ecological – that together make up the city. The relationship of the city to its natural setting is critical to its long-term ability to provide a healthy environment. The overall shape and evolution of the city need to be planned so as to offer a degree of choice and freedom to all social groups – in terms of shelter, work, accessibility to facilities and greenspace, clean air and water, healthy food. The avoidance of ghettos of poverty is essential. Every neighbourhood should enable those with less mobility to live full lives, prioritizing active travel and shared transport systems.

4 The responsibility of power

Those with the power to make decisions about urban infrastructure and major developments have a huge responsibility that they need to recognize. Health, well-being and quality of life provide powerful motives for improving the human habitat. The powerful include central government which makes the rules, local politicians who guide cities, public agencies and private companies who invest in the built environment. Just as they accept responsibility for sound building and engineering practices, so too should they for creating healthy, resilient urban environments. The pursuit of 'sustainable development' has not caught the public and political imagination. A switch of the rhetoric to 'health and well-being' could galvanize support for better strategies and designs.

Politicians, especially at state level, need to step up to the mark, recognize that many current policies make health *worse,* and guide the long-term evolution of settlements in the interests of the well-being of the people they represent, reducing the burden of poor health on society.

5 The role of planners

Professional planners of all kinds need to accept their moral responsibility, and gain the knowledge and skills to persuade decision-makers of appropriate actions. This applies not just to traditional town planners but others who affect the form of cities: those promoting economic development and regeneration, transport and housing planners, civil engineers, surveyors, urban designers, architects and landscape architects. All have a professional responsibility not just to their clients or political bodies, but to the users of the city – the people.

6 Achieving coherent, co-operative action

Healthy urban environments can only be achieved if the official bodies and major investors pull together, working collaboratively with communities. In a democratic and pluralistic society, recognition of a shared ethical position is important. The successful cities have a high level of financial autonomy and develop rational debate about spatial choices, with all interests involved. They rely on support from government, strategic agreement with neighbouring authorities, and co-ordinated programmes of public, private and voluntary sector investment.

7 Educating planners and designers

The training of planners requires a fresh approach, with the various linked professions sharing a deeper and more ethically informed education. Inter-professional activity, gaining a basic understanding of the relationship between people, the urban environment, development decisions and the wider natural environment, would assist. To a significant extent planning training in English-speaking lands has underplayed social, economic, ecological and design processes in favour of legal and procedural studies. This is false priority, because legal frameworks are different in every state or country, and can change frequently. Professional training should be focused on internationally transferable knowledge and skills, with an appropriate emphasis on practical planning and design exercises. From the outset there should be no question as to the professional ethical stance: that the purpose of planning is to facilitate/create places that are healthy.

Final thought

Just as doctors take the Hippocratic oath to preserve individual life, so planners (of many different varieties) could promise to promote healthy urban environments for all. Hippodamus, based in Miletus in the fifth century BC, is credited with the first attempt to establish and systematize the principles of good town planning. So a new promise for planners could perhaps be called the *Hippodamic oath.*

The original Hippocratic oath is worth reading. Physicians promise to practice medicine ethically and honestly, never intentionally to do harm or commit injustice, but work always for the good of the patients – avoiding any seduction and temptations of the flesh with men or women. The contemporary version, the 'Declaration of Geneva', is still sworn by many medical students. They promise to consecrate their lives to the service of humanity, to respect human life, and to put the health of their patients as the first consideration, irrespective of background.

Planners could promise to practise ethically and honestly, to work for the health and well-being of everyone irrespective of their status, and to enhance the quality and resilience of the human habitat. Six hundred years after Thomas More's *Utopia*, 2,400 years after Plato's reflections on a lost eco-paradise, is it time to make our dreams reality...?

I dwell in a fair city, with homes and bowers, domes and towers – a humane and healthy place in balance with nature, where green park-lands thread through the city, linking to a productive countryside; where convivial streets, safe cycleways and efficient, cheap trams give access to a diversity of work, play, educational, health and social settings; where vibrant urban neighbourhoods and quieter urban villages offer choice of affordable housing; an environment that encourages healthy physical activity, flourishing and diverse communities and creative entrepreneurial spirit.

INDEX